BROKEN PROMISES

CRITICAL STUDIES IN EDUCATION SERIES
Edited by Paulo Freire & Henry A. Giroux

EDUCATION UNDER SIEGE
The Conservative, Liberal & Radical Debate Over Schooling
Stanley Aronowitz & Henry A. Giroux

CRITICAL PEDAGOGY & CULTURAL POWER
David W. Livingstone & Contributors

LITERACY
Reading The Word & The World
Paulo Freire & Donaldo Macedo

THE POLITICS OF EDUCATION
Culture, Power & Liberation
Paulo Freire

WOMEN TEACHING FOR CHANGE
Gender, Class & Power
Kathleen Weiler

THE MORAL AND SPIRITUAL CRISIS IN EDUCATION
A Curriculum for Justice & Compassion in Education
David Purpel

EDUCATION & THE AMERICAN DREAM
Conservatives, Liberals & Radicals Debate the Future of Education
Harvey Holtz & Associates

POPULAR CULTURE & CRITICAL PEDAGOGY
Schooling & the Language of Everyday Life
Henry A. Giroux, Roger Simon & Contributors

BROKEN PROMISES
Reading Instruction in Twentieth-Century America
Patrick Shannon

□ BROKEN PROMISES □
Reading Instruction in Twentieth-Century America

Patrick Shannon

Introduction by Henry A. Giroux and Paulo Freire

BERGIN & GARVEY
New York • Westport, Connecticut • London

CRITICAL STUDIES IN EDUCATION SERIES

In Memory of Paul T. Shannon

Library of Congress Cataloging-in-Publication Data

Shannon, Patrick, 1951-
   Broken promises: reading instruction in twentieth-century
America / Patrick Shannon : introduction by Paulo Freire and Henry A.
Giroux.
      p.   cm.—(Critical studies in education series)
   Bibliography: p.
   Includes index.
   ISBN 0-89789-161-9 (alk. paper)
   ISBN 0-89789-160-0 (pbk. : alk. paper)
   1. Reading (Elementary)—United States—History.   2. Reading
(Elementary)—United States—Textbooks—History.   3. Reading—
United States—Aids and devices—History.   4. Reading teachers—
United States—Effect of technological innovations on.   I. Title.
II. Series.
LB1573.S466   1989
372.4'0973—dc19   88-27397

Library of Congress Catalog Card Number: 88-27397
ISBN: 0-89789-161-9
      0-89789-160-0 (pbk.)

First published in 1989

Bergin & Garvey, One Madison Avenue, New York, NY 10010
An imprint of Greenwood Publishing Group, Inc.

Printed in the United States of America

10 9 8 7 6 5 4 3

Contents

Preface

☐ When I first heard the title of this book, *Broken Promises*, I thought it was too sensational—more appropriate for a television mini-series or a romance novel. It was clear, at least to me, that my original title, "Managing Literacy," was descriptive of twentieth century reading instruction, in which reading experts, textbook publishers, and state officials attempted to manage, and continue to manage with ever increasing levels of sophistication, the instructional practice of teachers. In turn, teachers manage the literacy learning of their students. Moreover, "Managing Literacy" connoted the new skills of teaching reading, which teachers must now demonstrate if they are to be considered "effective" in their work. My title seemed an apt, even compelling, descriptor of what takes place in American classrooms in the name of reading instruction. Yet, Jim Bergin, the publisher, and Henry Giroux, the series editor, suggested *Broken Promises* without explanation. What can such a title mean?

American reading instruction is based on a series of promises concerning its audience, its delivery, and its benefit. Originally, reading instruction was supposed to lead Americans to salvation of the soul from that Old Deluder, Satan, in the Massachusetts Bay Colony in 1647, and of the spirit from political and economic tyranny, in the educational writings of Thomas Jefferson. The ability to read promised salvation by enabling the public to be aware of and to examine critically the religious and political temptations likely to lead a free people astray. Right from the start, however, the promise of reading instruction was broken for women, minorities, and the poor, who for one reason or another were excluded from formal instruction. Sadly, this promise is still often broken today, even though laws require compulsory school attendance. Minorities and the poor continue to lag well behind white middle and upper class students, and although women seem to fare somewhat better overall, they find themselves behind in the scientific and technical literacies required to gain power in the world of work.

Promises were also made and broken to those who wished to teach reading. Reading instruction was supposed to make a difference in the lives of their students. It was to enable students to gather and evaluate information necessary for them to live fulfilled lives (however defined), empowering them to have greater control over their lives. Implicit in this belief is the promise made to teachers that they would lead fulfilled lives and control their work at school. After all, teachers were already literate. Yet, I will argue that during the twentieth century teachers lost more and more control over their work, as textbook technology became more sophisticated and was expected to carry what is sometimes considered to be the burden of teaching reading.

The promise of benefit has been broken to all Americans—not just to women, minorities, and the poor. At present, American reading instruction does a good job of teaching students to decode words and to reproduce the meaning of texts. But we were promised much more. Reading as promised is supposed to enable us to read both the word and the world in ways that allow us to see through the mysteries, ambiguities, and deceit of modern living in order to make sense of our lives, to understand the connections among our lives and those of others, and to act on our new knowledge to construct a better, a more just, world.

I think these are some of the broken promises to which Bergin and Giroux alluded in their cryptic suggestion for a title change. The new title puts my concerns in a new light, one that might allow more people to see the importance of reconsidering and reconstructing American reading instruction. We have a right to expect reading instruction to fulfill its promises, and I hope my book illuminates some of the reasons why the promises have been broken in the past and illustrates some ways we can work to realize desired changes.

As are all authors, I am indebted to several people who helped me develop the arguments I offer in this book. Robert Smith helped me learn to think critically and historically, showing me that culture and history are human artifacts and that "things don't have to remain the way they currently appear." Robert Schreiner, P. David Pearson, John Cogan, Elton Stetson, Dick Abrahamson, Pose Lamb, Ed Kameenui, Peter Winograd, Peter Mosenthal, and Andy Effrat each helped by giving their time to read and comment on my writing or by allowing me time to pursue that writing. Jim Hoffman, Ken Goodman, and Henry Giroux offered opportunities to tie my studies together and to extend my argument. Joan Craig and Susan Sperling helped me prepare the manuscript. I thank them all. Most sincerely, I wish to thank my wife, Kathleen, who remains my most supportive critic.

Editors' Introduction

Reading Instruction and Critical Pedagogy
HENRY A. GIROUX AND PAULO FREIRE

☐ Theories of reading and reading instruction have fallen on hard times. Conservatives assert their ideological clout and forcefully embrace the old scientism as a model for reading instruction. Touted as a central element in the back-to-basics movement, reading instruction, as a discipline sorely in need of more stringent regulation and control, becomes a major target in the public schools. Relying upon research paradigms which display a passion for exactness, standardization, and rationalization, the federal government has initiated an educational reform movement that defines reading as a technological rather than a historical and social practice. Invoking a methodology that removes history, politics, and values from its formulaic principles, policy makers at the national and state levels have performed ideological surgery on reading programs across the country. Rejecting the notion that reading is a cultural practice inextricably related to the histories, experiences, and voices of the teachers and students—who engage it as a form of social and cultural production—the new technocrats of reading proceeded to develop and argue for forms of reading instruction that deny the active side of human understanding, social interaction, and human intentionality. Abstracted from history and the realm of public culture and power, reading instruction has been enlisted by the dominant culture as part of a wider political and pedagogical attack on the capacity of teachers and students to engage in critical thought as a meaningful form of teaching and learning. What is at stake in this position is not merely the ability of students to learn how to read critically, but also the even more radical pedagogical practice of teaching students to take risks and to engage in meaningful social action. In effect, the reading instruction that has dominated schooling is part of a wider thrust to undermine the possibility of public schools developing and educating an autonomous and self-motivated critical citizenry.

Consigned to the margins of the current debate on theories of reading and reading instruction, radical social theory in the United States has not been able to challenge the new conservatism effectively. Of course, the works of the Paulo Freire, Ken and Yetta Goodman, and others offer a progressive alternative as both a theory and a pedagogy of reading, but their influence has been limited to adult literacy programs and a few schools of education. A more serious problem has emerged in the influential discourses of postmodernism and poststructuralism that have begun to exercise considerable influence on the theory and practice of reading and text analysis in higher education in the United States. Celebrating the death of the subject and the infinite play of signification and difference, various theorists in these movements have played down the act of reading as historical, value laden, and political. Rejecting historical, ethical, and political practice as one of the crimes of modernity, the culture of postmodernity has largely refused to engage the act of reading and the construction of text as a pedagogical act that itself can only be seen as part of a wider historical and political project. Freire's notion that human beings read the world before they read the word has no place in a paradigm whereby human agents have been relegated to the ashcan of history.

It is to Patrick Shannon's credit that he avoids the ideological tenets and worst simplifications of both of these positions while engaging in a project designed to appropriate critically and advance the most important and empowering insights of the progressive tradition on reading and pedagogy.

For Shannon, the question of reading instruction is deeply implicated in issues of power, domination, and possibility. Rejecting the universalizing discourse of prevailing theories of reading instruction, Shannon attempts to develop a criticism of these positions by situating them in historical and theoretical analyses that combine three important considerations. First, he reasserts the primacy of the theoretical, the social, and the functional as central categories for a critical theory of reading and reading instruction. Specifically, Shannon argues that theory cannot be seen merely as a predictive or descriptive category in establishing a language of reading instruction. Theory is a productive category that is constitutive of the categories educators use to organize their views of pedagogy, texts, and students. As a self-reflective discourse, theory both constitutes and is reconstituted through its engagment with practice.

Similarly, Shannon recognizes that theory is always shot through with values and must be seen as both an ethical and political discourse. In addition, Shannon strongly argues that the social as an analytical unit cannot be replaced through an exclusive focus on the individual as the isolated referent for generating critiques and theories of reading instruction. In fact, the individual must be understood and analyzed in social terms, as these are uniquely constructed within larger historical and structural relations. Put another way, the material and ideological conditions that give meaning to human subjectivity and individual behavior as they unfold within particular social practices and cultural forms can only be understood as part of wider specific social formations that occupy a particular historical conjuncture. Instead of talking about the structure or the how of reading programs, Shannon focuses on their function, as determined by the interest they express and the effects they have on students and teachers, especially in terms of how they work to empower or disempower such groups. The language of technique which guides most reading programs is insufficient as a discourse and practice for referencing the theoretical, ethical, and political interests that structure and mediate the purpose and effects of existing approaches to reading and pedagogy.

Second, Shannon develops his own transformative project by examining existing reading instruction as historical and political practice. He attempts to reveal the ideologies and interest at work in current dominant approaches to reading instruction by first treating them as objects of historical analysis. He then critically examines the effects of these approaches on teachers and students through an analysis of how current reading approaches deskill teachers and disempower students at the same time. In effect, Shannon attempts to link questions of history, power, and knowledge through a critical perspective that brilliantly illuminates the ways in which school texts are produced as part of the wider commercialization of schooling, teachers are deskilled under the imperatives of management, and the voices and experiences of students from subordinate groups are silent or ignored as a result of the growing management pedagogies now proliferating in American schools.

Third, Shannon is not content to stay within the language of critique. He devotes the last section of his book to a project of possibility and hope. In doing so, he both provides a critical discourse for teachers to use to rethink their own theory and practice of reading and exemplifies his position by demonstrating how a number of teachers, researchers, parents, and students actually have struggled to reverse the current language and practice of management as it shapes educational policy in a number of public schools.

Shannon is not a bad utopian. On the contrary, he is an educator who believes that hope matters, that struggle must continue, and that schools are important sites of contestation and reform. His book combines history, theory, and practice in a manner that is unmatched by any other text on reading instruction in North America. His attempt to retheorize and reconstruct a theory and pedagogy of reading is courageous and much needed. Patrick Shannon provides the most illuminating and instructive critique of the historical development and current ideologies at work in existing dominant approaches to reading instruction to appear in years. More important, he lays the groundwork for educators to develop an approach to reading instruction which embraces the insight that schools should be places where a pedagogy of reading truly teaches students to read the world, and the word, in the interest of creating a more humane and justly democratic society.

Introduction

☐ Walk into any American elementary classroom during a reading lesson, and there is a 90 percent chance that you will observe a teacher and students working with commercially prepared materials. Most likely, the students in this classroom are divided into groups according to their abilities to read accurately and to complete written assignments successfully. Two of the groups will be sitting at their desks completing pages in appropriate workbooks or filling in the blanks of a worksheet, all practicing a reading skill taught to them earlier. When individual students finish their pages, they check the blackboard to see if all of their seatwork is completed. If so, they hand in their assignments and read a book, visit an activity corner of the classroom, or go to the library, if it's the proper day, while they wait for their turn with the teacher.

The teacher works with a third group as its members sit at a table somewhat separate from the students' desks. One of three activities is taking place at the table: students are reading and answering questions about a story from the group's anthology; they are listening to the teacher as she presents information on a new reading skill; or the teacher and students are correcting seatwork together as a group. Regardless of the activity in progress, the teacher is in control, or, at least, she appears to be in control: setting the page limit for reading and asking questions to check if students understood the passages if read silently or were paying attention if another group member read aloud; providing explanation and examples of the reading skill to enable students to complete their seatwork; or reading directions and calling on students to state their answers from their seatwork aloud. Close to the teacher's hand is a guidebook which coordinates the day's, week's, and year's events for reading instruction in this classroom. The teacher is patient but moves quickly because she divides her time equally among the three groups which only to the facts of the matter in their studies. Third is the belief that the social world is the summation of distinct systems of variables which can be analyzed, understood, and reassembled without injury to our knowledge of the social whole. The fourth assumption suggests that each variable has one precise definition which once discovered will hold across research studies, thus allowing researchers to establish controls within their studies. And finally, the search for context and value-free generalizations finds its most exact expression in mathematical logic and deductive reasoning. Taken together, these assumptions enable reading researchers to treat all questions as if they had single answers and to design true experiments which compare groups according to some measure of increase in a designated variable directly attributable to the variation of another specified treatment variable.

The empirical/analytic tradition is readily apparent in the type of questions most researchers ask: What is reading? What is the most effective means of reading instruction? What is the relationship between teachers and materials that will produce the greatest gains in students' test scores (Mosenthal, in press)? Each of these "What is" questions is assumed to have one absolute answer which, once discovered, will not be subject to interpretation. The empirical/analytic reading researchers' job is to hypothesize an answer or partial answer to the questions based on verifiable evidence from other experimental studies and then to design research that will test their new hypothesis. Of course, these example questions are too complex for one study, and few researchers would attempt to tackle them in a single experiment—there are too many undefined, uncontrolled variables for that. More likely, reading, instruction, and teacher/material relations would be divided into components for study. For example, reading might be divided into attention, decoding, comprehension, and information retrieval, and then each of these subsystems could be divided even further.

Some of the components have long histories as research topics upon which reading researchers would build their case through controlled studies in order to inch us closer to understanding all of reading and how it is learned. Other components require preliminary "fieldwork" before controlled studies can be profitable; here, nonquantitative research methods—interviews, observation, description—find their way into the empirical/analytic tradition because they can provide sufficient data to allow credible hypotheses for testing (Barr 1986a). These early descriptive studies become tied to experimental results through theoretical literature reviews which set the agenda for the next round of experimental studies.

Although empirical/analytic reading research has the advantage of producing theory that is easily translated into instructional practice, it has several shortcomings and it is quite limited in its usefulness in explaining the reversal of teachers' and materials' roles in elementary school reading instruction. First, the empirical/analytic tradition has generated multiple theories of reading without providing a means to choose among them because each has its own internal validity and system of verification. In fact, you must become unscientific and play your favorite in order to choose at all. Second, empirical/analytic researchers seem relatively unconcerned about the effects of their work on the total social framework of reading instruction; rather they seem most intent on fine-tuning existing systems, investigating individual cognitive processes, developing rational systems for testing, and validating their own hypotheses. Overall, empirical/analytic reading researchers suggest a restricted role for teachers—the follower of someone else's theory and plans—and an impoverished, overly psychological and individualistic definition of literacy. And although they claim neutrality in and for their work, empirical/analytic reading researchers really support the status quo overall because they attempt to shore up the sagging parts of the present conditions of elementary school reading instruction.

This support of the status quo represents the limited utility of this tradition for my purposes. Because empirical/analytic researchers accept the present conditions as given, immutable facts, they begin their work by assuming that my question is irrelevant to American reading instruction. That is, since empirical/analytic researchers do not consider the goals of reading instruction as scientific topics for research, they are unable to posit alternative situations and relationships among the participants and materials in school reading programs. They work only in the present and accept current circumstances as the parameters of their research. Perhaps that is why Beck and McKeown do not see the irony in asking teachers to be thoughtful and reflective as they follow someone else's theoretical principles while implementing someone else's plan. The blinders imposed by the empirical/analytic research tradition allow empirical/analytic reading researchers only to see the facts of reading instruction not the human action and consequences behind those facts nor the potential for what reading instruction might do for all participants under different conditions.

SYMBOLIC READING RESEARCH

The symbolic tradition shifts the emphasis of research from experimentation in order to verify lawlike generalizations of behavior to observation and interpretation of human interaction and intent. Rather than a search for objective facts which will hold across all contexts, symbolic researchers assume that the social world differs from the physical world in that the human participants determine what is real and valid through negotiations in which they reciprocally define rules of acceptable behavior within specific social contexts. According to the symbolic tradition, the social world is a constructed and socially maintained phenomenon rather than a naturally given entity as it appears to empirical/analytic researchers. In this way, the context in which symbolic research is conducted becomes very important because different social circumstances will most likely produce different rules for appropriate behavior. The task of symbolic research becomes the observation and interpretation of the symbols people create in order to negotiate these social rules in everyday interactions. And because symbolic researchers seek to understand naturally occurring rule making, they cannot disturb the ordinary social situation under study. That is, they cannot divide the context into parts, set artificial controls, or intervene because each act will necessarily affect the natural negotiations and subvert the external validity of the study.

The symbolic research tradition is just beginning to gain legitimacy within the reading research community (Mosenthal, in press). Although as yet symbolic studies do not comprise a significant percentage of the articles in reading research journals (Shannon 1987), symbolic researchers have found alternative outlets for their research and often present their work at professional conferences. In that work, they attempt to discover how participants in everyday typical reading events negotiate definitions of reading and rules to govern reading instruction in those specific contexts; they want to know how these participants make sense of each others statements and actions sufficiently well to enable children to learn to read and write. To accomplish this task, symbolic reading researchers immerse themselves in classroom or home reading activities, observe the participants' words and actions, record their interactions, and then examine these records to locate patterns of communication and behavior that might provide insight into how participants make sense of such social situations. Bloome's *Literacy and Schooling* (1987), the published proceedings of a University of Michigan multidisciplinary conference on literacy learning, offers several examples of symbolic reading research. Barr's "Classroom Interaction and Curriculum Content" (1987) most closely addresses the teacher/materials relationship during reading instruction from the symbolic perspective. Although depth of description is valued more highly than the ability to make generalizations from the conclusions from one situation to another, the intent of symbolic reading research is to develop theories about rule and sense-making processes (Green 1987). These theories are more sociological or sociopsychological than the purely psychological theories generated by empirical/analytic researchers.

Symbolic research satisfies some of the shortcomings of the empirical/analytic tradition for an investigation of reasons for the development and maintenance of the role reversal between teachers and materials in elementary school reading programs, but it also shares some of the limitations of the empirical/analytic tradition, and it has some limitations of its own. Certainly, symbolic research begins from an assumption that the present circumstances of reading instruction are socially determined, and this assumption would allow my question to be entertained as a legitimate topic for research. And symbolic research rests on interpretation of symbols and signs rather than on mathematic logic. However, the symbolic tradition still separates theory from practice, and it may even make theory more contemplative than empirical/analytic research because, in the symbolic tradition, theory is to describe and clarify rather than to affect practice directly. Moreover, symbolic research is frozen in the present because it must focus on the present rules as they are being negotiated for reading and instruction.[3] Along these lines, symbolic science requires a moral neutrality and a restraint from intervention—the interpretative theories of symbolic science are rarely seen as catalysts for change. Thus, like empirical/analytic reading research, the symbolic tradition can really only address "What is" questions concerning current reading instruction, never considering "Why it is" or "What it might become."

CRITICAL READING RESEARCH

The critical research tradition begins with the premise that the social negotiations concerning definitions of reality and validity are not conducted among equals because social, economic, and political circumstances have given certain groups license to assert undue influence over the outcomes. Consequently, these outcomes benefit the negotiators unequally, and the less dominant groups become dependent on the dominant group's definitions. Because these present conditions are rooted in the social relations of the past, they often seem opaque and immutable to present day negotiators, and the inequality of participation and benefit appears benign, appropriate, and "the way it is." The task of the critical researcher is to illuminate these past and current relations, to document their consequences, and to identify inconsistencies in the relations as opportunities for change toward more just relations. Critical research must be normative, substantive, as well as formal, because the critical researcher becomes an advocate in the political struggle over rules, definitions, and meaning in everyday life.

Theory and practice have a different relationship in the critical tradition than they had in empirical/analytic or symbolic research. Theory becomes individual self-reflection conducted during and in response to dialogues with other social negotiators concerning everyday events and how these events are connected to larger social issues. Self-reflection in this social context allows individuals to come to understand themselves and their situation more thoroughly, and thus, bringing this reality to consciousness, sets the stage for prudent practice in which individuals and researchers work together to combine ethics, morality, politics, and science to orient groups toward what is right and just in their social circumstances. Theory, then, provides an orientation for practice, not a prescription or description as in the other research traditions. In effect, theory and practice are united as the social negotiators make strategic, informed choices in the political negotiations which direct anew their daily lives.

The unit of analysis for critical research also differs from the other traditions. Empirical/analytic research assumes the social components of interest can be studied in isolation because they simply add up to reality regardless of their treatment. Symbolic research suggests that the social situation must be studied in its totality. Critical researchers reject these narrow focuses and assume that the isolated social situation forms a dynamic relationship to the whole of social existence. That is, the situation influences the whole as well as being influenced by the whole. This relationship is not linear or entirely rationally aligned as the empirical/analytic researchers insist, nor is it of secondary importance to the immediate observable context as implied in the symbolic tradition. Rather, according to critical researchers, social relationships are often fraught with contradictions which allow and at times invite change. To understand isolated events, then, critical researchers must consider the past, the present, and the possible future of the situation including its relationships to the large social context.

Causality in critical research becomes "the intersection of history, social structure, and biography" (Popkewitz 1984: 47)—that is, the regularities of present social action that result from past social relations, objective factors that are beyond the current negotiators' control, and subjective factors that individuals use to make sense and to modify their immediate situations. To investigate causality, critical researchers must combine research methods from historiography to access the past, survey and statistical analyses to gather information on social structure, and qualitative analyses to understand how individuals cope with their negotiations and situations. Because the critical tradition values an advocate's role for the researcher, who is expected to work toward identifying and overcoming constraints on negotiators' freedom, critical researchers can treat research methods as merely means to this moral goal, rather than as ends in themselves as the other research traditions must.

To date, the critical tradition has had little impact on the reading research community (Mosenthal, in press). Rarely does critical reading research appear in leading reading research journals, and there are few critical papers presented at professional meetings (Shannon 1987). This may be because of the strength of the empirical/analytic tradition in graduate schools of education and its assumption that open advocacy within research invalidates the usefulness of its results. With this assumption in mind, reading researchers are trained in the psychology and pedagogy of reading and writing and study quantitative and sometimes qualitative methods, but they rarely spend more than fleeting moments considering the philosophy and history of education. Within the empirical/analytic and even the symbolic tradition, these latter disciplines are nearly irrelevant since research must be conducted in the present with values in check. And thus, the lack of impact may be due to the fact that there are few critical reading researchers.[4]

Despite the lack of impact for whatever reason, the critical tradition presents the ideal conditions for the study of the reversal of teachers' and materials' roles in elementary reading instruction. First, this question can be considered of paramount importance within the critical tradition because of the importance of literacy in coming to understand the world and because the role reversal limits teachers' and students' freedom of thought and action; it imposes a definition of literacy from outside the social context and therefore cannot meet participants' needs; and it restricts students' and teachers' literate behavior to those acts prescribed in the teacher's guidebook. Moreover, the assumptions of critical research allow me to trace the development of these unequal negotiations and unfortunate consequences through the history of reading instruction in America and to connect the current classroom circumstances to the social, economic, and political structure of society. Furthermore, this tradition frees me to use whatever research methods are needed to identify impediments to just and constructive negotiations of definitions of reading in schools. However, the critical tradition also obligates me to discover seams in organizational fabric of elementary school reading programs that will provide opportunities for participants to change the status quo. By choosing this tradition for my research, my intentions for this book should be clear to all.

The book ends by suggesting that although the current situation of reading instruction in the United States seems bleak when examined closely, it is far from hopeless if students, teachers, researchers, and parents are aware of the reasons for the present conditions and are willing to work together to promote change.

□ PART I □

*The Role of Commercially
Prepared Materials*

1

Reading Instruction
Before the Turn of the Century

☐ Recently, Penguin Books published a thin paperback called *More Fun with Dick and Jane* (Gallant 1986), which satirizes the basal primers of the 1940s, 1950s, and 1960s by bringing Dick, Jane, and Baby Sally into the 1980s of divorce, designer clothes, and networking parties. Cleverly done, what makes this spoof so effective is the immediate familiarity of these names to millions of Americans who followed their lives while learning to read at school.[1] If you close your eyes you can almost see the faded water color pictures with short cryptic sentences like "Run, Dick, run" printed below them. Perhaps you can remember the routines of your reading instruction as well: reading aloud in turn to the teacher, memorizing flashcards, or receiving a star at the top of a perfectly completed workbook page. Although the materials and routines have changed a bit over the years, one thing has not changed since the 1920s—most reading lessons consist of teachers and students using commercially prepared basal materials. And it may appear to some that American reading instruction has always taken this form.

One way to gain some perspective on current reading instruction is to look at the past to see what factors contributed to the current relations and perhaps to see what opportunities for different arrangements might have been missed along the way. This is not an easy task since most analyses of reading instruction before the turn of the century consider only materials (e.g., Smith 1986), expert opinion (e.g., Mathews 1966), or educational policy (e.g., Cubberly 1934). Better evidence comes from

2

first-hand accounts of classroom practice from teachers' journals, students' diaries, or itinerant observers' reports. Although I risk misrepresenting the actual activities of reading instruction, I must rely solely on descriptions of materials and policy for the colonial period of American schooling.

In earliest colonial times, education was a family and religious matter in which children learned to sign their name and to repeat catechisms concerning the *Bible*. However, schooling was a priority for American colonialists; "it being viewed . . . as the most important bulwark after religion in their incessant struggle against the satanic barbarism of the wilderness" (Cremin 1970: 176–77).[2] Independent schools appeared as early as 1635 in Virginia and Massachusetts and 1642 in Connecticut, although literacy rates among colonists remained relatively low in comparison to those of England (Soltow and Stevens 1981). In 1642, the Massachusetts legislature passed a law requiring towns to make certain that all "youth under family Government be taught to read perfectly the English tongue, have knowledge in capital laws, and be taught some orthodox catechisms, and that they be brought up to some honest employment, profitable to themselves and to the Commonwealth" (quoted in Cubberly 1934: 18). By 1647, they enacted a second bill which established schools for larger communities.

> It being one chief project of that old deluder, satan, to keep men from the knowledge of the Scriptures, as in former times by keeping them in an unknown tongue. . . . It is therefore ordered that every township in this jurisdiction, after the Lord hath increased them to fifty households shall forthwith appoint one within their town to teach all such children as shall resort to him to write and read, whose wages shall be paid either by the parents or masters of such children, or by the inhabitants in general. (quoted in Cubberly 1934: 18–19)

Most New England and Mid-Atlantic colonies followed with similar laws within the next fifty years, although some Southern colonies took over one hundred years before they established publically funded schools (Cohen 1974).[3]

These petty schools, as they were called, were expected to render children literate in English, taking two or three years to complete the task using passages with religious themes. Graduates who could afford to were able to attend grammar schools which were to be available in towns of one hundred households in Massachusetts, according to the Old Deluder, Satan Act of 1647.[4] These grammar schools prepared students in classical languages in order to enable them to attend university. Although even in New England laws requiring petty schools were unequally applied (Murphy 1960), and teachers for these schools came from a wide variety of backgrounds—from literate mothers who taught in dame schools to college-educated scholars waiting for a ministry—the purpose for establishing these schools and the materials used for reading instruction in them were quite similar.

As explicitly stated in the Old Deluder, Satan Act of 1647, petty schools were designed to enable individuals to fulfill their Protestant responsibilities to know the word of God and to learn proper religious behavior. In a sense, schooling was viewed as a device for promoting uniformity of thought and character. This intent came through most noticeably in the materials used in these schools. Until the middle of the eighteenth century, there were few books published specifically for children (Huck 1976), and instructional materials for reading came in three forms. Hornbooks, paddles made of wood with a thin layer of cow horn stretched across to protect the writing, held the alphabet, a syllabary, and the Lord's Prayer on a three-by-five-inch paper. After being able to recite the hornbook upon demand, students began in a psalter, a book of spelling lessons. Here they listed syllables, words, and *Bible* verses, or they went directly to the *Bible* for instruction.

By the beginning of the eighteenth century, but as early as 1680 in Boston, the dominant reading text in the colonies was the *New England Primer* (Venezky 1987), which included both alphabet and syllabary and began with "A—In Adam's fall, We sinned all." For more than a hundred years, the *Primer* was the schoolbook of America, and it was a remarkably successful enterprise, selling over three million copies in its first 150 years of printing. The contents of the *Primer* give some insight into the expected relationship between teachers and students during reading lessons. Students were asked to memorize the following verse in the first few pages:

> I will fear God, and honour the KING.
> I will honour my Father & Mother.
> I will obey my Superiors.
> I will Submit to my Elders.

As best can be determined, memorization of *Bible* verses was the ultimate goal of reading instruction for most students, and teaching methods followed two forms: students' independent practice of lessons followed by recitation before an overseeing master or the master leading students in choral drills of lesson content.

To be sure, not everyone was satisfied with the religious and authoritarian overtones of the petty school and the solely classical content of the grammar schools. For example, in 1749 Benjamin Franklin proposed a different kind of grammar school which would include a useful education for average citizens and would include tracts like *Cato's Letters* (Levey 1971) within its curriculum. These letters, essays really, argued that freedom of thought and speech was essential for economic and social development, a freedom which was incompatible with schools dominated by religion.[5] Franklin was a leading proponent of such freedom for people of means through his establishment of the first subscription library in the United States.

> These libraries have improved the general conversation of the Americans, made the common tradesman and farmers as intelligent as most gentlemen from other countries, and perhaps have contributed in some degree to the stand so generally made throughout the colonies in defense of their privileges. (Lemisch 1961: 72)

With John Newbery's *A Little Pretty Pocketbook* in 1744, the publishing of children's books began in earnest, and some of these books were published for the first time in America during the War of Independence.[6] Their contents demonstrate a general change in the childrearing philosophies of the times from instilling a fear of God to developing a positive moral character and entrepreneurial spirit in children. There is little evidence that these books were widely used in reading lessons, but the instructional materials of the period reflect a similar change in tone. For example, Noah Webster's *Blue Backed Speller*, first published in 1793, included lessons which were patriotic and morally didactic, and the 1800 edition of the *New England Primer* began "A was an angler who fished with a hook." The goals for education were also modified, as suggested in Thomas Jefferson's words: "If a nation expects to be ignorant and free, in a state of civilization, it expects what never was and will never be" and he proposed universal schooling for white males in literacy, arithmetic, and history "at common expense to all" as the primary protection against tyranny (Jefferson 1893: 221).

READING INSTRUCTION IN THE NINETEENTH CENTURY

Although for the colonial period, I relied primarily on descriptions of materials and policy to develop a sense of reading instruction in that period, for the nineteenth century, there are sufficient numbers of first-hand accounts of teacher and student interaction to get a more exact picture of what actually transpired on a daily basis. Perhaps the best source of this information is Barbara Finkelstein's dissertation, *Governing the Young: Teachers' Behaviors in American Primary Schools, 1820–1880, A Documentary History* (1970), in which she synthesizes nearly one thousand diaries, journals, and reports from that period and devotes nearly one-seventh of her discussion exclusively to reading instruction. The problems of relying on policy statements become readily apparent when, for example, you look closely at Finkelstein's remarks on the word method in reading instruction. While Smith (1986) and

Mathews (1966), two of the most widely quoted sources on this subject, suggest the word method became popular in the 1840s and 1850s, Finkelstein does not find much mention of it until the 1870s and 1880s.

During this period, reading instruction emphasized word identification over meaning, required oral reading rather than discussion, and was largely directed by the available textbooks, most of which were developed more according to their authors' whim than according to a study of pedagogical principles. Finkelstein (1970) concludes that "the descriptive literature suggests that most teachers of reading confined their activities to those of the overseer and drillmaster" (p. 26). Overseers left learning almost entirely to students, limiting the master's role to defining assignments and later listening to recitation. On the other hand, drillmasters organized exercises that would help students memorize information but without teacher explanation. A third, atypical type of master was the "interpretor of culture" who sought to clarify and elaborate on textbook materials. Regardless of the means of instruction, the goal remained the same because "[teachers] proceeded as though learning had occurred when their students could imitate the skills or reproduce the knowledge contained in each of the assignments" (p. 25).

During the first half of the nineteenth century, the spelling method predominated as reading instruction—students learned the names of letters (lowercase, capital, and italic), spelled and pronounced lists of two- and three-letter nonsense syllables, and then spelled and pronounced lists of words of various lengths before they begun to road sentences orally. In Webster's *American Spelling Book*, the most popular spelling method textbook of this time, reading of sentences did not begin until page 101. In schools with students of various ages, teachers grouped students into classes according to their ability to spell lists. In rural areas, most lessons were conducted orally with students perhaps copying letters in the dirt; in cities where materials were more plentiful, students used slates, blackboards, and sand. The following excerpts from students' reflective journals as quoted in Finkelstein provide glimpses of, first, the overseer's technique and then that of the drillmaster in a so-called loud school.

> The class, composed of eight or ten scholars, takes its place on the floor, each one toeing the mark. The master commands "attention" then "obedience," the boys bow their heads and the girls curtsey. . . . One end is called the head, the other the foot, of the class. . . . The teacher opens the book, which is of course Webster's *Elementary*, and turning to the lessons, pronounces the words, beginning at the head. If a scholar misspells a word it is given to the next one. . . . (J. S. Minard, *Recollections of the Log School House Period*, 1905)

The teacher had a queer contrivance nailed to a post set up in the middle of the room. It was known as a "spelling board." When he pulled the string to which the board was fastened, the school could spell out words in moderate tones. . . . If he proceeded to pull the board uptight everybody "spelled to themselves." When he gave the cord a pull until down dropped the plank and the hubbub began. Everything went with a roar. Just as loud as you pleased, you could spell anything. People along the road were happy to know the children were getting their lessons. (Fenton, *Country Life in Georgia in the Days of My Youth*, 1919)

By the 1860s, most urban teachers had shifted the emphasis of their reading instruction from the letter and spelling to the syllable and pronunciation. Many rural teachers, however, continued with the spelling method for several decades (Mathews 1966). By far the most successful textbook promoting this phonics method was William Holmes McGuffey's *Eclectic First Reader for Young Children*, in which he removed spelling as a prerequisite to reading and used it as a means to aid and assess students' mastery of the recognition of words. In the phonics method, teachers directed students' attention first to the alphabet, then to the pronunciation guide for words, and finally to simple sentences and stories. This approach and sequence proved unquestionably satisfying for teachers as over 120 million copies of the *Reader* were purchased between 1836 and 1920. To help teachers concerned with the lack of correspondence between symbols and sounds in English spellings, a *McGuffey's Reader* was published with a modified alphabet (Leigh's *McGuffey's New England Primer and Pronouncing Orthography*, 1868). According to descriptions collected by Finkelstein (1970), this phonics method lent itself easily to a similar set of oral drills and individual learning activities as were experienced with the spelling method.

Just as the content of the *New England Primer* and Webster's spelling books were reflective of the moral tenor of their times, the McGuffey's *Readers* represent the popular moral philosophy of beginning industrialization and increased immigration. Beyond the primer and spelling book, the *Readers* offered five volumes of progressively more sophisticated readings including essays on nature and history, descriptions of manufacturing, and stories concerning appropriate deportment. These stories suggested that women should be tidy, appreciative of learning, and submissive, while men should be industrious, thrifty, and charitable. Moreover, these stories attempted to foster a respect for private property, a religious rationale for the contemporary class structure, and a distrust of Jacksonian democracy (Mosier 1965).[7] According to Finkelstein's (1970) interpretation of the first-hand accounts that she gathered, teachers' "tendency to rely almost completely on the texts meant that students, as they learned to read, write, cipher, and draw maps, imbibed the moral maxims, the political pieties, and the economic and social preachments of the writers whose books the students were commonly asked to memorize" (pp. 142–43).

Writing instruction of this period involved basically three kinds of activities: use of the pen and letter formation, copying words and passages from textbooks, and recopying hastily completed work. Quite often writing instruction was hampered by a lack of supplies, which teachers had to fashion out of available materials. (Over one hundred of Finkelstein's (1970) documents discuss pen-making at some length.) The teacher's role in these activities was often limited to that of overseer and drillmaster, and "in no instance could I find a description of a teacher who even hinted to his students that writing was an instrument for conveying thoughts and ideas" (Finkelstein, p. 56). Motivation for both reading and writing lessons was seen as a disciplinary rather than an instructional matter. "Throughout the period under discussion, we find that teachers more or less consciously devised a variety of rewards and punishments which reflected the belief that the route to literacy was neither interesting nor stimulating" (p. 102).

Despite Horace Mann's advocacy in the 1840s and 1850s, the word method made little headway as a teaching method until the late 1860s and 1870s. Finkelstein (1970) argues that the method failed to attract teachers' enthusiasm because it required teachers to become "interpretors of culture" rather than overseers or drillmasters. That is, the word method in its pure form eliminated the alphabet, syllabary, and spelling exercises from reading textbooks, beginning instead with familiar words complete with discussions concerning their meaning. Perhaps the earliest large scale attempt to implement the word method was Edward Austin Sheldon's "objective system" for primary education, which became the mainstay of the Oswego Movement from the 1860s until the mid-1880s. During an inspection of Toronto schools, Sheldon, then Superintendent of Schools in Oswego, New York, discovered the English Home and Colonial Institution's methods and materials, which were oriented "not to communicate knowledge but . . . to lead the children to take an interest in all objects that surround them; to cultivate attention, the power of accurate observation, and correct expression" (Dearborn 1925: 44). From his experiences in Toronto and his subsequent examination of the $300 worth of English Home and Colonial materials (objects, pictures, and teacher's manuals) he purchased, Sheldon rewrote the Oswego Course of Study to include the following statement on reading instruction:

The children first begin by reading words, without spelling, as printed on the board by the teacher. At first, they only learn the names of animals, or objects, or actions perfectly familiar to them, and as far as possible, these objects or pictures of them, should be presented to the children and made subjects of familiar conversation that they may become interested in them before the words are put upon the board. (as quoted in Barnes 1911: 121)

Acceptance of the word method, then, required teachers to redefine their goals of education from the reproduction of the facts within textbooks to the examination of objects from their daily experience and then the interpretation of textbook facts in light of their observations.

In 1861, Sheldon established the Oswego State Normal and Training School to train teachers to provide instruction in all subjects using the objective system. Sheldon's Normal School became immediately popular with hundreds of teachers enrolling over the next twenty-five years and graduates finding employment in most states of the Union and several foreign countries. Although the objective system created much enthusiasm within the educational community, the system was not without its contradictions and its critics. And reading instruction was at the center of the controversy. It seemed that while the word method was the official position of the methods and materials advocated at Oswego Normal, the sample lessons developed by Oswego teachers to direct reading instruction dealt primarily with the phonics method. "A few simple words were permitted to be learned as words, but in the main, the reading proceeded from the use of letters and phonetic combinations of letters" (Dearborn 1925: 80). According to the critics of the system, teachers followed these sample lessons to the letter (Cuban 1984a). Thus, two forms of reading instruction coexisted within the objective system of the Oswego Movement—a word method of vocabulary study conducted during science and social studies lessons and a formal phonics program during separate reading lessons. By 1872, the Oswego schools began to withdraw some support for the objective system (Dearborn 1925), and by 1900 the system was virtually indistinguishable from the lessons of overseers and drillmasters (Cuban 1984a).

In fact, most teachers who used the word method textbooks combined it with a phonics method—pronouncing the word, requiring students to repeat it in unison, breaking it immediately into its phonic elements, blending those sounds to its original pronunciation, and finally discussing its meaning. In this combined method, definition of the word was the main treatment of meaning, rather than a discussion of the word in relation to students' lives. In this way, the word method was rendered acceptable to overseers and drillmasters. Finkelstein (1970) summarizes her analysis of the first-hand accounts of reading instruction prior to 1880 by stating:

The evidence suggests that whether [teachers] taught in urban or rural schools in the North, South, East, or West, whether they instructed students according to the literal, syllabic, or word system, they typically defined reading as reading aloud—an activity which required the teacher to do little more than assign selections to be read, and if he chose to correct the pronunciation of his students.

THE BEGINNINGS OF THE NEW EDUCATION

Lest this account of nineteenth-century reading instruction seem overly pessimistic, it is important to remember that there were some "interpreters of culture"—to use Finkelstein's (1970) phrase—who sought to extend children's understanding of their world beyond the memorization of textbook information. In fact, their numbers increased slowly during the latter half of the century (Cremin 1961). These teachers sought to integrate literacy instruction into elementary curricula based on children's interests, needs, and inclinations; that is, to make literacy a natural consequence of children's study of their physical and social environment. What distinguishes this position most from that of contemporary school norms was the teacher's acceptance, at least in principle, of Rousseau's rejection of the doctrine of child depravity, which supplied the rationale for authoritarian didactic moral training. Rather than constrain children's curiosity and urges in order to overcome original sin and to instill a proper moral attitude, these teachers sought schools organized to foster and develop children's natural goodness. Teachers who accepted this philosophy became known as New or Progressive Educators.

Perhaps the best example of an attempt to organize an entire school district according to these atypical principles is Colonel Francis Parker's superintendency at Quincy, Massachusetts. After having studied for three years in Europe, where he became acquainted with the work of Comenius, Pestalozzi, Froebel, and Herbart, Parker was given full responsibility to examine and improve the seven schools of Quincy. In his initial report to the Quincy Board of Education in 1875, Parker commented that he was appalled that children came to school after five years of successful development in "Nature's great methods, object training, and play," only to find imagination, curiosity, and love for mental and physical activity destroyed "by dull, wearisome hours of listless activity upon hard benches." Parker began immediately to reorganize the primary grades into a "pleasant, cheerful home" by providing demonstration lessons and inservice education for Quincy teachers and by rewriting Quincy's Course of Study.

For reading, Parker proposed the word method because he believed that students should learn to read as they learn to talk, by discussing topics of interest in a supportive atmosphere. Moreover, he suggested that the language arts should be integrated—with the rules of grammar being replaced by drills for constructing sentences, writing letters, and short compositions concerning the day's events; spelling being developed through these writing exercises which stressed the children's own vocabulary; speaking being exercised through activities in which children shared their day's work; and listening being cultivated through short lectures which supported students' examination of everyday objects. Charles Adams, president of the Quincy School Board, remarked that "in all, children were being taught to read, write, spell, and think all at the same time without really taking notice" (Adams 1935: 500). The rules of grammar and phonic analysis were to be considered formally later in the curriculum after students had literacy well in hand, and they were intellectually able to embark on the detailed study of the English language. All students were to be allowed to progress through this curriculum at their own pace rather than according to their age, and slower students were expected to receive more of the teacher's attention than the students who caught on quickly.

Observers of Quincy teachers, and there were many,[8] reported that Parker's policy was indeed implemented in classrooms. The most detailed account of the "Quincy System" in practice is Lelia Patridge's *The Quincy Method Illustrated* (1880). Patridge, a former teacher and "teacher of teachers," spent much of 1880 and 1881 observing classroom instruction and recording actual lessons. Her first observation was that there was no Quincy System, wherein teachers were expected to follow one set plan as befell the Oswego Movement; rather Patridge observed unity of principle without uniformity in classroom practice. For example, in the lowest primary class, Patridge observed a lesson centered on Jumbo, P. T. Barnum's circus elephant, which had passed through Quincy by train the previous day. The lesson began with a listless group of students and a teacher's remark, "This is what I'm thinking about," as she drew a clumsy figure of an elephant wearing a blanket inscribed with JUMBO. When finished, the teacher asked "What is it?" and with that she had the attention of all her students. They replied, "Jumbo!" "Yes, that's its name, but what is it?" "An elephant," came the reply. "Tell me something about him?" To which the students responded with a long list of sentences which the teacher wrote on the blackboard to provide the text for reading and context for further discussion.

In another classroom of more advanced children, Patridge found children "talking with the pencil," a practice in which the students discussed a picture, "first with their tongues and afterwards with their pencils." The talking with the pencils did not immediately follow the conversation about the picture because then students might memorize their sentences and copy them in their essays, thus limiting the benefits of the exercise in composition and reducing the number of different texts for other students to read later. In all, Patridge describes scores of these lessons, each holding to Parker's principles.

To be sure, not all visitors to the Quincy schools were as impressed with the "Quincy System" as Patridge, and Parker met almost immediate opposition from parents and even some school board members. As early as 1877, only the second year of his tenure, the town council entertained a resolution to dismiss Parker as superintendent. Most critics questioned the possibility of students being asked to think, read, and figure without first memorizing the skills to do these tasks, and in fact, students did poorly in year-end examinations which stressed memorization of textbook facts. Other critics wondered aloud about the cost of Parker's expansion of the curriculum to include practical topics such as sewing and gardening, when so few students seemed to know valued academic information. And at times even Charles Adams and Parker showed concern about their project. Adams was shocked that at one school only one in six students could read a common book at sight (Adams 1878, as quoted in Campbell 1965) and Parker referred to the primary program as "fairly a success" and the grammar school changes as "by no means a failure" (Campbell 1965: 92). In 1880, Parker resigned his position in Quincy to accept a post as a supervisor for Boston Public Schools, and in 1883 he began to train teachers to move the child to the center of education and to unify the curriculum as director of the Cook County Normal School in Chicago.

THE PUBLIC SCHOOL SYSTEM OF THE UNITED STATES IN 1892.

One way to determine Parker's and the European influence on reading instruction is to look closely at Joseph Mayer Rice's (1893) survey of elementary schools in thirty-six cities conducted in 1892 as a prelude to a series of articles published in *Forum Magazine*. Rice, a New York City pediatrician, had become so interested in education that he had spent two years studying the "science of education" at Jena and Leipzig, and he had subsequently published several short critiques of American instruction in small weekly journals. These articles brought Rice to the attention of *Forum Magazine*'s editor who offered to sponsor Rice's first-hand appraisal of schooling from St. Paul to Washington, D.C. and from St. Louis to Boston. During his survey, Rice placed "no reliance whatsoever on reports published by school officials" (p. 2), rather he visited several classrooms in each city and interviewed over 1200 teachers. He returned in June of 1892 with notebooks crowded with observations, statistics, and illustrations detailing his tour. His articles first appeared in October of 1892 and ran for nine consecutive months during which time *Forum*'s circulation quadrupled (Cremin 1961).

In the best muckraking tradition, Rice reported that reading instruction in nearly 90 percent of the schools in these cities was outdated, mechanical, and totally ineffective. "I found the results in reading and writing language almost universally poor in schools where reading matter, at least during the first two years, consisted of nothing but empty words, silly sentences, and baby-trash, and where the time spent writing was devoted to copying such words and sentences from the blackboard or reading book" (Rice 1893: 26). Even Quincy schools did not escape Rice's criticism because they abandoned the unified curriculum established thirteen years before by Francis Parker. In all, he divided the schools into three categories based on their integration of literacy instruction with regular subject areas and whether or not students' interests were taken into consideration during classroom instruction.

Rice offered numerous examples of "mechanical reading instruction," the least effective programs, according to Rice, including the following observations from Baltimore with an overseeing teacher attempting the word method and from Chicago where a drillmaster attempted phonics instruction.

The reading was fully as mechanical as the arithmetic. It amounted simply to calling off words. Not only was there no expression, but there was not even an inflection, or a pause at a comma or a period. Nor did the teacher ever correct mispronounced words, or make any attempt to teach the pupils how to read. Before the children began to read the designated lesson, there was a ludicrously mechanical introduction, including the calling off of the words placed at the top of the page, then: "Page 56, Lesson XVIII, the Dog and the Rat. Dog, Rat, Catch, Room, Run, Smell, Wag, Jump." And then came the story. (pp. 57–58)

After entering the room containing the youngest pupils, the principal said to the teacher, "Begin with the mouth movements and go right straight through. . . . " About fifty pupils now begin in concert to give utterance to the sounds of a, e, and oo, varying their order, thus: a, e, oo; a, e, oo; e, a, oo, etc. . . . When some time had been spent in thus manoeuvering the jaw, the teacher remarked, "Your tongues are not loose." Fifty pupils now put out their tongues and wagged them in all directions. The principal complimented the children on their wagging. (pp. 176–77)

Rice characterized the second group of schools as programs in transition, wherein children's interests were considered in some, but not all classes, and the supervisors were attempting to elicit change. However, the language arts curriculum was separated into isolated subjects of reading, penmanship, and grammar. In most schools in this second group, Rice attributed lack of progress toward unification of curricula to political interference, to poor execution of reasonably progressive plans, or both, as in these examples from Rice's description of Philadelphia schools:

> The public schools of Philadelphia offer a striking example of the difficulties involved in advancing schools, when those in authority use their offices for selfish motives, whether political or other, instead of for the purpose of furthering the welfare of the children intrusted to their care. (p. 147)

> The influence exerted upon the schools by the new course of study, together with the attempt on the part of the superintendent and his assistants to break up the mechanical work without materially increasing the professional strength of the teachers, has been a most peculiar one . . . so that we find the instruction at the end of ten years of supervision neither mechanical nor scientific. What we do find, however, in very many instances, is the weakest teaching conceivable. (p. 153)

Although Rice drew roughly the same general conclusions about reading instruction in 1892 as had Finkelstein in her analysis of the one thousand journals, diaries, and reports from the 1820s to the 1880s, Rice did not blame teachers alone for the problems of reading instruction as Finkelstein does. Rather, Rice attributed blame to unconcerned parents who did not acquaint themselves with the principles of scientific education or the practices of schooling, to meddling politicians who appointed cronies as superintendents and teachers and tampered with school budgets, to uninformed and overworked supervisors and superintendents who could not possibly overcome the problems of schooling, and to poorly educated teachers who were not well versed in either content or pedagogical knowledge. While Rice cajoled parents to take an active part in their children's education, he offered three "laws" that must be obeyed if schools were to improve: (1) "the school system must be absolutely divorced from politics in every sense of the word, (2) the supervisors of the schools must be properly directed and thorough . . . the principle aim of which is to increase the professional strength of the teachers, and (3) the teachers must constantly endeavor to grow both in professional and in general intellectual strength" (pp. 17–18).

In contrast to these mechanical schools and isolated literacy instruction, Rice described the schools in four cities to be "scientific" and "progressive" in their approach to reading and education in general. These schools, which comprised Rice's third category, attempted to implement principles of Rousseau, Pestalozzi, Froebel, and Herbart in their primary programs and were often quite successful in reorganizing their grammar school curriculum to approximate unification of subjects. Rice argued that in these schools "it is no longer the textbook or the arbitrary will of the superintendent but the laws of psychology, that now became the ruling spirit of the school" (p. 21). Concerning reading instruction, Rice reported that:

In schools conducted upon the principles of unification language is regarded simply as a means of expression and not a thing apart from ideas. Instruction in almost every branch now partakes of the nature of a language lesson. The child being led to learn the various phases of language in large part incidentally while acquiring and expressing ideas (p. 223). . . . And, strange as it may seem, it is nevertheless true that the results in reading and expression of ideas in writing are, at least in primary grades, by far the best in those schools where language in all its phases is taught incidentally. (p. 224)

Rice based these comments on his testing of students' sight reading, the results of which demonstrated the superiority of the unification method as taught in Indianapolis, Minneapolis, St. Paul, and the Cook County Normal School.[9] For writing assessment, Rice collected first drafts of compositions from each child in the schools in "several cities" and compared the seven or eight thousand examples he received. He found the compositions from the third category of schools so superior to the others that he devoted the final seventy pages of his subsequent book based on the *Forum* articles to several examples.

Combining moral indignation against partisan politics, the public's fascination with science, and optimism about the future, Rice's articles in the *Forum* were generally accepted as fact (Cremin 1961). Despite educators' protests to the contrary, it was clear to most citizens after reading Rice's report that public schools were unprepared and unable to help Americans adapt to the changes caused by rapid industrialization, urbanization, and immigration. Although there was general agreement that schools needed change and that science was the best tool for directing that change, there was little agreement concerning the goals of that change. Businessmen sought vocational education and efficiency, settlement workers recommended instruction in hygiene and childcare, and "patriots" of every stripe demanded a curriculum based on American values. For the local superintendents of schools whose jobs depended on public support, the problem was one of degree—should schools be completely overhauled, abandoning the traditional emphasis on teachers and textbooks in order to adopt the New Education's emphases of children's needs and unified curriculum, or should the traditional emphases be technically fine-tuned?

2

Early Attempts
to Reform Reading Instruction

☐ In order to understand why the technical fine-tuning of traditional reading instruction ultimately won out over the unified curriculum of the New Education, it is necessary to digress for a brief consideration of the spirit of the times in which this recognized crisis in school literacy took place. During the latter part of the nineteenth century and the early decades of the twentieth, many Americans enjoyed the prosperity brought about by the industrialization of production,[1] and as a result, they became enamored with the businessmen, values, and practices that they believed were responsible for this progress. Of course, Americans had been prepared to admire these values through the implicit message of their school textbooks, particularly the McGuffey's *Reader*, but the "captains of industry" also cultivated their image as models and benefactors.

> This, then, is held to be the duty of the man of wealth: . . . to consider all surplus revenues which come to him simply as trust funds . . . for his poorer brethren, bringing to their service his superior wisdom, experience, and ability to administer, doing for them better than they would or could do for themselves. (Carnegie 1900)

The overwhelming productive change and the fortunes amassed for Carnegie, Rockefeller, Morgan, and their like directed the public's attention to how the principles of business could be applied to social institutions and private life. Schools did not escape this public scrutiny, which Callahan (1962) suggests came in a standard form—unfavorable comparison between schools and business using economy and efficiency as the criteria, followed by suggestions that schools be more businesslike in their organization and instructional methods.[2] Perhaps the introduction to William C. Bagley's popular *Classroom Management* (1911) gives some indication of how quickly educators adopted the language and practices of business: "Primarily [classroom management] is a problem of economy; it seeks to determine in what manner the working unit of the school plant may be made to return the largest dividend upon the material investment of time, energy, and money" (p. 2). One result of these comparisons was that superintendents, supervisors, and educational leaders began to consider themselves businessmen rather than scholars, thus seeking to separate decision making, curriculum development, and evaluation from the instructional practice of teachers, just as administration and labor had been in industry.

In several ways, science was also influential in the development of America's institutions. First, it provided a rational explanation for several apparent problems of industrialization. That is, science "dis-enchanted" the things of nature by relying on physical rather than metaphysical explanations. Because all things were made up of atoms—not spirits—there was little reason to worry about the soul of the environment abused by industry, especially when science and industry brought vast material progress. Additionally, when Herbert Spencer and others applied this "dis-enchanted" view of science to society (in what later became known as Social Darwinism), there thrived an emotionless explanation for inequality of standards of living (as described by Riis 1893)—it was due to the survival of the fittest, a natural consequence of the evolutionary process. The notion of natural selection was similarly interpreted for schools. For example, Spencer and his American disciple, William Sumner, suggested that schools could do little to meliorate this inequality, and furthermore they should not try. "At bottom, there are two chief things with which government has to deal. They are property of men and the honor of women. These it has to defend against crime" (Sumner 1883: 101). According to these conservative social Darwinists, the rest should be left to nature.

Second, science (understood as technology) seemed to be the driving force behind the material progress in American society. Prior to industrialization, most goods were produced locally by craftsmen and the process of production was familiar to most citizens, but with the advent of machines, production became a bit mysterious because people seemed confused concerning how machines were invented, how they worked, and how they were able to be so productive. To many, it seemed that the machines themselves were responsible for production. In education, this led to the notion that both instructional materials and methods could be designed scientifically.[3]

A third way in which science influenced social institutions was that science promised a rational explanation of any thing or phenomenon through the discovery of its compliance with the laws of nature. These laws, it was argued, are discoverable through the scientific process, involving the inductive procedures of gathering initial detailed information about a phenomenon, observing systematically the phenomenon across time, and developing generalizations concerning the observed change in the phenomenon. These generalizations or "laws" of nature allow scientists to explain the current state of nature, to hypothesize about its past, and to predict the future with precision previously unknown. As early as 1883, G. Stanley Hall in the *Contents of Children's Minds* implied that educators could improve both the methods of instruction and the contents of curriculum based on scientific inquiry into the laws of child development. Most educational research of the following four decades (that would later be accepted as scientific) (Judd 1934) used quantitative methods of data analysis adapted from agronomy and physics. This practice of science required educational experts to develop mathematical scales in order to measure accurately the change in social and mental activity directly attributable to experimental treatment. In fact, Harold Rugg (1941) describes educational research during the first two decades of the twentieth century when he began his career as "one long orgy of tabulation."[4] By 1918, E. L. Thorndyke felt confident writing:

> Education is concerned with changes in human beings; a change is known to us only by the products produced by it—things made, words spoken, acts performed, and the like. To measure any of these products means to define its amount in some way so that competent persons will know how large it is . . . and that this knowledge may be conveniently recorded and used. . . . We have faith that whatever people now measure crudely by mere descriptive words . . . can be measured more precisely and conveniently if ingenuity and ardor are set at the task. . . . This is obviously the same general creed as that of the physicist, or chemist, or physiologist. (p. 16)

The search for a science of pedagogy was directed primarily by the emergence of the new academic discipline of psychology. Although initial efforts to study the development of the mind were informed by the Darwinian notion that ontogeny recapitulates phylogeny (e.g., Spencer's and Hall's work), American educational psychology found its most influential and proactive voice in Edward L. Thorndyke. Thorndyke accepted the views of Frank Ward and William James, arguing that schools ought to intervene in the natural development of individuals to avoid past problems and to make learning more efficient. "We ought to change what is to what ought to be, as far as we can" (Thorndyke 1898: 105).

Through his experiments on animals, Thorndyke concluded that learning could be studied scientifically by the examination of outward behaviors because these behaviors appeared as the organism's total response to its environment. The mind and body were connected through a reflex arc. Learning could be explained, then, by the connection of a specific external stimulus to a specific stimulus which was stamped into the neural system of an organism that is continually rewarded for a desired consequent behavior. Thorndyke's conclusions simultaneously rejected the *Bible's* explanation of human nature through original sin and Rousseau's idea of a natural state of grace, replacing them with the notion that personality, will, or inclination—good or bad—were learned phenomena depending on how people's environment responded to their actions. That is, Thorndyke challenged the contemporary views of teaching as a battle against evil within children (the traditional approach) or as an impediment to children's natural development (the New Education). In his *Principles of Teaching*, Thorndyke (1906) asked teachers to be cognizant of the aims of education set by higher authorities in the school organization, but suggested that they "should often study how to utilize inborn tendencies, how to form habits, how to develop interests, and the like with reference to what changes in intellect and character are to be made" (p. 3).

From the results of his experiments and the work of others, Thorndyke fashioned laws of learning by which he described how knowledge was composed of stimulus and response connections and how teachers could best manage their students' learning environment in order to evoke the desired changes: (1) From associationist psychology, Thorndyke took the notion that learning is ordered and that efficient learning follows one best sequence (later to be called the law of readiness). (2) From James Watson's work, he accepted the idea that practice strengthens the connection between a stimulus and a response and leads to habit formation (the law of exercise). (3) From his own experiments, he concluded that rewards influence the stimulus-response connection; that is, positive rewards increase the frequency and the strength of the response and negative rewards decrease the frequency (the law of effect). And (4) in collaboration (Thorndyke and Woodworth 1901), Thorndyke developed the idea that education has a specific rather than a general effect on students' knowledge, thus, challenging the notion that certain subjects, such as Latin or Greek, generally facilitate intellectual development. Thorndyke and Woodworth found little transfer of training and argued generally for the effectiveness of specific instruction toward desired goals and suggested that learning can only be tested in situations similar to how the connections are formed (law of identical elements).[5]

In this general milieu of business, science, and psychology, the philosophy and radical changes required to implement the New Education seemed inefficient, sentimental, and overly optimistic concerning both human nature and learning. Indeed, Francis Parker, whom Rice had celebrated at the end of his article in 1893 as leading the ideal school, was forced to resign from Cook County Normal School in 1899 amid rising public criticism of his pedagogical principles, and he spent his last few years before his death in 1902 working in a private school connected with the University of Chicago. According to Cremin (1961), even John Dewey was concerned about the lack of rigor in many schools subscribing to the New Education at the turn of the century. He questioned whether or not teachers from these schools had a strong sense of the character of the graduate they wished to produce or a sufficient understanding of academic disciplines to truly recognize the teachable moments in children's development and experience.

Certainly, the New Education, as championed by Dewey and William Kirkpatrick generally, and by Laura Zirbes and Jeanette Veatch in reading, flourished in some schools, although "in small, mostly private schools" (Cuban 1984a: 31). Its major effect came from the ability of some traditionalists to accommodate some elements of the New Education into their methods and language without really threatening traditional educational goals. Accordingly, classrooms became less formal and rigid, but teachers and textbooks remained at the center of schooling. This ability to incorporate elements of innovative methods into traditional methods is how elementary education has appeared to change with the times while remaining essentially the same (Cuban 1984a).

Perhaps the best example of how the spirit of business, science, and psychology combined to influence education away from the New Education is found in the development and implementation of scientific management, first in industry and then in schools. Developed at the turn of the century by Frederick Taylor as a method to increase workers' productivity, and therefore industrialists' profits, scientific management required the analysis of the labor activities of the most able workers so that the best of their models could become standard practice for all workers. To begin, the able workers' procedures were studied to determine which parts were most effective, next the most effective procedure was analyzed to its parts, each part was timed in order to eliminate nonessential movements, and then, these streamlined parts were reassembled into a series of activities performed by groups of workers. These new procedures were learned in a step-by-step fashion, each worker practicing his part while being timed; and financial incentives (piecework wages) were offered to those employees who performed their tasks according to these administratively approved plans. Taylor's intentions for scientific management were by no means modest, as his remarks before a House of Representatives subcommittee suggest:

Scientific management would bring about the substitution of peace for war; the substitution of hearty brotherly cooperation for contentions and strife; of both pulling hard in the same direction instead of pulling apart; of replacing suspicious watchfulness with mutual confidence; of becoming friends instead of enemies. (Taylor 1912, quoted in Kliebard 1986: 96)

By 1910, scientific management was front-page news; in 1911, the National Society for the Study of Education's Department of Superintendents appointed the Committee on the Economy of Time in Education; and in 1914, Joseph Mayer Rice published his second book, *The Scientific Management in Education.*

THE EARLY SCIENCE OF READING INSTRUCTION

The Committee on the Economy of Time in Education was charged with responsibility to make recommendations to eliminate nonessentials from the elementary school curriculum, to improve teaching methods, and to set minimum standards for each school subject. Among the Committee members were Frank Spaulding, then superintendent of Minneapolis schools who boasted that he "landed the job by cleverly convincing the school board that he was an efficient, business-like, cost conscious administrator" (Callahan 1962) and J. F. Bobbitt, an assistant professor of educational administration at the University of Chicago and author of "The Elimination of Waste in Education" (1912). Spaulding and Bobbitt argued for a three-step procedure in order to design curriculum and instruction scientifically: First, analyze the learning environment during instruction to identify instructional methods: second, measure the effects of various methods with specifically designed tests: and third, adopt the methods that yield the highest results. Their plan is scientific management with test scores as a substitute for production, and this is precisely the approach that the committee used in their four reports published as Yearbooks for the National Society for the Study of Education (NSSE) from 1915 to 1919.

The *14th Yearbook* (Wilson 1915) begins with the results of a questionnaire returned by fifty school districts and includes four essays specifically addressing reading instruction. According to the survey, reading instruction was offered in all fifty cities which represented Northeast, Midwest, Northwest, West, and Mid-Atlantic states, and it comprised an average of 26.3 percent of the time allotted for instruction (from a high of 30.6 percent in first grade to a low of 9.6 percent in eighth grade) (Holmes 1915). Language, spelling, and penmanship (composition was not considered a subject on the questionnaire) were treated as separate lessons; and if combined, all language arts activities occupied an average of 53.4 percent of the school day.

The four essays in the first Committee report concern vocabulary, reading rate, formal testing, and literacy content, and each in its own

way offers recommendations on how teachers could improve the efficiency of their instruction. For example, in an attempt to explain how
to design and use a vocabulary test, Jones (1915) describes a method
based on the recurrence of words in ten commonly used primers as the
ideal procedure for teachers to decide where to devote their attention
during instruction. He cautions teachers to attend to the potency of words
because "it is a greater error for a pupil to miss the word 'man,' which
has a recurrent value of 633, than it is to miss the word 'cap,' which has
a recurrent value of only 104" (p. 13). S. A. Coutis (1915) offers similar
scientific encouragement in his description of an attempt to establish
average reading rates for each level. He concludes that there is a great
range of reading rates at any one grade level, but that there is a constant
rate for any large group at a given grade. "The great range of individual
variation is a sign of inefficient teaching . . . it is the duty of elementary
school to see that each individual attains this optimum degree of skill.
Otherwise he does not know how to read" (p. 46). William S. Gray (1915)
and James Fleming Hosic (1915) offer annotated bibliographies concerning practical tests of reading ability and studies of elementary school
literature respectively. Their advice seems to be that teachers must be
regular readers of scholarly journals if they hope to stay informed concerning effective means to provide reading instruction.

The second Committee report (the *16th NSSE Yearbook*, Wilson 1917)
divides language arts into essays on reading, literature, handwriting,
spelling, and grammar (again composition is not considered a subject),
each written by a different author and each packed with charts, graphs,
and tables attesting to its scientific validity. W. S. Gray (1917) describes
the importance and economy of silent reading, the most appropriate
periods of schooling in which to provide silent reading instruction, and
the methods to improve students' silent reading. Relying totally on experimental data, Gray argues that silent reading is more practical, more
efficient, and more effective than the regular regime of oral reading. To
determine the optimal times for silent reading instruction, Gray reports
the norming data from his first iteration of his Standardized Oral Reading
Paragraphs and Silent Reading Tests, and he concludes that there should
be a gradual transition from the legitimate use of oral reading in primary
grades to silent reading during the third grade. Moreover, Gray maintains
that intermediate and high school years should be devoted exclusively
to silent reading, with grades four, five, and six being most appropriate
for silent reading instruction.

In the final portion of his essay, Gray suggests necessary modifications
for reading textbooks if the new scientific emphasis on silent reading is
to be profitable. "Most of the reading texts in current use have been
organized for purposes of oral-reading instruction" (p. 31), and in order
to improve them publishers must reduce the difficulty of the vocabulary

to diminish the chance that students will stumble over words and lengthen the stories in order to provide easy and extended practice to help students increase their reading rate. Additionally, Gray offers brief suggestions for instruction—emphasize speed and purpose before assignments and prepare teacher-directed assessment to determine if students comprehended important information from the passage read.

The literature essay included in this second Committee report presents a list of the library books and reading textbooks recommended for each grade level in the courses of study from fifty cities across the United States (Munson and Hoskinson, 1917). Including only titles that were mentioned more than five times, 817 library books and 95 different reading textbooks were listed by grade level in what appears to be an inverse relationship. That is, first grade recommendations include the largest number of textbooks (38) and least number of library books (8), and this ratio switches as you move down the table to eighth grade. Library titles begin to outnumber textbooks at fourth grade. The authors caution "while this tabulation of books cannot be considered an absolute standard of practice for all schools, it is sufficiently extensive to represent the prevailing practices with a fair degree of approximation" (p. 33).

The third Committee report (the *17th NSSE Yearbook,* Wilson 1918) contains only a six-page essay on the recurrence of words in second grade reading textbooks (Housh 1918). During his study, Housh found great variability among vocabularies included in the readers, and he warns teachers that some textbooks may be incompatible with others because their vocabularies overlap so little that students who were trained in one would not be able to read the other text independently. Based on this finding, Housh recommends that teachers would find it more efficient to use only one set of textbooks for at least the primary grade years. However, he states that his most startling finding is the fact that over 50 percent of the words in any textbook appeared less than three times, "thus failing to develop drill on these words" (p. 45).

H. B. Wilson, chairman of the Committee, stated succinctly the purpose of the fourth report (the *18th NSSE Yearbook,* Horn 1919a): "Its effort throughout has been to put its recommendations in simple, direct language, that its report may constitute a handbook and guide for the use of teachers and supervisors who are interested in planning classroom procedures with due regard for both economy and efficiency in teaching and learning" (Wilson 1919: 7). In fact, each of the six essays in the report was to serve as a "clearinghouse for [published and unpublished] experimental data" on one elementary school subject (Horn 1919b: 8).[6] This fourth report, with its emphasis on instruction, was by far the most widely circulated and implemented of the Committee's reports (Cremin 1961).

Three of the report's essays were directed toward improving literacy instruction: "Principles of Method in Teaching Writing as Derived from Scientific Investigation" (Freeman 1919), which offers twenty-eight "rules" for penmanship concerning posture, stroke, development, and materials as well as tips on testing and record keeping; "Principles of Method in Teaching Reading, as Derived from Scientific Investigation" (Gray 1919); and "Principles of Method in Teaching Spelling as Derived from Scientific Investigation" (Horn 1919c), which presents forty principles for spelling instruction which Horn reduces to five "rules—pretest all words to be taught, teach only those words that students spell incorrectly, provide rigorous review, show students progress continuously, and keep up the interest." Each essay concludes with a bibliography with 22, 35, and 133 citations respectively.

Gray's (1919) forty-eight principles cover norms for student progress across grade levels, suggestions for oral and silent reading instruction, even specifications for the printing of books to maximize the economy of reading—all in twenty-six pages. Gray emphasizes that experiments had not shown one textbook method of teaching reading to be necessarily superior to all others regardless of circumstances; rather he maintains instructional effectiveness varied according to how teachers used the materials, the backgrounds of the students, and the amount of materials available for instruction. As in the second report, Gray stresses the relative efficiency, utility, and overall superiority of silent reading in developing students' reading rate and comprehension, as measured by standardized tests, and in preparing them for adult life. Although Gray acknowledges that science confirmed the importance of oral reading in primary grades, he adopts a moral tone concerning how it ought to be used: "Oral reading exercises should emphasize the content of what is read" (p. 30); "Two different types of oral reading exercises should be provided for second and third grades" (p. 37); and "The oral reading which is required in the fourth, fifth, and sixth grades should be conducted under the stimulus of real motive" (p. 37). However, Gray returns to a voice of scientific authority when he later addresses rate and comprehension: "Much reading of simple interesting materials is effective in increasing rate of reading" (p. 41) and "knowledge, while reading, that the material is to be reproduced improves the quality of the reading" (p. 41).

Clearly, Gray's essay demonstrates the Committee's intent to improve the typical patterns of instruction in public schools through the application of scientific findings, but a close analysis of Gray's words suggests that these changes were not to be at all radical. To be sure, influences of the New Education are present in Gray's rhetoric—"emphasize the content of what is read," "a real motive," and so on. However, there is no mention of the student-initiated project method (very popular at this time), learning to read incidentally while pursuing an interest, or a unified curriculum. Rather teachers were to direct formal lessons according to the principles Gray abstracted from the experiments on reading. Moreover, the goal of reading instruction is not the evaluation or use of information, rather it is the ability to retell, or to answer questions about the content of a passage—"the material is to be reproduced." While Gray recommends a considerable number of changes for the routine of reading instruction that Rice and others had found so objectionable for the preceding twenty years, Gray's use of science fits well with the fundamental conditions of traditional reading instruction.[7]

A TECHNOLOGY FOR SCIENTIFIC READING INSTRUCTION

If scientific reading instruction was to improve classroom practice by reorienting it toward silent reading and evaluation through standardized testing, then in some way Gray's modest but numerous suggestions had to penetrate the classroom door in order to alter the day-to-day interactions between teachers and students. Curiously, the Committee on the Economy of Time in Education was silent on this matter. Since many elementary school teachers were poorly educated, knowledgeable superintendents and supervisors were in short supply, and teachers already relied heavily on textbooks, one means for change was the alteration of the reading textbook. Some of these changes are suggested in the NSSE Yearbooks previously mentioned in the discussion of the Committee reports (e.g., reduction in multisyllabic words, greater repetition of words), but by far the biggest change to reading materials was the advent of teacher's guidebooks designed to direct instruction.

Although some previous textbooks had included brief directions for teachers within the student's books (Venezky 1987),[8] the number and the specificity of the new scientific maxims could no longer be accommodated in this manner. "Every author of new reading textbooks furnished generous instructions for the use of his materials. Furthermore, authors of texts which had appeared during the preceding period without detailed instructions now came forth with manuals . . . to furnish rather definitely prescribed instructions" (Smith 1965: 169). These guidebooks usually were separately bound for grade levels, provided specific information on appropriate instruction for each lesson, questions to test students' comprehension of each story, and brief explanations of the science of reading instruction. In a survey of the teacher's guidebooks from ten textbook series at this time, Smith found that the size of the first grade guidebooks ranged from 219 pages to 434 pages in length. This explicit attempt to redirect teachers' interactions with students on a daily basis through the medium of a scientific teacher's guidebook is the beginning of the basal reading materials as we know them today.

The logic of a teacher's guidebook for reading instruction makes perfect sense within the context of this time. First and foremost, the guide-book was an expression of educators' and the public's deep faith in the power of science to explain the mysteries of the universe and to solve the practical problems that they faced. Not only were the guidebooks' originating maxims the results of scientific investigations, but their entire rationale was founded on the idea that theory should direct practice; that is, that universal principles were preferable to the idiosyncratic behaviors of particular teachers and students. The directions to teachers, then, were offered as facts to be followed regardless of the social context of the instruction or the abilities and attitudes of students or teachers. If teachers would use the materials according to the directions in the guide-books, all students would learn to read efficiently and effectively. This general tone of scientific authority was important to the eventual ac-ceptance of the teacher's guidebook because its directions required teach-ers to change their previous instructional practice, and few teachers were eager to alter procedures that seemed successful previously (Cuban 1984a). But who could argue with scientific facts?

The guidebooks also incorporated principles from business. After all, the guidebooks were the explicit attempt to standardize teachers' practice according to methods found to be most productive and economical during experimentation. Certainly, the directions in the guidebooks were not as restricting as the scientific management in factories, but in a direct way, these teacher's guidebooks provided a scientific management of reading instruction. They separated the planning of instruction from the practice of instruction, they implicitly quantified the goals of reading instruction as standardized test scores, and they provided objective criteria for judg-ing the adequacy of a teacher's performance through comparison of practice with prescriptions for practice.[9] These effects required a dis-tinction to be made between the roles of teachers and administrators during reading instruction. While teachers remained the primary instruc-tors, someone at a higher level of authority had to select the instructional goals and plans from among the many sets of basal materials available; someone had to ensure that teachers followed those selected plans. Thus, the teacher's guidebook contributed to the formalization of roles and rules for the business of teaching reading.

If we look at the crisis in reading instruction as a problem of provoking more scientific reading instruction from classroom teachers, as the read-ing experts of this time apparently did, then it is easy to understand the teacher's guidebook as a direct application of Thorndyke's psychology. The guidebook was the correct stimulus that would evoke the appropriate response from teachers. Because the guidebooks provided a daily lesson plan for instruction, they afforded sufficient opportunity for teachers to practice scientific instruction. Teachers' subsequent reward for making this desired connection would come from the satisfaction in seeing their students learn to read faster and better, achieving higher scores on tests because, as demonstrated in the Committee reports, some of the tests were based on basal content and procedures. In short, the guidebook provided an appropriate environment to ensure that teachers learned to teach scientifically.

In fact, Thorndyke's laws of learning were also incorporated in all of the components of basal materials. For example, the law of readiness was demonstrated in the rough sequencing of the directions for instruction in the mechanics of reading which corresponded to children's levels of development and prepared them for subsequent learning. Because silent reading is an individual task not conducive to the organization of reading instruction solely around group drill, individual seatwork had to be invented to provide students with sufficient practice (law of exercise) to make desired connections. Accordingly, publishers supplied workbooks with passages and questions and directions for drawing and construction, which quickly became a necessary part of daily instruction. Finally, the law of identical elements was met through specified instruction on the utilitarian aspects of reading—silent reading for the author's message—instead of oral reading instruction which promised transfer to purposeful reading at some time later or a generalized effect on students' oral language.

In summary, basal reading materials met the expectations of a public and educational community enthralled with business, science, and psychology as they tried to find a remedy for the apparent crisis in reading instruction in schools at the turn of the century in order to prepare students for the rapid changes of an industrialized America. Moreover, basal materials required little additional tax expenditures, bypassed or effectively bolstered weak supervision by providing the criteria and materials for scientific reading instruction, and taught poorly educated teachers to provide that instruction. Promoted as the results of scientific study, basal materials promised that all children would learn to read well if teachers and students would simply follow the directions supplied in teacher's guidebooks. And although the contents of these directions would change a bit from time to time during the next sixty years, the rationale for and the format of basal reading materials were set by the spirit of the first two decades of the twentieth century.

3

The Rise of the Reading Expert
and Commercial Publishers

☐ In 1908, Edmund Burke Huey, the first American to summarize experiments on reading instruction, offered a challenge to the newly emerging group of reading experts: "After all we have thus far been content with trial and error, too often allowing publishers to be our jury, and a real rationalization of the process of inducing the child with the practice of reading has not been made" (p. 9). In this statement, Huey implies that there was little direction in teachers' use of reading textbooks beyond their own opinion and that their instructional practice could be greatly improved if it was subjected to scientific scrutiny. Twenty years later, reading experts were certain that they had the answer to these problems in basal reading series, the proper technology for introducing scientific reading instruction into public schools.

> One of the most potent factors in spreading the results of research is through a well-prepared set of readers and their manuals (p. 106); yet we find teachers still instructing children as they themselves were taught, absolutely ignorant and oblivious that science had discovered for us truths and that little children are entitled to the benefits of these discoveries. (Donovan 1928: 107)

Right from the start reading experts and commercial publishers recognized that they needed each other if reading instruction was to be rendered scientific. The experts needed the basal publishers to spread the results of their research and their opinions concerning the implica-

28

tions of that research across the country. That is, if most teachers already used textbooks as the stimulus for their instruction, then no amount of talk from reading experts was going to change their practice. Reading experts who were intent on implementing a science of reading instruction had to change that stimulus from teacher-directed use of reading text-books to scientific guidebook-directed use of basal reading series.

Commercial publishers needed reading experts to gain legitimacy for their materials which they hoped to sell to as many customers as possible. If science was to be the order of the day, then reading experts who conducted experiments would appear as the authors of the basal series. And commercial publishers have been very successful in employing lead-ing reading experts from major research universities across the country. For example, Ernest Horn, Arthur Gates, and William S. Gray were basal authors beginning in the 1920s and 1930s; Emmett Betts, David H. Russell, and Paul McKee in the 1940s and 1950s; Guy Bond, Albert J. Harris, and Russell Stauffer in the 1960s; Kenneth Goodman, P. David Pearson, and Robert Ruddell in the 1970s; and Richard Allington, Donna Alvermann, and Robert Tierney in the 1980s.

The problem facing these and other reading experts since the late 1920s was how to induce teachers, who were already using textbooks according to their own ideas, to follow the scientific directions included in teacher's guidebooks. Most reading experts set at this task with a vengeance, using all the tools at their disposal. And over the next sixty years, the control of reading instruction passed from teachers' hands to those of the reading experts and commercial publishers as basal use became more and more prevalent in elementary schools across America— so prevalent, in fact, that it often seems that the materials are using teachers rather than teachers using the materials.

EXPERT OPINION

NSSE Yearbooks

The National Society for the Study of Education's Committee on Reading began to report on reading instruction, materials, and research in the 24th NSSE Yearbook (Gray 1925) and continued to report at twelve-year intervals until 1961.[1] Directed largely by William S. Gray, who chaired the Committee until his death in 1960, these reports chronicle reading experts' efforts to place the teacher's guidebook at the center of elemen-tary school reading through what has been considered the most influ-ential source on the policy of reading instruction (Smith 1965). In their first report, the Committee was careful not to recommend one set of books over another because they lacked sufficient scientific data to sub-stantiate their opinion. This was not for lack of trying since experiments comparing various textbook methods for silent reading and phonics were characterized as inconclusive in reviews of literature published in the *18th* (Gray 1919) and *20th* (Theisen 1921) *NSSE Yearbooks*. However, by making this statement the Committee did give its implicit endorsement to the use of any basal which met their five simple criteria for acceptable materials. Among their statements concerning interesting stories and balance between skill and comprehension comes the first reference to the teacher's guidebook—"there should be a brief, simple, efficient manual" (Gray 1925: 185)—which was to direct teachers' and students' use of the basal materials.

In their second report (*36th NSSE Yearbook*, Gray 1937), the Committee on Reading was much less reserved in their endorsement of the use of basal materials over the teacher-directed instruction of the New Education or the traditional use of supplemental readers based on teacher's judgment. For instance, Gray (1937) challenges "experience-based" instruction by detailing its benefits and limitations in comparison to the use of "commercially prepared materials," and he concludes that "prepared materials are, as a rule, more skillfully organized and are technically superior to those developed daily in classrooms. Because they follow a sequential plan, the chance for so called 'gaps' in learning is greatly reduced" (pp. 90–91). Gray makes similar remarks concerning reading instruction during intermediate grades, suggesting that the thoroughness with which the basals are prepared makes them much more efficient and effective than teachers' or students' choices. Finally, Gray implies that teachers should not deviate from the arrangement of lessons in the guidebook if they wish to be scientific in their instruction. "[The stories] may be read in the order in which they appear in the book. This is not only a safe procedure, but also one that reduces the possibilities of unexpected handicaps in progress" (p. 102).

A second essay in the *36th NSSE Yearbook* deals with teachers' use of basal materials, and it is perhaps most remarkable because it was prepared by a sub-committee which included representatives from the three leading publishers of basal reading materials—Ginn, Scott, Foresman, and Macmillan. While other NSSE yearbooks had been devoted exclusively to instructional materials (*19th NSSE Yearbook*, Whipple 1920 and *20th NSSE Yearbook*, Whipple 1921), this was the first time that publishers were formally represented on an NSSE committee. To begin their report, the subcommittee presents its interpretation of an informal survey of elementary schools in which they estimate that 90 to 95 percent of all teachers used basal readers during their reading instruction. Accordingly, the subcommittee directed its comments to the appropriate use of the materials during reading instruction. Among their suggestions, they warn teachers to avoid using different sets of basal readers, library books, or supplemental materials within and across grades because the vocabularies do not match sufficiently well to allow beginning readers to practice their reading independently. Finally, the subcommittee suggests that "individual and local groups of teachers are increasingly unlikely to improve upon the product of professional text-book-makers" (p. 211). Using words like "perfected to such a degree," "can be used effectively," and "systematic" to describe basal readers and "seldom justified," "scattered," and "aimless" to characterize teachers' independent instruction, there seems to be little room for interpretation of the Committee's position on basal use; moreover, they suggest that basals are indeed a closed, but complete system for beginning reading instruction.

By comparison to the *36th Yearbook*, the subsequent reports are absolutely tame in their support of basal use according to the teacher's guidebook. But each is firm in its support. For example in the *48th NSSE Yearbook* (Gates 1949) contributors suggested that "improvements in the construction and use of basal reading materials have contributed appreciatively to the improvement of primary grade reading instruction" (Hildreth 1949: 56); "the teacher is referred to the manuals accompanying whatever readers are to be used. . . . it should be remembered that as a rule, pupils gain most from the use of a reader when the selections contained in that book are taught as the authors of the reader intend them to be taught" (McKee 1949: 131); and "the teacher who attempts to prepare substitutes for basic readers ought to make the substitutes better than the readers available" (Whipple 1949: 152). In fact, in *Innovations and Change in Reading Instruction*, the *67th NSSE Yearbook* (Robinson 1968), the Committee acknowledges that the only thing that won't change in reading instruction in the 1970s and 1980s is that "basal readers will continue to be used . . . " (Wittick 1968: 124).

Textbooks

Professional books on reading and methods textbooks for training teachers also carried the message that scientific reading instruction depended on the use of basal reading materials according to the directions in the teacher's guidebook. In *Supervision and Teaching of Reading*, Harris, Donovan, and Alexander (1927) suggest that teachers follow the publishers' suggestions for instruction because "the authors of the newer readers have grouped the materials for instructional purposes" (p. 446). They list fifty-two different sets of basals which they regard as acceptable for teachers' use. Later textbook authors became much more emphatic in their endorsements and clear about *what* was to direct instruction.

> The advantage of orderly procedures in reading instruction is such that few, if any, teachers can serve all pupils well by incidental or improvised reading methods. . . . The well planned basal-reading

> systems presented by experienced textbook publishers have many advantages. . . . A detailed study of the manuals of basal-reading systems is the first step to learning how to teach reading. (Durrell 1940: 22)

> A basic reader is really one part of a 'system for teaching reading.' This system includes the basic books themselves, the workbooks that go with them, and the teacher's manual, which tells what to do with the textbooks, what to do with the workbooks, and also tells all the other activities a teacher should go through in order to do a complete job teaching reading. (Dolch 1950: 319)

Most recent reading methods textbooks offer three reasons for their relatively unqualified support of teachers' reliance on basal materials: the reading selections are of high quality, the teacher's guidebooks offer suggestions for comprehensive and systematic instruction, and the materials are based on scientific investigations of the reading process (Shannon 1983b). In six textbooks randomly selected from the thirty textbooks available with copyright dates after 1980, authors demonstrated their commitment to basals by their allotment of page space and the language they used during their descriptions of the materials. For example, these textbooks included between eleven and thirty-six pages of explanation with between six and nineteen reproductions directly from basal materials to illustrate points, but they alloted only between 0 and 1.5 pages to discussions of comprehending the main idea while reading. Moreover, terms like "best routines," "developed by teams of reading experts," and "objective tightly structured and logically ordered" in the rationale for basal use can leave little doubt in prospective teachers' minds concerning how to conduct their reading instruction. Perhaps the most extreme example of a methods textbook's endorsement of basal readers and their use is Robert Aukerman's (1981) *The Basal Reader Approach to Reading*, in which he describes the fifteen leading sets of basal reading materials for 333 pages.

Even when some reading experts believe that recent basals lag behind the rapid expansion of scientific information concerning reading instruction, they continue to recognize that they are reliant on basals to spread this new information. For example, consider the stance of the contributors to *Learning to Read in American Schools: Basal Readers and Content Texts* (Anderson, Osborn, and Tierney 1984), the proceedings from a conference held by the Center for the Study of Reading funded by the United States' National Institute for Education, who suggest that "currently there would appear to be a lag as long as 15–20 years in getting research findings into practice" (p. x). However, rather than call for a large-scale educational program to provide prospective and in-service teachers with this scientific information so that they can change their reading instruction accordingly, the contributors argue that because teachers follow teacher's guidebooks "it stands to reason therefore that researchers who wish to have scholarship influence practice ought to give high priority to interacting with publishers" (p. ix). In this way, recent professional books as well as most methods textbooks advocate using basals according to a teacher's guidebook as the appropriate vehicle for scientific reading instruction.

Journals

The articles published in professional journals suggest more complexity in reading experts' support for basal readers than do the NSSE yearbooks or methods textbooks. During the late 1920s, through the 1930s, and into the 1940s with few exceptions, journal articles provided unquestioned advocacy of basal use over other methods. By the late 1950s and the early 1960s, however, it became apparent to some reading experts that the balanced relationship between experts and basal publishers had tipped in favor of the publishers and that profits rather than science directed the contents of basal series in their increasingly more frequent revisions. Yet within the logic of the science which they sought to employ and behaviorist psychology, these experts lacked many alternative means to express their dissatisfaction, except to attempt to beat basals at their own game by proposing alternate, "more scientific" methods which would produce greater gains in test scores. Perhaps an example of the articles published in one journal will illustrate this point.

Consider the articles which appeared in *Language Arts*, the National Council of Teachers of English's elementary school journal which has published continuously since 1924, making it an ideal candidate for this illustration and the oldest American journal devoted exclusively to literacy instruction.[2] Until 1984, *Language Arts* published three types of articles concerning basal readers: analyses of content of the anthologies and other basal components, descriptions of teachers' use of these materials, and arguments concerning appropriate methodology.[3] Although these themes are represented in most volumes of the journal, the analyses of content type of articles were most prominent during the first two decades of publishing when reading experts were eager to explain the contents of basals to teachers and other school personnel and to prepare teachers for changes to come in the materials. For example, Gray (1933) comments on the possibility of "blocs, strikes, and even religious and racial persecution" without proper attention to the selection of readings in basal anthologies, and Emmett Betts (1939), E. L. Dolch (1936), and Arthur Gates (1936) discuss the appropriate vocabulary for basal readers. By the thirtieth anniversary issue of *Language Arts*, the use of basal readers had become so commonplace that Gerald Yoakam (1954) challenged reading experts to find the most effective balance "between basal, curricular, recretory, and corrective reading" (p. 430) in order to prepare students for the future.

During the most recent three decades of publishing, contributors to *Language Arts* have stressed the other two themes in their articles. In 1958, Ralph Staiger, then director of the International Reading Association, presented the results of his survey of 474 school districts from forty-eight states and Hawaii, which suggested that 99 percent of the school districts responded that teacher's guidebooks directed reading instruction in elementary classrooms. By 1972, A. Byron Calloway, then director of the University of Georgia reading clinic, rejected all nonbasal forms of teaching reading because Georgia teachers would simply not use them. In a similar way, most descriptions of teachers' practice suggested that reading experts and publishers had convinced most teachers to follow the teacher's guidebooks.

In the third type of articles, the experts' ambivalent support of basal use becomes apparent as many contributors to the journal compared students' achievement as determined by standardized tests following instruction from an alternative, "more scientific," nonbasal method of reading instruction and after guidebook-directed instruction (e.g., Frame 1964; Hill and Methot 1974; Veatch 1967). On every occasion the results provided unintended support for teachers' continued use of basals because contributors found no statistically significant differences between the alternate and the basal method. Although the contributors suggest that this is good news and that teachers now have little to lose in trying the new method, within the scientific logic on which their studies were based, the opposite is also true. Teachers could and do infer from these reports that they have little to gain from such a switch.

The largest program comparing methods for teaching reading is the United States Office of Education's Cooperative Research Program in First-Grade Reading Instruction, which included twenty-seven separate studies conducted in various regions of the United States and which was discussed in several *Language Arts* articles (e.g., Bond 1966; Fry 1966; Sheldon and Lashinger 1968, 1969, and 1971). Initiated by Donald Durrell, an author for Ginn and Company, this project sought to determine once and for all which method was superior to all others in terms of raising students' scores on several standardized tests of letter and word recognition, oral reading, and sentence comprehension. Of the twenty-seven studies, twenty-one explicitly compared nonbasal approaches—initial teaching alphabet, phonics, language experience, and so forth—to "the basal reader method" during an entire year of instruction (1964–1965). Four of the studies were designed to test various methods of supervision of teachers using basal materials, and two studies used primarily experimentally designed materials.

In a summary of results from all the studies, the coordinators of the project, Guy Bond and Robert Dykstra (1967), concluded that the only clearly superior alternative in comparison to a strict regimen of guide-book-directed instruction was a basal plus formal phonics approach. All inconsistent superiority concerning comparisons on various test scores was described as being "not of much practical significance in terms of actual reading achievement." In short, the largest research project ever conducted on reading instruction, without really trying to, confirmed scientifically what reading experts had said unconditionally before the 1960s, and which publishers had said all along—guidebook-directed reading instruction was as good or better than any alternative. The results of the First Grade Studies had a significant impact on instructional policy at the time and are still used today to dismiss alternative nonbasal methods of teaching reading in the United States (Anderson 1984).

This positive ambivalent support for basals is also evident in James Hoffman and Nancy Roser's recent special issue for the *Elementary School Journal* (1987), which includes essays on the history, selection, and use of basal readers. The tone of the issue is set in Jeanne Chall's introduction in which she attempts to quell any dissenting views concerning the importance of basal readers by suggesting that much of criticism is directed toward teachers' use of the basal rather than at the basals themselves and by proclaiming "and we know that basal readers are perhaps the most effective way to improve students' reading achievement" (1987: 244).[4] Most contributors to the issue are more subtle and often seem apologetic in their support.

For example, Duffy, Roehler, and Putnam (1987) report that their attempt to help teachers use guidebooks more rationally ended in frustration because "neither the content nor the instructional design (of basals) offered much structure for decision making" (p. 360) and that teachers complained about the time and the effort it took to render basals substantially useful according to the researchers' definition. Yet, Duffy and his co-authors conclude that "the solution does not lie with abandoning basal textbooks" because "all teachers appreciate the guide" (p. 362). In the same issue, Farr, Tulley, and Powell (1987) conclude their essay, which enumerates the foibles of textbook selection committees who are frequently duped by extravagant claims and promises from publishers and often appear compromised by the lavish gifts publishers provide, with the statement "by and large, however, American educators are fortunate to have available such a large quantity of high quality textbooks and other materials to support reading curricula" (1987: 281).

If these articles in *Language Arts* and *Elementary School Journal* are typical of other journals' treatment of basal materials and their use, then despite the occasional critical essay, reading experts present a favorable review of basals and perhaps a slightly less charitable view of teachers' use of this technology in their journal reports. Their tone is always conciliatory and when surrounded by the large quantity of paid advertisements in the most popular reading journals, they suggest to readers of these journals that basal use is necessary for scientific reading instruction.

Professional Organizations

As some reading experts became concerned about the scientific validity of basal materials in comparison to current scientific knowledge about reading and instruction, one way in which commercial publishers maintained their scientific credibility with school personnel was through their participation in the International Reading Association (IRA). Established in 1947 with six members, the IRA boasts a current membership of over 72,000 teachers, administrators, and reading experts. The publishers' influence on the IRA has come in three forms. First, most of the presidents and many of the members of the Board of Directors since its beginning have also been basal authors or associated with basal publishers. Second, publishers often cover the expenses of their authors and consultants to speak at local, state, regional, national, and world IRA conferences. Frequently local, state, and regional conferences must rely on publishers' generosity in order to secure speakers because the groups cannot afford speakers' fees by themselves. Moreover, the publishers are always well represented at these conferences by sales personnel who emphasize the connection between the scientific rhetoric of the speaker and his or her association with their basal materials, even if the speaker does not mention this connection.

The presence of sales personnel with their basal wares also supplies much needed capital for conferences and IRA organization in general. According to Kenneth Goodman, a former president of the IRA, this third type of publisher influence was responsible in one year for a $300,000 surplus of receipts over expenses after an annual conference (Goodman, Shannon, Freeman, and Murphy 1988). In return for this money supply, publishers seek certain license in advertising their materials and time and space at the conferences. Most recently, this financial connection between the publishers and the IRA has become even more direct as the IRA Board sought and received sustaining contributions from publishers of as much as $5,000 a year. In return for their "donation," publishing companies receive special membership status in the IRA.[5]

Thus, wherever teachers and other school personnel turned in search of information on elementary school reading instruction since the late 1920s—whether they consulted research yearbooks, read methods textbooks, perused journals or professional books, or attended conferences— they found reading experts advocating the use of basals according to the directions in teacher's guidebooks in order to render reading instruction more standard and scientific. Even when they witnessed infrequent complaints about the contents of the basals, teachers were told and continue to be told that only minor technical modifications are needed to renew basal readers' service as the science of reading instruction.

DISSENTING VOICES

Not all reading experts favored the association of scientific reading instruction with the growing influence of basal reading materials during the twentieth century, and their opposition was presented on theoretical, practical, and moral grounds. Perhaps four examples will provide the flavor of this small but persistent dissent. First, Laura Zirbes, whose career spanned six decades (publishing articles from 1918 to 1961), began by developing textbook materials (1927) and stating "major recommendations which rest upon fundamental (experimental) studies are and should be the directing influence in the reorganization of current practice" (1928: 13). However, for the last thirty years of her work she promoted the ideals of the New Education in reading programs. Her critical review (1937) of the *36th NSSE Yearbook's* "abiding and unquestioning faith" that science would uncover the laws of reading instruction demonstrates her disdain for the Committee's attempt to place the teacher's guidebook rather than the teacher and child at the center of reading instruction. According to David Moore (1985), Zirbes refused to work with William S. Gray on several publishing ventures. Additionally, she (1949) supplied the first controversy in an IRA publication when she recommended research projects, language experience, and individualized reading lessons as superior to guidebook-directed instruction. To do otherwise, according to Zirbes, is to deny students' and teachers' individuality.

Claude Boney, then superintendent of schools in New Jersey, also took exception to the *36th NSSE Yearbook* and the Committee on Reading under the direction of William S. Gray (1938: 1939). Boney found three overriding problems with basal materials: library books had better content; basal materials were too expensive ($1.37 per pupil in 1934), and worst of all, the guidebooks did not ensure thoughtful instruction. Rather than supporting good teaching practices of the best teachers and improving the instruction of the worst, as publishers maintained, Boney argued that following the guidebook supplanted good teaching and poor teaching alike, replacing them with bland lessons ill fit for any individual student. After defending individualized reading methods with testimony that students' test scores had not suffered under their use, Boney (1938) offers two reasons for the longevity of basal readers.

> There are teachers and administrators who do not know how to rely entirely upon extensive reading for developing the reading skills. . . . And lastly, the publishing of a popular set of basal readers is, perhaps, the most lucrative pedagogical business. Estimates by

bookmen of the royalties of popular sets are from ten to five hundred thousands of dollars. It is hard for those who receive these sums to give a true evaluation of sets of books. (p. 137)

Rudolph Flesch (1955, 1981), whom Venezky (1987) characterizes as a public relations specialist, offers a different set of criticisms of the pervasiveness of basal materials and the scientific basis of the methods most suggested. All tolled, he blames basal publishers and authors for the literacy crisis he says now faces America. In an emotional plea, Flesch (1955) charged that the directions in teacher's guidebooks of the leading basal series were responsible for students not learning to read properly and that for those fortunate few who did happen to learn to read at some later date, he maintained that they would not enjoy reading like their parents because they had missed the golden years in which to appreciate children's classics. While some of the emotional tone remains in his second book—basals are listed as the "Dismal Dozen" because they contain "window dressing phonics"—Flesch (1981) cites considerable research on reading and instruction which he suggests scientifically demonstrates the superiority of a phonics-first method for beginning reading instruction. He implores parents to force schools to drop basal readers and to adopt an early phonics program that will enable students to read literature by the end of first grade.

Beginning from an exactly opposite set of assumptions than Flesch, Kenneth Goodman (1974, 1979, 1986), a former basal author and previous president of the IRA, combines theoretical, practical, and moral concerns to argue that basal readers prevent students from becoming literate because "literacy in this competency-based, highly structured, empty technology is reduced to a tight sequence of arbitrary skills. The teacher becomes a technician, part of a 'delivery system' " (1979: 663). Furthermore, he calls for "either replacing or turning around (basals)" (1986: 363) in order to bring reading instruction more in line with a modern interpretation of the ideals of the New Education. In his most recent writing (Goodman, Shannon, Freeman and Murphy 1988), Goodman questions the over 100 to 1 ratio in school budgets which is spent on basal materials and paperback library books ($350,000,000 to $3,000,000 in 1985), the questionable marketing practices of basal publishers including lavish parties and free trips for representatives of teachers and students from large districts and state agencies, and the connection between basal publishers and professional organizations (e.g., IRA and the National Council of Teachers of English).

SURVEYS OF ELEMENTARY SCHOOL READING INSTRUCTION

Despite these persistent, but peripheral, objections, by 1960 all but a small minority of elementary school teachers had accepted the authority of reading experts and basal publishers when they taught reading. This fact is verified in three large surveys of American reading instruction funded by the Carnegie Foundation. First using questionnaires collected from 1,847 school districts across the United States, observation in 65 school districts from all fifty states, and interviews with 2,000 classroom teachers, 225 principals, and 271 central administrators, Mary Austin and Coleman Morrison (1963) concluded that "the basal reader was used as the major instructional tool in reading by almost every system in the field study" (p. 21). Austin and Morrison found that teachers seldom used supplemental materials, that they followed the teacher's guidebooks "slavishly" (p. 224), and that most students spent their time completing workbook assignments. In short, they lamented that the basal series were in fact the reading program in most schools.

Anthony Barton and David Wilder (1964) sought to trace sources of scientific information which school practitioners relied on to make decisions about reading instruction. Using the medical profession as a model, they posited a top-down flow of information wherein research scientists would publish the results from their latest studies in professional journals which in turn would inform school policy and classroom practice. During a survey of all reading experts with doctorates in the United States and of principals and teachers from 221 school districts, Barton and Wilder found something altogether different. In summarizing their data, they characterized reading experts as "marginal researchers" who relied on the research and opinions of a very few people in order to form their positions on reading instruction. In this research void, Barton and Wilder were not surprised to learn that high percentages of school personnel (over 70 percent) believed that basal reading series were essential for reading instruction, that teacher's guidebooks were based on scientific truths, and that elementary school teaching was a profession. Moreover, they found that over 90 percent of all teachers used basal materials and teacher's guidebooks on all or most days in the year. They were quite disturbed to find that this regular use of basals favored children from upper- and middle-class homes.[6] They conclude that "teachers think they are professionals—but want to rely on basal readers, graded workbooks, and teachers manuals, and other materials prefabricated by the experts" (p. 382).

Chall (1967) examined the research, materials, and practices of beginning reading instruction. Among her many conclusions, she found that publishers often unduly influenced how children were taught to read by convincing school administrators which basal program to purchase for their schools and by providing "propaganda" for their product during in-service programs once the basals were in place. Rather than blame the publishers (whose actions Chall accepts as part of good salesmanship), she questions the training school personnel received at colleges of education which would allow them to be duped so easily—

"doubtless these people have been oversold by the publishers. However, if they never actually look at the research evidence, the job of overselling cannot have been too difficult" (p. 307).

By 1977, according to 11,918 teachers' self-reports, the percentage of teachers teaching reading according to the directions in teacher's guidebooks was over 94 percent (EPIE 1977). Since that time, a number of observational studies involving fewer teachers over greater lengths of time have confirmed the results of the early surveys. For example, in a series of studies Dolores Durkin (1978–79, 1981, 1983) argues that teachers use basal materials consistently, but that they skip certain parts of the suggested lessons to keep their classes running smoothly. Rebecca Barr (1986b) agrees that teachers do in fact make decisions concerning which parts of a basal to use during reading lessons, but that all of their instructional actions are influenced by the suggestions in the teacher's guidebook. Even when class size is reduced to below a 20 to 1 student/teacher ratio, teachers still find the directions of the guidebook compelling and 90 percent follow these suggestions faithfully (Shannon 1987). In fact, teachers now define their instructional role during reading lessons as that of being the monitor of students as they work their way through the basal series (Duffy and MacIntyre 1980).

Clearly, reading experts and commercial publishers have been successful in exerting their authority on classroom practices, a fact to which these quantitative and qualitative studies attest. The authors of *Becoming A Nation of Readers*, the most current state-of-the-art report on reading instruction, report that the most consistent research finding in the field of reading over the past twenty-five years has been the one stating that teachers conduct their reading instruction according to the directions in teacher's guidebooks in a nearly uniform way and that students spend their reading lessons using basal materials (Anderson, 1984). When teachers do deviate from the directions as Durkin (1983) found, typically they delete the basal author's few suggestions to move beyond the anthology and workbooks, suggestions that teachers apparently consider unnecessary for students to proceed successfully to the next basal lesson. What is left for students is a dulling tedium of reading groups, skill work, and tests; and what is left for teachers is a profession without professional activity.

Summary

American reading instruction before the twentieth century was really quite different from today; in fact, it seems accurate to say that really there were no good old days when it comes to reading instruction. Before the Great War, instructors came primarily in two forms—overseers who gave assignments to memorize spelling words, poems, or textbook content and then expected students to learn the information on their own, and drillmasters who led students through a series of exercises to help them memorize these facts. Reading textbooks were arranged to facilitate these types of instruction regardless of whether their authors thought the letter, syllable, or word was the appropriate place to start instruction. A very few teachers—interpreters of culture—attempted to extend students' understanding of their world through their reading instruction. These teachers worked directly from students' everyday experience in order to help them grasp the meaning and the significance of what they were expected to learn. In a survey of public schools in 1892, Joseph Mayer Rice found a nine to one ratio of overseers and drillmasters to interpreters of culture. Labeling this circumstance deplorable, Rice suggested that contemporary reading instruction could not prepare students for the rapid changes of industrialization, urbanization, and immigration.

This perceived crisis in reading instruction (it was really the instruction which existed for over two hundred years in American schools) was attributed to underfunded schools, poorly educated teachers, and overworked supervisors. The solution to this reading problem was the same

41

as it was for other institutions which were criticized at the time—superintendents and efficiency experts would promote a greater use of business practices, the application of scientific procedures to discover the laws of appropriate action, and the organization of learning within the maxims of behaviorist psychology. Accordingly, reading programs became formal bureaucracies with supervisors planning procedures and goals and teachers executing those plans in order to reach those goals, standardized tests objectively and scientifically arbitrated which students were making the most progress under what program, and teacher's guidebooks presented the proper stimulus to evoke the correct response from teachers while they used the basal technology during their reading instruction.

In this way, reading experts, basal publishers, and school personnel sought to overcome the paucity of good children's literature, the poor education of teachers, and the problems of teacher supervision through anthologies of stories and essays considered scientifically appropriate for students of various reading levels, a scope and sequence of objectives reflecting child development and skills necessary for children in order to learn to read, detailed directions for instruction and practice activities to meet these stated objectives, tests to determine whether the objectives have been met, and marking systems to enable teachers, supervisors, and parents to keep track of student progress. Together, these materials comprise the basal reading series, a technology developed to standardize the teaching practices in elementary schools according to the science of reading instruction.

After reading experts' prolonged and multichanneled attempt to promote teachers' use of this technology, the standardization of reading was virtually complete by 1960. Consistently over the last twenty-five years, surveys and observational studies have demonstrated not only that teachers use basal materials religiously, but that they rely on the teacher's guidebook to inform themselves about the science of reading instruction and that they define their instructional success according to the parameters established in the materials. The predominance of basals has even worked its way into state legislation as twenty-two states have statewide textbook adoptions, and at least in Texas, teachers are subject to a $50 fine if they are caught teaching without an approved textbook.[7]

However, of late, some reading experts have begun to feel uneasy about the marriage of the science of reading instruction with the commercial publishings of basal materials. Although only a very few advocate abandoning the use of basal readers during reading instruction, they recognize the power of the market economy in the development of this technology of reading instruction. That is, whenever new scientific discoveries are made that contradict the directions or materials already incorporated in the basal series, publishers are reluctant to change their product that already has a proven track record in the marketplace.[8] Rather, publishers are more likely to assume the rhetoric of the new discovery in order to attract new customers without changing the traditional basal programs.[9] Thus, several reading experts find current basals to be well behind the latest scientific information and consider them to be more a product of the 1920s and 1930s than the present.

In this first part, I have attempted to establish that American reading instruction is a historical, social construct; that is, it has changed across time according to contemporary social, political, and economic circumstances. Moreover, I sought to explain that since 1920 reading experts and commercial publishers have exerted more power than school personnel and the public during the negotiations of what is to be considered the proper definition of reading and the appropriate way to teach reading. This unequal participation seems to have rendered school personnel dependent on the dictates of reading experts and basal publishers as demonstrated in the fact that over 90 percent of elementary school teachers rely on teacher's guidebooks and basal readers during 90 percent of their instructional time. And although the experts and publishers may be well-intentioned in their use of this undue power, in the second section of this book I attempt to unravel the consequences of these unequal negotiations for teachers and students.

□PART II□

The Role of the Teacher

4

Why Teachers Use Commercial Reading Materials

☐ Most elementary school teachers use commercial reading materials during most of their reading instruction on all or most days during the school year. Moreover, teachers find support for their actions in most reading experts' efforts to inform school personnel concerning scientific and professional reading instruction. However, teachers' heavy reliance on basal materials and teacher's guidebooks makes outside observers of reading instruction skeptical concerning teachers' professionalism. Professionals control their work and make critical judgments about what procedures and materials are most suitable for specific situations (Lortie 1975). By this definition, teachers do not appear to be professionals during their instruction because they apply the guidebook directions and assign basal materials regardless of their instructional circumstances, apparently ignoring the range of students' abilities and interests.[1] Yet, while teachers stridently covet the status associated with the label "professional," few teachers seem willing or able to move away from the major obstacle to their attaining that status—the use of basal materials according to the teacher's guidebook.

To understand this paradox, it might seem simply necessary to talk to teachers about why they act so apparently irrationally. In this commonsense approach, researchers assume that teachers are fully aware of why they rely on the guidebooks and basals so often and that they are willing and able to articulate all the contributing factors. These assumptions may prove faulty, and there is some controversy over whether teachers are accurate in their assessment of their work because observations rarely confirm teachers' statements about what they do during reading instruction (Duffy 1982; Rosenshine 1978). Perhaps, a more productive procedure to discover why teachers rely on commercial materials is to treat teachers' thoughts and beliefs about their work as sincere and to seek to identify situational constraints—administrative expectations, tradition, curricula—which prevent teachers from acting on their convictions (Sharp and Green 1975). In this way, teachers' subjectivity, factors within their control, is considered legitimate and important; and objective factors, those beyond teachers' control, can be identified in order to develop a more accurate picture of teachers' work.

AN EMPIRICAL STUDY

To date, few researchers have attempted the commonsense, the more productive approach, or any other method to find out why teachers rely so heavily on basals. However, without an answer to this question, the reading instruction provided for most children in the United States cannot be fully understood or changed in any substantial way should it prove inadequate. In an attempt to discover an answer, I sought to identify subjective and objective factors that might contribute to teachers' dependence on commercial materials during reading instruction in one large school district which had served as the model for the Right to Read program in Minnesota.[9]

To investigate teachers' subjective reasons, I developed a questionnaire and follow-up interview to test four hypotheses offered without benefit of specific research, to explain teachers' behavior. Durkin (1978–79) implies that teachers do not take sufficient time to make rational instructional decisions concerning individual students because they are unwilling to manage their time more constructively (Hypothesis 1: Teachers are not involved in their reading instruction). Austin and Morrison (1963) suggest that teachers act as if they believe that basal materials do all the work during reading instruction because they follow the guidebook "slavishly" and use few supplemental texts, leaving students to work their way through the basals page by page (Hypothesis 2: Teachers believe commercial materials can teach students to read). Barton and Wilder (1964) hypothesize that teachers might justify their instructional behavior by referring to the putative scientific validity of the format of the materials and the directions in the teacher's guidebooks (Hypothesis 3: Teachers believe that the materials embody scientific truth). Finally, Chall (1967) found teachers who thought ("incorrectly") that their administrators expected them to follow the teacher's guidebook and to use all the materials during their instruction (Hypothesis 4: Teachers think they are fulfilling administrative expectations when they use these materials). To elicit subjective reasons beyond these hypotheses, three open-ended questions which asked teachers to describe why, how, and when they used basals during their reading instruction were included in both the questionnaire and interviews.

Because teachers do not participate in reading instruction uninfluenced by others, I sought objective factors which provided opportunities for and constraints on teachers' instructional behavior in the organization and policy of the reading program in the school district. To gather this information, I solicited administrators' and reading teachers' opinions on the four hypotheses in appropriately altered survey instruments. Moreover, I informally observed administrators', and administrators' and teachers' interactions concerning reading instruction during one school year and read the district's published policy documents to obtain the official position on reading instruction. I mailed 591 questionnaires to classroom teachers, reading teachers, and administrators (with over an 81 percent return), held over thirty formal interviews, observed eight formal meetings and dozens of informal meetings of principals, central administrators, and teachers, and read over three hundred pages of policy documents.

Objective Factors

At the time of the study, the school district was served by twenty-six elementary schools with student enrollments between 371 and 676 in the first through sixth grades. Each school was directed by a principal, at least one reading teacher, and between fifteen and twenty-five classroom teachers.[3] According to all administrators and faculty who were interviewed, the school staff was organized hierarchically, with the superintendent and the Board of Education at the top and classroom teachers at the bottom, with a director of elementary education, a supervisor of elementary curricula, a reading coordinator, principals and reading teachers in between. The reading coordinator described the roles and organization of personnel most succinctly:

> Central administrators are responsible for decisions. This is a large district and the coordination of efforts is a big job. . . . Principals are instructional leaders in the (school) buildings. They are responsible for carrying out district policy. They carry it out and interpret it to an extent. Reading teachers are there to help coordinate the building program. . . . They explain the policy to teachers and facilitate the classroom instruction. . . . Teachers are the strength of the program. They provide the instruction on the basic skills of reading that all children need to know. . . .

A textbook selection committee comprised of the reading coordinator, "several principals, reading teachers, classroom teachers, and parents" reviewed the reading curriculum on a five-year cycle. One member reported: "The charge to the committee was to select a basal that matched our needs. This meant, we looked at how they taught the skills, then the goals of our program became the scope and sequence of objectives in the basal." According to the reading coordinator, "once the basals were selected a review of the scope and sequence of objectives is impossible before the next textbook adoption is considered." *Notes on Pacing Instruction,* a district policy publication, affirmed the followers' role for teachers in setting goals for instruction—"teachers cannot change the pupils, or the materials, or the scope and sequence of skills. . . ." And the district's *A Course of Study to Guide Reading Instruction* stated that all teachers would follow a single scope and sequence of goals for all students because the skills program provided by the basal series "includes all those skills which are generally considered to be essential. . . ."

The district was officially committed to the idea of mastery learning and to teaching for skill mastery before proceeding to the next set of skills. The practical definition of mastery learning among teachers was quite different than the theoretical work of Benjamin Bloom (1976). All twenty-six teachers who were interviewed stated some paraphrase of "mastery means a student reaching the critical score on the book tests." That is, a student was considered to know a skill only after he or she answered 80 percent or more of the questions correctly on the tests supplied by basal publishers. In order to reach the critical score on these tests, teachers were expected to and did follow the directions in the teacher's guidebook, by their own admission, in order to ensure "the continuity of the program across classrooms, grades, and schools."[4] The reading coordinator explained that "because of the size and mobility of the student population, it is necessary to use one set of goals and procedures."

Since the basal materials set the goals, procedures, and criteria for success in the reading program, the process for the selection of the basals was particularly important to all participants in the reading program. Officially, the process involved representatives from all groups except students, and it consisted of several months of study of recent reading research literature, formal presentations by publishing company representatives, and finally, detailed study of three sets of materials, first by the committee and then by classroom teachers at schools.

> The selection process was an open one. Anyone had an opportunity to provide input. . . . We did not take a democratic vote. But we did try to reach consensus. [The basal] was the most acceptable program to everyone concerned. (The Reading Coordinator)

Teachers felt quite differently about the procedure. During interviews, over 80 percent of the teachers informed me that the district had used the previous editions of the same reading series for ten years prior to the study and had just selected it for a third time.[5] Apparently, these teachers considered this less than coincidental because there had been several complaints about the series prior to the last selection process yet the same series was selected again. One teacher who had worked for the last selection committee explained:

> First, teachers were underrepresented on the committee and those who were on the committee were selected by administrators. Second, I feel, and others agree with me, that the major decisions were made before the committee was called together. We did pick the same materials as the last time, you know. Most teachers would like a choice of materials, so that they can match students to the materials.

Although *A Course of Study to Guide Reading Instruction* listed consideration of individual differences as a high priority for the program, *Notes on Pacing Instruction* limited those provisions to one aspect of instruction. Since the students, materials, goals, and procedures for instruction were set by the single basal selected for use during reading instruction, teachers could only adjust their reading instruction through their pacing of their delivery of the content. However, eighteen of the twenty-six teachers interviewed suggested that there was pressure within their schools to cover a certain amount of materials during specified marking periods. The main source of that pressure was the reporting system devised to keep track of students' progress centrally. In this system, "(teachers) are required to record the criterion test scores and the dates on file cards. These cards are reviewed every other week by (our reading teacher). Sometimes the principal looks at them and announces whose class is doing well over the loud speaker."[6] One teacher summed up the other eighteen teachers' feelings:

> Obviously, if we have to turn in test scores every two weeks, students are supposed to make some progress every two weeks. You know and I know that students don't progress regularly by the calendar. It comes in fits and spurts, and sometimes it doesn't come at all for a long time. But try telling that to the central office.

The central administrators were aware of students' progress generally throughout the district. And most students in this district did make progress. The director of elementary education reported that according to the last standardized achievement tests over 80 percent of the third and sixth grade pupils read at or above grade level according to national norms. But some schools in the district were identified as "slow schools" because their biweekly reports failed to show progress consistently. Since these schools served students and families with largely similar economic and social backgrounds to the other schools, the supervisor of elementary curricula hired reading experts from a local university to work with the teachers on their pacing and brought in a consultant from the basal publisher to make sure that the teachers were using the materials properly.

Subjective Factors

In light of these findings concerning the district's organization and policy for reading instruction, it was not surprising to find that the 445 classroom teachers who responded to the questionnaire believed foremost that they were fulfilling administrative expectations when they used the basal according to the teacher's guidebook (Hypothesis 4). This opinion held across the forced choice items, the open-ended why question (64 percent), and the interviews. Some teachers even ridiculed me for considering any other rationale for their use. The typical response to this question was a quick "because I want to keep my job." The strength of teachers' acceptance of this hypothesis seemed based on two aspects of the program—resentment over the textbook selection process which several teachers considered inadequate for their purposes, and anxiety concerning the test-driven reporting system which was used to monitor students' progress. During interviews, all twenty-six teachers mentioned one or both of these factors during their discussion of the why question, and on the questionnaire 78 percent mentioned one or both.

However, teachers agreed strongly (but not quite as strongly) that basal reading materials can teach reading (Hypothesis 2) and that the materials are based on scientific fact (Hypothesis 3). With the exception that teachers believe that anyone could do their job just as well, teachers did consider themselves involved with their instruction (Hypothesis 1). In a first analysis, classroom teachers' opinions were compared with those of twenty-three (of a possible twenty-six) reading teachers and eighteen (of twenty-six) principals. There was little disagreement concerning Hypotheses 1 and 2 on the questionnaire, each group agreed moderately that these factors contributed to teachers' reliance on basals. However, administrators were more likely than either classroom or reading teachers to agree strongly that basals were based on science (Hypothesis 3). Although both reading teachers and principals agreed that administrators expected teachers to follow the guidebooks, the strength of their agreement did not approach that of the classroom teachers on this matter. In response to the open-ended why question, 35 percent of the reading teachers and 55 percent of the principals suggested that teachers should use the materials because the materials can teach reading.[7]

At first glance, it seems obvious that Hypothesis 4 explains teachers' reliance on basals in this district. The analysis of both subjective and objective factors points toward administrative expectations as the appropriate conclusion. Administrators offered Hypotheses 2 and 3 as justification for their expectations, implying that the materials can teach reading because they are based on scientific investigations of the reading and instructional processes. Administrators reasoned that if teachers followed the directions in the teacher's guidebook, then all students would master the basic skills of reading. And in fact, a closer look at classroom teachers' responses suggested that teachers shared this opinion.

First, over 25 percent of the teachers offered Hypothesis 2 as the only rationale in response to the questionnaire's "Why do you use the basal materials," and another 14 percent offered Hypothesis 2 as a second rationale. That is, nearly 40 percent of the classroom teachers acknowledged the basal series' instructional powers. Moreover, when asked during interviews what they would do if administrators did not require guidebook-directed instruction, 84 percent of the teachers offered Hypotheses 2 and 3 as their justification for continuing to use the basals in much the same way, with only one slight deviation—they would include more sets of commercial materials in order to meet students' individual needs while remaining within the parameters of the original program.

Beyond the controversy over the textbook selection and the reporting system, teachers and administrators agreed concerning the goals and procedures of appropriate reading instruction. And my initial attempt to understand why teachers rely so heavily on commercial reading materials ended with a question instead of an answer: Why do administrators and teachers believe that commercial reading materials can teach students to read?

A TECHNOLOGICAL IDEOLOGY

In an attempt to answer this second question, I sought an explanation that would relate school personnel's thoughts about their reading instruction to the way in which others view their work. Although elementary grade teachers work with children and their product is not necessarily tangible, as a group they are not that different from other workers in the United States. At the very least, they are subject to the same social, economic, and political influences as other citizens. Basing my work loosely on Georg Lukacs's Theory of Reification (1970), I developed a model of reading programs that suggests that teachers' and administrators' beliefs about basals and instruction can best be understood as a natural development of the "rationalization" of everyday life in Western society. Lukacs argued that, in order for countries to prosper materially, all parts of their society, both public and private, must be made or considered predictable in order to reduce the risk of capital investment. Accordingly, along with standard laws, social norms, and other institutions, schooling became organized and its success measured by business and scientific principles.

For Lukacs, the process of rationalization could be explained by the relationship of reification, formal rationality, and alienation. My point in developing such a model of reading programs based on a dialectic among these three factors is to demonstrate that school personnel's apparently irrational opinions and behaviors about commercial reading materials during reading instruction are really not irrational at all but deeply ingrained in the fabric of American culture.

Reification

Reification is the treatment of an abstraction as a concrete object or immutable procedure. In my study, school personnel reified reading instruction as the application of commercial reading materials, rather than engaging in any of the other possible ways of teaching reading. This act is neither willful neglect of their work as Durkin (1978–79) clearly implies nor the mistaken interpretation of administrative expectations as Chall (1967) contends—it is the way that these teachers and principals defined their work. "It's the way it is" in American reading instruction. An explanation of why this happens is not so straightforward as some reading experts would like.[8]

School personnel have confused the commercial materials' contribution to students' reading development in a way similar to the way in which others confuse the contribution of capital to the commercial production of any commodity. In both cases, what are really transactions among people (past and present labor) are understood as transactions among things. For example, in a factory the machines appear to do the work, rather than the craftsmen who designed the routine, the tool makers who developed the machine, and the worker who keeps the current run of production flowing smoothly. Or, in an office the word processor and computer seem to run the operation, not the programmers, data processors, secretaries, and clerks. In my study, rather than a collaboration among author, teacher, and student, reading instruction was understood as an exchange between basal materials that have the power to teach and students who can absorb that instruction. Thus, administrators and teachers are not being irrational when they over-rely on commercial reading materials, they are acting quite rationally within the logic of reified instruction.

This general confusion about commodities, I believe, underlies school personnel's conception of reading instruction. Basal reading materials are at their core simply commodities produced to make the largest possible profit for their publisher.[9] The psychological, intellectual, and physical distance from the basal production, coupled with the everyday confusion over the properties of commodities and the dazzle of advertising, leaves school personnel with the illusion that the basal materials applied according to the guidebook's directions—not the labor of authors, artists, typesetters, and so on—can teach students to read. Of course, no participants in my study used these terms to describe their work, but their actions, the examples they offered from their classroom practice, and their comments on the materials pointed in this direction. Consider, for example, teachers' reluctance to leave the closed logic of their reading program even to entertain other methods of meeting students' needs under hypothetical circumstances during interviews. Moreover, their response to problems which fell outside the parameters of the single available basal series was to find more basal materials to remedy the situation. And then, compare all this to the nonreified reading instruction of Herbert Kohl (1974) which suggests "that all you really need to help someone learn to read and write is something to write with and something to write on" (p. 163).

When asked during interviews to justify their beliefs from the questionnaires, most respondents offered the scientific nature of the materials as the basis for their materials' instructional powers. In fact, teachers' and administrators' responses were significantly correlated concerning the questionnaire items dealing with instructional capabilities of the materials (Hypothesis 2) and their scientific base (Hypothesis 3). This deference to science also fits Lukacs's (1970) explanation of rationalization of Western society because it is based on two generally accepted ideas: an understanding, or rather misunderstanding, of science as technology and a use of science as the major form of evaluation of social institutions or customs.

Aldous Huxley (1963) and C. P. Snow (1959) commented on the gulf between the scientific community and everyday life, each suggesting that people who are not directly engaged in scientific investigations do not understand the human process of scientific inquiry. Rather than recognizing the intuition and effort involved, most people see only the material results of scientific endeavors—increased quantity, standard means, and efficiency (Habermas 1970). Science does not appear to them as human activity, but as an object or unalterable process which seems to make life easier. In other words, most people reify science as technology. During my study, this meant that school personnel treated the directions in teacher's guidebooks as the science of reading instruction, making the basal series the technological solution to the problems of teaching students to read.

The reification of reading instruction as the application of commercial materials and of the scientific study of reading as the format and directions of those materials has important consequences for school personnel: they become uninformed spectators of the scientific, instructional activity of the basal series, and they see no need or way to alter the course or content of their reading instruction except to change the type of materials they use. Rather than consider long-range goals for their school's reading program, they let the basals set those goals. Rather than puzzle over the logic of the skill sequence and direction, they push ahead because "you can't understand it, you can only follow it" (Duffy, Roehler, and Putnam 1987: 362).

A second consequence of the misunderstanding of science is the increased role that measurement and efficiency play in our daily lives. In earlier times, most social institutions were judged primarily in ethical and moral terms; people wondered if an institution was just or good. However, with the rise of industrialization, with its requirement that all aspects of life become predictable, more and more public and private matters have come under the scrutiny of scientific principles (Heilbroner 1985). Currently, it seems that everything is judged in terms of quantity and efficiency. In fact, science is considered the sole method with which to define and solve the problems we face. For example, the problem of equal opportunity for employment is defined as the number of various groups in the workplace, and scientific studies are conducted to isolate factors that encourage or impede achievement of that balance.

In a similar manner, the administrators in my study attempted to solve the problem of teaching large numbers of students to read by defining reading as verified competence in the basic skills of reading (i.e., achieving certain scores on tests) and by requiring all teachers to use the technology of reading instruction. Of course the problem could have been addressed in any number of other ways—from relying on college educated teachers to devise their own plans to embedding literacy instruction in students' pursuit of their own interests. However, these alternatives emphasize teachers' and students' subjectivity too much, if predictable progress is the goal, and therefore, these alternatives seem beneath consideration.

Reification, then, explains that three social forces are working when school personnel believe that commercial reading materials can teach. First, when they reify reading instruction, teachers and administrators lose sight of the fact that reading instruction is a human process. Second, their reification of the scientific study of the reading process as the commercial materials means that their knowledge of reading and instruction is frozen in a single technological form. Third, school personnel's reification of science requires that they define their work in terms of efficiency of delivery and maximization of students' gains in test scores.

Formal Rationality

This use of science to reorganize reading programs explains in part administrators' interest in teachers following the directions in teacher's guidebooks and teachers' recognition in my study that they were expected to use them. These school personnel were simply describing their respective roles in a scientifically arranged organization in the same way that any worker who is employed in a large modern corporation would explain his or her work. In other words, they all have internalized a system of thought that Max Weber (1964) called formal rationality in his attempts to describe the impact of capitalism on everyday life. Formal rationality is distinguishable from traditional uses of reason because the former, like science, excludes all consideration of values and moral questions. Reorganization of production processes according to the principles of formal rationality emphasizes the development of the most efficient means with which to maximize the production of each worker in a coordinated unit rather than according to the "qualitative, human, and individual attributes of the workers" (Weber 1964: 99).

Several organizational theorists maintain that schools are "loosely coupled" organizations based on public confidence in the certification of teachers, students, and curricula (e.g., Lortie 1975; Meyer and Associates 1978; Weich 1978). John Meyer and Brian Rowan (1978) report that within schools which enjoy public confidence "structure is disconnected from technical (work) activity, and activity is disconnected from it effects" (p. 79). "Education comes to be understood by corporate actors according to the 'school rule': Education is a certified teacher teaching a standardized curricular topic to a registered student in an accredited school" (p. 294). Although the notion of "loose coupling" may be accurate when schools are examined in total (particularly high schools), it does not explain the organization of sub-systems which fail to inspire public confidence. Reading instruction has been traditionally and remains such a sub-system in American elementary schools (Flesch 1955, 1981; Kozol 1985; Huey 1908; Postman 1979; Rice 1893).

In order to regain public confidence in reading programs schools seek mechanisms to assure the public that their standards are high and that their methods are efficient and effective. This search originally lead school administrators and reading experts to Fredrick Taylor's scientific management system (which Lukacs considered the culmination of bringing science to social institutions) at the turn of the twentieth century as I explained in chapter 2. Those who might doubt that it still has considerable effect on reading programs even today should consider carefully the implications of Richard Anderson's (1984) statement in *Becoming a Nation of Readers*, a national report on reading instruction funded and endorsed by the United States National Institute of Education—"America will become a nation of readers when verified practice of the best teachers in the best schools can be introduced throughout the country" (p. 120). "Best" and "verified" are defined as instructional practices which produce the highest test scores consistently, and "introduced throughout the country" sounds very similar to Taylor's calls for standardization of labor practices for industry.

The adaptation of scientific management to reading instruction has a profound effect on reading programs. First, it reduces the goals of reading instruction from the development of students who love literature and can use literacy effectively in their daily lives to a standard identifiable level of reading competence (Artley 1980; Brown 1978). Second, the process of reading is segmented into discrete skills so that increments of progress can be identified across grades (Winograd and Smith 1986). Third, objective tests replace teachers' judgment concerning whether or not a student is to be considered literate because teachers' judgment is unpredictable (House 1978; Rivlin 1971). Next, a search is made for the most efficient instructional means to move students through the levels of reading (Huey 1908; Rosenshine and Stevens 1984). And finally because few teachers would originally choose this organization for their instructional behavior, a formal hierarchy of authority is established within reading programs.

According to the survey, observations, and policy documents, each of the five elements of formal rationality was apparent in the reading program in my study. The goals of the program were clearly stated as students' mastery of basic skills. Although love of literature was mentioned in the district goal statements, it was listed as goal 23, while mastery of basic skills was listed third. The remainder of the program was organized to deliver this goal most effectively. The official definition of reading for the program was simply the summation of the "basic skills which are generally considered necessary." The basal scope and sequence of skills distributed these basic skills within and across grade levels to ensure systematic progress. Officially, teachers were unable to deviate from this sequence—"teachers cannot change ... the scope and sequence of skills" (*Notes on Pacing Instruction*).

Perhaps the strongest pieces of evidence of formal rationality in the reading program I studied were the attempts to standardize practice and the monitoring system of pupils' progress. There was an acknowledged separation of roles in the program—administrators were to set policy and teachers were to follow that policy. Policy was translated into practice through a single set of basal materials, selected by a committee of administrators, reading teachers, parents, and classroom teachers. Several teachers interviewed were suspicious of the motives of these classroom teachers ("looking to get promoted") or their independence ("they're hand-picked"). Actually, once the basal was selected, the publishers did the actual planning of goals and instruction because according to district policy every teacher was supposed to pursue one set of goals through one sequence using one set of basal materials according to the directions in the accompanying teacher's guidebook. "The systematic use of (the basal series) ensures the continuity of the program" (one principal). Although administrators could not tell which skill each teacher was covering on any particular day, they could predict with some certainty where most students would be in the basals on any given week.

While the biweekly monitoring system kept track of student progress through the curriculum, it also kept track of teachers' instructional practices. Because the chapter and book tests were tied closely to the basal series (Johnson and Pearson 1975), administrators could determine if teachers were following district policy and were applying the materials successfully. Two-thirds of the teachers interviewed expressed concern about the pressures which the monitoring system applied to their instruction. Since pace was all that teachers controlled in the program, this pressure to maintain a steady pace suggests administrators' intent to deliver a predictable reading program for their public.

The attempt to implement this formal rationality was not without controversy. Teachers questioned the fairness of the textbook selection process and the monitoring system, the most obvious point of contention. But some teachers also resisted the more subtle forms of control. For example, a third of the teachers interviewed related a story about a group of third grade teachers' conflict with the Reading Coordinator over the scope and sequence of skills at their level. These teachers requested that certain skills be postponed until later grades because most of their students failed the criterion-referenced test several times before "actually memorizing the answers on the multiple choice test well enough to get 80 percent correct without really knowing what they were doing." The Reading Coordinator rejected their request because "with proper instruction any objective can be reached. It's not the objective's fault when students fail a test." These teachers appealed to an author of the basal series, who reported that the skills would be "moved back in the curriculum" in a later edition upon the request of many teachers. Armed with this information the teachers renewed their request, to which the Reading Coordinator replied that when the new edition was adopted the skill could be taught later, but until that time the curriculum was to remain unchanged. "One change would bring a flood of such requests."

Alienation

Alienation is the process of separation between people and some quality assumed to be related to them in natural circumstances. This process can be consciously recognized (subjective alienation) or beyond the control of the individual (objective alienation). If teachers were related naturally to the totality of reading instruction—supplying the goals, means, and assessment of their work, for better or worse—prior to the advent of basal materials, then alienation becomes a relevant concept for discussion of current reading programs. In chapters 1 and 2, I have tried to build a case for this argument, suggesting that the drillmasters, overseers, and especially the interpreters of culture (later the careful practitioners of the New Education) did in fact control the totality of reading instruction as they defined it. In this sense, the organization of reading programs according to the principles of formal rationality and school personnel's reification of reading instruction as the application of commercial materials suggest that the teachers in my study were alienated from their reading instruction.

First, the fact that school personnel's roles, by their own accounts, did not include goal setting or directions for regular instruction means that teachers were objectively separated from their work. This form of alienation from their work seemed to prevent school personnel from recognizing that their organization of the reading program was but one of many possible arrangements that would accomplish the task of teaching children to read. This may be the lack of involvement about which Durkin hypothesized as her explanation of teachers' actions during reading instruction. However, it's not that teachers are uninvolved that is the problem—it's that they cannot be totally involved that explains their behavior. Like the workers in factories (Noble 1983) and in offices (Howard 1985), the teachers and administrators assumed that their present circumstances are "just the way it is."

This sense of fatalism was apparent in many teachers' answers to the open-ended questions on the questionnaire and during interviews. Although teachers complained loudly about the textbook adoption process and the monitoring system, very few teachers and no administrators challenged the separation of planning of the reading program from the process of teaching. By accepting their roles with only minor complaint, teachers acknowledged that they were subjectively alienated from their work. Granted this is modest evidence for such a conclusion, however, teachers' statements during the survey must be taken in the context of their reification of instruction as the following of the directions in the teacher's guidebook. That is, teachers defined their work teaching students to read primarily through the application of basal materials in order to lead students to mastery of the basic skills of reading. Since the district's program was so organized, it is unlikely that many teachers would describe themselves as alienated from such a program. Teachers' strong agreement with the item, "Anyone can teach reading in the same way I do," lends support to the notion that teachers saw themselves as interchangeable parts in a large technology. Only when you step outside of the reified instruction to see what reading instruction could be, is it apparent that teachers are separated from the totality of their work. Within this logic, reification decreases the likelihood of teachers recognizing this fact.

In summary, my model of reading programs is based on the notion that school personnel understand and describe reading instruction in a manner similar to how workers in other occupations discuss their work because they all are subject to the same societal influence—the process of rationalization. The model suggests that school personnel believe that commercial reading materials can teach because they have reified reading instruction as commercial materials. This illusion of instructional power is supported by school personnel's reification of the scientific inquiry concerning reading instruction as the directions for lessons in teacher's guidebooks and by the use of formal rationality in the organization of reading programs. According to the model, this combination of reification and formal rationality alienates school personnel from a central feature of their work in elementary schools—the development of students' literacy. Thus, administrators expect the use of commercial reading materials and teachers use them because they have internalized the process of rationalization; and like other workers, they apply its business and scientific principles to the task of teaching reading. From this point of view, it would be more startling if teachers and administrators thought reading instruction was a human transaction rather than an interaction between objects—commercial reading materials and students.

5

Recent Attempts to Refine
Reading Instruction

☐ As I found in my original study, administrators require and teachers use commercial materials during most of their instruction because they believe that the scientifically valid materials are the direct technology developed during research on reading and instruction. According to the model I developed to explain this phenomenon, school personnel's thoughts and actions are really an expression of the rationalization of social institutions in twentieth-century America, a process intent on bringing predictability into the economy and one used to legitimize school systems in the public eye. The results of this process for reading instruction are an elementary school staff who reduce all possible ways to teach reading to the application of basal materials and who run as a bureaucracy to maximize the bottom line of reading instruction—test scores—and a teaching faculty who are separated from the goals and means of their work.

In that first school district, teachers' application of the directions from basal guidebooks was sufficient to accomplish its goals of raising students' test scores and consequently regaining public support for the school district. However, in many other districts around the country, this typical pattern of teaching has not produced a supply of verifiably literate students adequate to ward off public concern (*A Nation at Risk* 1983). In these districts, school administrators attempt to refine reading instruction by controlling the use of teacher's guidebooks even further in order to make teachers' use of the materials predictable throughout a school

61

district and, in some cases, student progress calculable. I studied three such school districts in order to test the utility of my model in explaining school personnel's thoughts and actions in these recent attempts at reform. In each district, reification, formal rationality, and alienation combined in quite different ways to explain the changes in typical reading instruction. The first study demonstrates a contradiction between the egalitarian rhetoric of advocates of refinement and their desire to use reading programs to legitimize their schools for the public. The second study provides some breadth to the previous remarks I made about the effects of rationalization on teachers and their instruction. And the third suggests conflict between teachers and administrators concerning ideal reading instruction.

MASTERY LEARNING

Mastery learning is a recent method of reaching the attractive, but illusive, goal of teaching everyone to read at school. Advocates maintain that this universal literacy can be reached if schools reorganize themselves in order to meet three assumptions whereby: 1) reading is segmented into separate skills which are arranged in a curriculum hierarchically according to difficulty; 2) teachers engage in a teach/test/reteach/retest instructional cycle; and 3) students are given unlimited time to learn one skill before progressing to the next skill in the hierarchy (Block and Burns 1977; Bloom 1976). "Provided that mastery learning is placed productively within its larger instructional setting, and provided that serious attention is paid to predictable problems in implementation, mastery learning will result in impressive improvements in the quality and effectiveness of instruction" (Levine 1985: x). Because of its much reported success (e.g., Hyman and Cohen 1979; Levine and Associates 1985), mastery learning procedures have been incorporated in elementary school reading instruction across the United States.

However, if policy statements from the Chicago Public School District, home of the most celebrated mastery learning literacy project of the early 1980s (Arricale 1983; Levine 1982), are indicative of the translation of theory into classroom practice, mastery learning and reading instruction may not be as compatible as advocates maintain.[1] In a study of published statements made by Michael Katims, then director of the Chicago Mastery Learning Reading Program (CMLR), and his associates and superiors, I found a contradiction between Chicago school administrators' interest in teaching all students to read through mastery learning and their attempts to assuage public concern about their reading program by verifying students' reading competence at various intervals throughout their school careers.[2] Basically, the pressure on teachers to have their students meet these time constraints negated the mastery learning assumption of unlimited time to learn to read.

As suggested in the model, school administrators seek to regain public confidence in schools through the documentation of student reading progress. Mastery learning with its optimistic philosophy and its ideology of tight control of skill development through curricula and test-driven instruction is an attractive alternative. By designing a reading program around the teach/test instructional cycle, schools believe they can produce test results that will certify that all students have become masters of reading before they graduate, relieving public concern about school literacy (Cohen 1981). Moreover, school administrators come to echo the businessman's complaint that low teacher productivity is the culprit concerning ineffective reading instruction and call for improved supervision and technology as the solutions to this problem. Chicago was particularly vulnerable on this point since its average test score for reading hovered around the 25th percentile of national norms. As the statements below attest, Chicago administrators adopted mastery learning for utilitarian reasons as well as for its philosophy.

> The system is based on a theory that has been successful in other areas, a system that has as its explicit goal the achievement of reading success for all students. (Smith and Katims 1979: 201)

> Each summer Chicago girds itself for its two regularly scheduled disasters; the Chicago Cubs and the newspaper publication of reading test scores. Though the overwhelmingly complex and arduous task for improving the Cubs is readily comprehended by the Chicago citizenry, they do get testy from time to time about those scores. (Smith and Katims 1979: 199)

The solution to the problem of low scores was obvious at least to superintendents Joseph Hannon and later Ruth Love. What was needed was a new reading curriculum and a specially designed district developed set of instructional materials and tests to direct teachers' actions in the delivery of that curriculum. This new technology was to meet the first two assumptions of mastery learning—a sequential set of skills and a teach/test instructional cycle. However, the goal to assuage public concern presented problems for the realization of the third assumption—unlimited time to learn.

Since the turn of the century, schools have typically segmented instructional time in several ways—daily class periods, marking terms, grade levels, and types of schools (e.g., primary, intermediate, and so forth). Each segment limits the time for reading instruction, and as school administrators become more concerned about demonstrating students' reading competence at each interval, the criterion for passing from one stage to the next becomes more rigid, limiting the time students have to master parts of reading curriculum. In turn, this failure to meet the third assumption of mastery learning—unlimited time—distorts the reading program's ability to meet the first two assumptions.

First, because even the slowest students must become masters of reading within established time limits, reading goals are set at a minimum level and are restricted to easily definable and testable skills. With this act, some reading goals usually associated with mature reading ability are excluded from the mastery learning curriculum because they are time consuming to teach, many students may not be able to master them, and they are difficult to test. In Chicago, "mastery learning instruction in elementary reading is not practical if 50 to 60 percent of the pupils cannot achieve mastery by the time of the formative test" (Katims and Jones 1981: 4). Ultimately, this reductionist view subverts Bloom's (1976) notion that mastery learning would enable students to reach a "higher level" of learning heretofore denied them because of poor instruction on basic skills. If all students are to reach mastery within set time limits, basic skills are all that are possible.

Second, as time and demonstrated competence become more precious, the instructional cycle becomes distorted as tests take precedence over teaching. Because each skill must be tested separately in order to ensure mastery and instructional time is limited, a greater number of tests with a lesser number of test items—most in multiple choice format—are needed to demonstrate student competence. Since reduction of the number of items reduces the test's reliability (many of which are already of questionable validity: Johnson and Pearson 1975; Kavale 1979), there are many false positives in test results, leading to students being passed on incorrectly through the curriculum only to be discovered as beyond their depth on a later test. As the Chicago administrators suggest below, time and tests figure prominently in the CMLR program.

> In Chicago, promotion to high school has been limited to progress through the matrix of reading objectives. The promotion policy specifies that pupils who have not mastered 80 percent of the objectives in each of the 13 reading levels shall be retained in elementary school an additional year. (Hannon and Katims 1979: 122)

> Even a more vexing problem was the citywide dilemma that students were not making appropriate progress through the matrix of objectives and tests. . . . So a system of administratively imposed expectations or goals and accompanying monitoring procedures were instituted. (Katims and Jones 1981: 3)

> Under the program on the other hand, the teacher instructs the entire class, the pupil then works on related activities, and then a

formative test determines what the pupil does next. (Katims 1979: 11)

Theoretically, mastery learning requires each teacher to design and develop his or her tests and instruction for both initial and subsequent attempts at each skill (Block and Burns 1977; Bloom 1976). This procedure, although time consuming, is essential in order to ensure that teachers are clearly aware of the instructional goals and the formats in which those goals will be tested (Knight 1981; Mueller 1976). However, schools attempting to legitimize themselves through their reading programs cannot afford this luxury of time, nor can they rely on teachers' subjective procedures because they need predictable judgment to present to the public. In this context, reading instruction becomes a management problem—how to allocate resources (teachers, students, and materials) to produce the maximum number of certified literate students within the designated time. Since all students are expected to learn the same skills, Chicago administrators developed a packaged set of objective tests, books, and instructional lessons as the only acceptable instructional practice throughout the district. In the following five statements Chicago administrators describe the need and method to control teachers' behavior during reading instruction.

Under traditional teaching, students are usually placed in reading groups. The groups primarily spend time reading. There is no real instruction in reading. (Katims 1979. 32)

Moreover, teachers had constant problems in preparing, storing, grading, and organizing the diversity of appropriate instructional materials each day. (Katims and Jones 1981: 6)

Providing materials that were centrally developed and successfully field tested would 1) reduce greatly the time needed to prepare and organize materials; 2) require little inservice time; 3) be economical for schools in Chicago and elsewhere to implement; 4) avoid some of the problems associated with exclusive reliance on basal reader instruction; 5) allow teachers to focus on teaching the students the content of these materials; 6) reduce greatly the time needed to develop lesson plans; and 7) be easy for substitutes to use. (Katims and Jones 1981: 7)

No prior grouping is required on the part of the teacher, instruction is laid out in detail, identification of pupils who need remediation and what skills they need help on is done by objective testing, and the amount of remediation and materials for the remediation are provided. (Smith and Katims 1979: 201)

> Remedial exercises are designed to provide additional instruction, additional practice, and something similar to additional testing. They are designed to be done by pupils alone with the teacher roving the classroom to assess progress. (Smith and Katims 1979: 201).

Clearly the model of reading programs suggesting a dialectic among reification, formal rationality, and alienation is useful in understanding the organization, logic, and even some resistance to the CMLR program. In an explicit attempt to regain public support for their schools, Chicago school administrators sought greater control over instructional events than basal guidebooks could afford. They reified reading as a set of essential basic skills and instruction as the application of a district-developed set of tests and materials. Accordingly, they arranged a reading program to deliver improved scores on criterion-referenced and norm-referenced achievement tests, and in the process alienated teachers from all important decisions traditionally associated with teaching (curricular, instructional, and evaluative).

The resistance they encountered to the implementation of this plan (Schmidt 1982) might best be explained by teachers' rejection of the materials as scientific.[3] Whereas the teachers in my first study accepted a similar mastery learning program based on commercially produced basals as the scientific technology of reading instruction because of their psychological, intellectual, and physical distance from the development of the materials they were required to use, Chicago teachers—by participating in the field testing and initial changes—recognized the problems the materials included and engendered in their reading instruction. As a result of this closeness to the development and the arbitrary availability of the materials in the stages of development, teachers doubted the scientific validity of the materials. However, these same materials when sold commercially to other school districts have met with virtually no resistance (Robb 1985).

MERIT PAY

In order to overcome public concern for student literacy, some schools have turned to merit pay programs as another alternative method to increase teacher effectiveness. Traditionally, teacher effectiveness has been defined by instructional input factors—service to community, professional activity, and instructional innovation (Levit 1972). However, with the charge to ensure that all students learn to read, teacher effectiveness has been tied to an instructional output factor, student achievement test scores (Otto, Wolf, and Eldridge 1984; Rosenshine and Stevens 1984). In a second test of the model of reading programs, I sought to describe teachers' and administrators' thoughts about reading and reading instruction within the context of a merit pay program based on student test scores which was initiated in a school district in a large metropolitan area.[4]

In this merit pay program, both input and output factors were included. Teachers could receive merit pay for input factors not related directly to reading instruction or student outcomes (e.g., improved work attendance, working in a perceived need area). Output money was awarded to all teachers and the principal in schools in which the collective reading and arithmetic achievement test scores exceeded goals set mathematically by central administrators. Schools, not teachers, were in line for merit pay if schools exceeded their quota. Merit pay consisted of approximately 5 percent of a starting teacher's salary, and the school was allowed to fly a flag to signify to the public that the school had received the award. In addition, schools were rank-ordered by average test score, and teachers and principals from the top 10 percent were given another 3 percent of a beginning salary.

Prior to the merit pay program, individual schools selected which of the state-adopted basals teachers would use in their classrooms, and some teachers taught from two or three different sets of materials. However, to assist schools in reaching these quotas, central administrators devised a five-step procedure for how to use the teacher's guidebook for a single basal series. They defined the teacher's role in reading instruction as using the materials and guidebook according to this prescribed procedure and the principal's role as ensuring that teachers performed their role. According to all involved in the district's reading program, the merit pay system had increased students' scores on achievement tests significantly.

However, according to the model of reading programs based on a dialectic among reification, formal rationality, and alienation, there should be two (perhaps unintended) side effects to this increased productivity. First, the confinement of administrators' and teachers' perceptions concerning reading and reading instruction to the prescribed administrative plan should reduce teacher's abilities to confront situations in which they cannot react mechanically because they fall outside the parameters of the basal materials (Anderson, Mason, and Shirley 1984; Jackson 1968; Mosenthal 1987). With the planning of goals and procedures beyond their control, teachers should gradually become accustomed to following someone else's planned routine, and they should replace their own interpretation of instructional events and problem-solving strategies with those prescribed by the central administration (Johnson 1984). Second, the introduction of an external reward like merit pay for effective reading instruction, which traditionally has been considered to have intrinsic rewards for teachers (Barton and Wilder 1964; Lortie 1975), should reduce or eliminate this psychological satisfaction that teachers experience. That is, as Notz (1975) observed during experimental tasks, financial incentives should decrease the joys of teaching reading, reducing it to another job requirement.

The combination of merit pay and reading instruction should entail a practical contradiction, according to the model. Although originally designed to improve teachers' reading instruction, the program instead creates teachers who have limited instructional repertoires, who are unable to make instructional decisions outside their planned routines, and who find reading instruction laborious. Moreover, this combination should create tension within teachers: they have the opportunity to increase their incomes and achieve a narrow sense of accomplishment, but to do so they may have to forfeit thought, insight, feelings of control, and broader feelings of accomplishment and responsibility.

In order to test these predictions from the application of the model for this merit pay reading program, interviews, questionnaires, and observations were used with twenty-four teachers, five principals, and two central administrators from the district. Because of the sensitive nature of the study—asking school personnel to comment on the effects of a policy still in place—eight trained teachers conducted the surveys and observations of teachers, one itinerant administrator surveyed the principals, and a central administrator in a similar position in another school district interviewed the central administrators. Through these precautions, all levels of personnel were typically candid in word and act. Although the survey results are not always consistent, when taken in the context of the classroom observation, they show that school personnel did accept the administrative definitions of reading and reading instruction and that most teachers found their work less fulfilling since the advent of the merit pay program.

While teachers and administrators disagreed concerning the effects of the merit pay program on teacher instruction and student reading—administrators were more convinced that the effect was positive—both groups acknowledged that the goal of the program was to raise student tests scores in order to stem public criticism of the district for low standards and effectiveness. Two teachers explained:

> The district was under so much criticism for falling short of certain nationwide standards in the field of reading. They had so much bad press. This was simply a method to inspire teachers to achieve better in (standardized tests). . . . The five step procedure, (the basal materials), and the stipend are all ways to raise the scores.

> Why else would we hang a flag from the school, if we weren't trying to improve our public image through this program. Principals take every opportunity to mention our success to parents. . . . But we never talk about anything but test scores. Our scores are high, God is in his heaven, and everyone is happy.

Administrators' responses suggested that they had the necessary attitude to fulfill their roles of supervising teacher instruction in order to ensure that students were learning to read. In fact, their responses to questionnaire items testing their thoughts on the effects of the merit program on student learning and teacher instruction were highly correlated, suggesting that they believed that their efforts in supervision of teachers using the five-step procedure would result directly in marked improvement in student progress. Several administrators offered strategies they used to help keep teachers on the right track for merit pay.

I tell my teachers to focus on the high ability students because they will raise the average score more than bringing up the bottom.

All my teachers follow the five step procedure each day, and they use all the (basal) materials available.

I have teachers prepare mini-tests based on the same format as the (standardized test) for every skill they teach.

One central administrator explained one incentive used to heighten principals' interest in raising student test scores:

Let's say the scores are down in a school. That principal is brought in for a meeting where we discuss methods to remedy the situation. It's all very informal. Principals are evaluated on their school's reading scores, and if the scores are not high next year, they are put on a growth plan, just like their teachers will be. It's like the domino theory.

Although the results from the questionnaire and interviews are somewhat ambiguous as to whether or not teachers accepted their role in the program—teachers seemed to resent the monitoring functions of the merit program on the questionnaire, but few mentioned them during the interviews—the observational data leave little doubt that most teachers accepted their role as implementers of the administrators' plans. In fact, the observation data were remarkably consistent with earlier, larger observational studies of teachers' instruction (e.g., Austin and Morrison 1963; Durkin 1978–79) because 93 percent of the observed lessons were guidebook-directed. However, there was one major difference. In only 20 percent of these lessons did the teachers make decisions about which parts of the guidebook to use as Barr (1986a), Durkin (1983), and Mason (1982) had observed. Rather, during 73 percent of all lessons in my study, teachers used the five-step procedure to direct their use of the teacher's guidebook and the basal materials. That is, they taught by applying the district's definition of reading (the skill in the basal scope and sequence of goals) and instruction (the five-step procedure) regardless of grade level, ability of student, background of student, or teacher's knowledge, suggesting that they were unable or unwilling to confront the complexities of reading instruction in their multi-abilitied, multicultural, and multilingual classrooms.

Just under one-third of the teachers found that the merit pay program improved their attitude toward reading instruction. It focused their attention on what their superiors considered most important and allowed them to use their time more efficiently and effectively. As a group, this third thought the merit program could be improved even further if awards were calculated on individual classes rather than entire schools. One teacher explained:

> I think the effect has been a positive one. Teachers are highly motivated. I think the teachers are improving their own reading instruction. . . . I became highly motivated—more interested in reading. . . . The goal became to try and see that children's scores were raised. While I prepared my lessons, I thought about the reward I would get financially. . . . I hope that doesn't sound too mercenary.

The other two-thirds of the teachers were less positive about the effects of the merit pay program on their feelings of fulfillment during reading instruction. All teachers acknowledged that central administrators set goals, materials, procedures, and rewards, and this two-thirds felt this loss of control:

> We have to show all five steps on our lesson plans and the principal checks these every week. I'm pushed harder to get my kids through (the basal). I have to be at a certain point in (the basal) by the end of the year. Otherwise I'm in trouble. I have to make my lessons quicker. I'm pushed so I push, and we do get there whether we're ready or not. . . . That sounds terrible I know . . . but what else can I do?

> I find myself teaching to the test. It's test, test, test at my school, and I caught the fever I guess. I heard about (these commercial materials) that will help kids with test-taking skills. . . . Well, I asked my principal if she would get some for our school. She said that we couldn't afford it, so we bought them ourselves. We're going to get that stipend.

Teachers mentioned several factors from the merit pay program that affected their disenchantment with their work. Principals applied intolerable pressure (posting test scores on classroom doors, requiring in-service for teachers who were "behind" in their basals, announcing test scores over the public address system, and conducting surprise observations). Because the merit pay program grouped all teachers into one merit-risk pool, other teachers were cited as making instruction less enjoyable through peer pressure. In fact, several teachers mentioned (and two principals and a central administrator confirmed) that some teachers cheated on the standardized tests in order to gain unfair advantage toward receiving merit pay.

In summary, the model again worked well to explain school personnel's thoughts and actions in the design and implementation of this reading program based on merit pay for higher test scores. Although this study might appear to be a setup for the application of the model, the district's success in raising reading test scores has been cited on national television shows for its improvement, and it was acknowledged as one of the "schools that work in America" by President Ronald Reagan.[5] Clearly, the use of a central administrator's quota system coupled with financial incentives is an expression of formal rationality, as are the separation of decision-making and implementation of reading instruction. Administrators and most teachers seemed to reify reading as the scores on standardized tests and instruction as the use of teacher's guidebooks according to the five-step procedure. Although test scores did rise, the program led teachers to disregard individual differences among their students as they applied prescribed procedures according to their roles. This left two-thirds of the interviewed teachers subjectively as well as objectively alienated from their work, as demonstrated in the following statement.

> At my previous school (in another school district) I felt no pressure about reading instruction. I felt good at my job and gave 100 percent. At this school, the principal stresses that it is important to teach tested skills. "Adapt your instructional time to raise those scores with your top group," she says. "Worry about your low group, but you need those high scores to bring them up." I do feel pressure from the principal and the other teachers. When the scores came in, we had a faculty meeting and the scores were distributed to all faculty listed by room number. . . . It's quite evident who has done the best. For example, the third grade teachers felt that the second grade teachers must have cheated to get scores that high because there was such small growth from second to third grade. All of this is unprofessional. . . . On my Christmas card that the principal sent me she did write, "I know that your (standardized achievement) scores will be better this year." I swear to God.

TEACHER AND SCHOOL EFFECTIVENESS PROGRAMS

In a third study, I sought to investigate more than just the existence of the three elements of the dialectic from the model. I wanted to see if a major presupposition of "effective" reading programs—that all school personnel shared the same conceptualization of goals and means for reading instruction—was correct. What I found was a suburban-rural school district which had recently reorganized itself in a manner similar to Larry Cuban's (1984b) "effective" school formula: a) the school board, superintendent, and central administrators established general district-wide goals for reading instruction in terms of student achievement; b) school and classroom goals were officially aligned with these district goals; c) a district curriculum and instructional materials were purchased because they were consistent with the generally stated goals; d) evaluation of principals and teachers was linked to these curricular objectives; e) the tests which accompanied the materials served as a monitoring process of staff and student performance; and f) a staff development program was established to help principals and teachers adjust to the new system. The results of this reorganization, according to an assistant to the state's superintendent for instruction, was a "model school district with test scores among the highest in the state."[6]

Previously, Ignatovich, Cusick, and Ray (1979) found that superintendents and state officials favored such formal rationalization of instructional programs, but that principals and teachers by-and-large, preferred what Ignatovich and his co-authors called "a traditional orientation" toward more local—building and classroom—control over instruction. Using questionnaires and interviews, I surveyed 421 elementary classroom teachers, 20 reading teachers, and 20 principals to probe their perceptions of an ideal reading program.[7] The results from this survey present an interesting challenge for my model. While all the elements of the dialectic were present, they combined in a very different way than they had in the three previous studies.

Principals described a program much like their own program. Sixty-seven percent favored district or school level decision making. Ranking the elements of formal rationality as essential in an ideal program, principals suggested that a single set of administratively arranged goals were necessary to ensure the continuity of student progress toward literacy, that one set of commercial materials were needed to deliver instruction toward those goals effectively, and that teachers' instruction had to be monitored closely in order to ensure that the program ran smoothly. Because principals were rarely involved directly in actual instruction, most considered reading instruction a management problem concerning large numbers of students and teachers and articulation of various parts of the program (classroom, chapter 1, the library, remedial classes, and the like) into a coherent whole while remaining within a fiscal budget. From their administrative vantage point, the organization of the reading program according to the elements of formal rationality and the reification of reading and instruction seemed to be the most efficient way to run a program. The reading coordinator stated this perspective clearly.

Reading programs should be designed so that you can keep track of the developments of students as they move from grade to grade, or school to school as in our district. Research shows that students need continuity in their reading program, if they are to successfully learn the basic skills. Our program while not ideal by any means, is the closest we can come given our circumstances. It is the work of many fine people. Our recent success is due to the careful selection of a curriculum and the materials and the hard work of our faculty. Our students learn to read! . . . Of course, we expect teachers to follow the curriculum and to use the materials we supply, but that doesn't mean that's all they should do.

Most classroom teachers projected a decidedly different idea for an ideal program, one where decisions were made at a local level—in individual classrooms or at grade levels "because teachers are most knowledgeable about what students do or do not know and what they should or shouldn't learn." Sixteen of the twenty teachers interviewed suggested that the district's curriculum (a basal scope and sequence of skills) was too narrowly focused on cognitive skills and not enough on affective aspects of reading—reading motivation and children's literature. As Walter Doyle (1983) has pointed out in other circumstances, these teachers seemed to recognize that student cooperation is a key to successful instruction and teachers' and students' psychological well-being, and they considered administrative overtures for change to be counterproductive to their establishing these cooperative relationships with their students. One teacher remarked:

There is too much outside interference. The curriculum is set, the groups are set, everything is set for the teacher and students. . . . They say that teachers should adapt to students' needs, but how can we, we only have time to go over the basics. . . . On Fridays, I try to work in a little free time reading, but it's like pulling teeth to get them to read on their own. I used to joke that we teach students to read but not what to do with books. . . . Now, I'm not sure that's funny, but you know what I mean. . . . I have to yell at them to get them to stop working in their math books, but they have their books away before I even open my mouth after reading period. I don't really blame them; there aren't many fun things to do in reading in this district.

Teachers' thoughts concerning the ideal means of instruction were closely aligned with administrators' views. Both considered basal materials to be the ideal way to teach students to read. Nineteen of the twenty teachers interviewed suggested that in an ideal program, they would use the basal in nearly the same way that they currently used it, but that they would have more freedom to mix and match basal materials in order to meet student needs. Despite their expressed interest in children's literature and reading motivation when speaking of goals, nearly all teachers were unable or unwilling to incorporate them into their ideal means for instruction. Although one primary teacher spoke of using children's writing, most offered remarks similar to the following:

> You have to have a basal to teach reading. Who has the time to find stories on the right level and to make up all the practice activities. Teachers have used them since I was in school—don't ask how long ago that was—and most kids learn how to read from them. I just don't think [the specific basal series] is the answer to everything. Many of my students have a lot of trouble with skills that aren't handled very well in [the specific basal series]. If I had other materials, I could get the job done right.

Their difference of opinion with administrators over goals, but near agreement concerning means of reading instruction created a paradox for teachers when they considered the elaborate monitoring system administrators used to keep track of students and teachers. Although teachers resented administrators' intervention into what they considered their "territory," and particularly complained about the pressures created by recording scores from criterion-referenced tests in students' files in the principal's office, they thought the tests were necessary in order for them to keep track of student progress through the materials. One teacher explained: "I'd use them to tell me which objectives I could skip without students missing any of the basics." It seems that because the criterion-referenced tests were tied closely to the basal, they would be included as a "necessary evil" in the teachers' ideal reading programs.

In this district, administrators saw formal rationality of the reading program and the reification of reading and instruction as integrally related, inseparable conditions of an ideal reading program. Most teachers, on the other hand, rejected much of the formal rationality when given the opportunity, preferring more effective goals and democratic organization; but they reified reading and reading instruction as the scope and sequence of goals in a basal and the directions in teacher's guidebook. Teachers did not seem to realize the contradiction of rejecting the administrators' acceptance of the basal goals as being too narrow and their own acceptance of the same basal goals as necessary and effective. That is, teachers separated reification from formal rationality.

Ignatovich, Cusick, and Ray (1979) explained their findings—superordinate school officials favored rationalized goals while school personnel closer to actual instruction preferred affective concerns—by referring to Ferdinand Tönnies's (1957) characterization of the resistance small, insular communities (individual schools and classrooms) offered the advances of modernization (administrative intervention, business principles, and accountability schemes) in the late nineteenth century—

what Tönnies called a confrontation between *gemeinschaft* (community) and *gesellschaft* (society). The responses of school personnel in this district suggest that the rejection of rationalization within schools organized according to school and teacher effectiveness research has decreased significantly to a point at which the forces of *gesellschaft* now include most building principals and some classroom teachers, reducing *gemeinschaft* to a simple majority of teachers. This progressive increase in rationalization of reading instruction is consistent with my model based on Lukacs's interpretation of social forces in modern life.

These three studies, along with the original investigation, suggest that the model of reading programs based on a dialectic among reification, formal rationality, and alienation will account generally for school personnel's actions and beliefs in a variety of situations. A central goal of each reading program was the notion that in order to regain public support teachers' subjective reliance on basal materials had to be controlled by some external technology in order to render it sufficiently predictable in the production of verifiably literate students. In all cases, this technology was found in a routine to standardize teachers' application of instructional directions written outside the classroom context, which ultimately separated teachers from the substantial decisions of reading instruction and made them managers of packaged lessons and tests. In most cases, school personnel reified reading as the goals of these materials and instruction as the managerial role. However, in each study, many teachers recognized, at least tacitly, that they had to give up some thing in order to get the full benefits of the rationalized program and the time-savings and instructional power of the technology. Although they were not always certain what they were giving up or to whom to affix the blame, these teachers were uneasy about the circumstances of their reading instruction.

6

The Deskilling and Reskilling
of Teachers of Reading

☐ Schools are not factories; they do not produce tangible commodities which they sell for a profit in order to attract more capital investment to maintain and expand their operations. The success or failure of a factory is easy to determine by a quick look at the color of the ink in its ledger. Without such an easily identifiable indicator of success, it seems that schools should have escaped the logic of production which seeks to increase profit margins by manipulating variables in the productive process—workers, machines, and raw materials—as if they were substantially equal to keep expenses at a minimum and productivity high. Early in this century, as I discussed in chapter 2, this logic was realized in Taylor's scientific management, in which the labor process was reorganized as mechanical behavior without thought or feelings. While the excesses of Taylorism are seldom evident today, more subtle forms of this logic find expression in factories, offices, and, if the data from my studies is generalizable, in reading programs throughout the United States.

Although school superintendents need not answer to stockholders concerning questions of profit and loss, they are accountable to and dependent upon local taxpayers for a major portion of school operating funds. These taxpayers, like investors, expect a reasonable return for their investment. Of course, taxpayers do not enjoy the same freedom to invest elsewhere should they find their local school lacking. However, as a group they can reject school budgets and bond issues, and as individuals they can move their households to another school district more to their liking. Recently, these expectations for school effectiveness (return on investment) have been exacerbated by town and city governments' attempts to attract new businesses and industries to their communities. Most often these heightened interests in school effectiveness come in two forms. First, management executives seek a literate, highly employable local workforce and "good" schools for their children. Second, few regular or potential taxpayers have sufficient time to evaluate the effectiveness of schools in detail, and they look for a quick, but reliable, way to judge the success of a school system—for a bottom line.

Being graduates of schools which featured reading instruction from basal materials and tests as the determiners of ability and being subject to the same social forces that led teachers and principals to reify reading and instruction, most taxpayers consider students' scores on standardized reading achievement tests to be the legitimate measure of school effectiveness (Postman 1979). Consequently, most local newspapers publish articles and stories describing the relative success of local schools in terms of students' scores and state and national norms on reading and mathematics tests. In this way, these scores become the equivalent of the profit and loss statements in business ledgers. To be perceived by their investors (taxpayers) as a viable concern, worthy of financial and moral support, school superintendents must arrange the educative means at their disposal to produce sufficiently high test scores to meet local expectations, which seem to vary according to economic class.[1] With this tangible goal, reading instruction becomes subject to the same logic of production found in the factory.

Two additional factors influence the public's and, therefore, school personnel's interest in scores. First, there is a concern that the demands on literacy are increasing faster than schools can keep pace as America moves from a production economy to one based on information and communications technology. It seems to many that the standards of literacy today will be considered marginal in a generation or two (Resnick and Resnick 1977). In light of such demands, it appears necessary that virtually everyone must learn to read in order to be a productive member of society; and, thus, each student's progress should be monitored early and often to ward off problems quickly.

Second, there is a perception that student test scores have fallen steadily over the past twenty-five years (Stedman and Kaestle 1987). In fact, while primary grade students have demonstrated progress, more challenging tests have indeed proven to be increasingly difficult for intermediate and high school level students. Moreover, when these scores are compared to those of students from other countries, American students never placed first or second on any tests of achievement and sometimes ranked at or below international averages (Guthrie 1981). These notions that America is falling behind other countries at the very time when the economy is making greater demands on literacy, adds considerable urgency to school administrators' attempts to find the correct arrangement of teachers, materials, and students to produce the greatest number of literate students as verified by standardized test scores (*A Nation at Risk* 1983).

As the results of my studies suggest, school administrators sought to solve this problem by establishing routines to reduce the variability among teachers' and students' performances. Since administrators thought they could do little concerning the student raw materials for their reading programs and because they considered the directions in teacher's guidebooks and basal materials to be the scientific means of reading instruction, the prime variable for manipulation was the teacher.[2] Accordingly, administrators sought to control teachers' use of the teachers's guidebook and materials in order to limit the choices they had to make before and during lessons. For example, in the Chicago Mastery Learning Reading Program, teachers were to teach the same lesson to their class according to a prepared script and then let the accompanying tests decide which students understood the lesson and determine whether the student entered the reteaching phase of the scripted lesson or went on to the next skill. When teachers' pacing of their students through these lessons seemed unduly influenced by individual teacher's opinions, Chicago administrators developed a pacing schedule to make the pace more uniform across classrooms, schools, and area districts. In this way, administrators who devised the program and those who set and monitored the pacing schedule made all the major decisions concerning the reading instruction delivered in every public school classroom throughout Chicago.

THE DESKILLING OF TEACHERS

The consequent uneasiness that many teachers experienced in the reading programs I studied should be considered a typical reaction to the control required in the rationalization of an institution like schools (Marcuse 1964). In reading instruction, as in most institutional work, this control comes in three forms: simple, bureaucratic, and technical (Apple 1982). Simple control is one person persuading others by whatever means to follow his or her directions concerning their work behavior. For example, in the Right to Read school district, the reading coordinator's insistence that the third grade teachers continue to follow the basal curriculum even though a basal author agreed with the teachers' complaint is a form of simple control. The teachers, as a group, had little legitimate recourse but to comply with the reading coordinator's dictates; there was no further appeal possible. Of course, as individuals, these

teachers could shut their classroom doors and follow their own con-
science.

Bureaucratic control, the establishment of a line of authority based on
explicit rules, regulations, and roles, is designed to prevent this individual
type of evasion of simple control. As most school districts and reading
programs grew larger, the development and sophistication of these face-
less bureaucratic policies overshadowed the simple individual forms of
control and legitimized the separation of duties within programs.

Individuals were no longer responsible for all aspects of the reading
program, rather these duties were officially distributed among various
levels of the hierarchy of authority to maintain some levels of uniformity
and efficiency within these larger organizations. To continue the previous
example, when the teachers first recognized that many students had
difficulty mastering a particular set of skills in the basal curriculum, they
appealed to the reading teacher and principal, who referred the teachers
to the policy statement in *Notes on Pacing Instruction*, "Teachers cannot
change . . . the scope and sequence of goals." The monitoring system
based on the chapter and book tests from the basals allowed the reading
teachers and principals to ensure that these teachers did in fact continue
to follow policy. In accordance with district policy, but deviating from
district norm, these teachers appealed to the reading coordinator, from
whom they received a response of simple control.

For several reasons schools pose considerable problems for simple and
bureaucratic types of control. First, teachers consider themselves professionals and often resist being told directly what to do when it is against
their better judgment. During interviews in all four studies, teachers
reported what they considered injustices that they had suffered at the
hands of administrators. Most objected to the arbitrary nature of administrative decisions and a lack of understanding of classroom conditions
in district policy. Foremost in this lack of understanding was administrators' failure to recognize that students do not always follow a rational
sequence in their development, their learning, or their behavior, which
causes great stress for teachers attempting to play by the bureaucratic
rules.

In the merit pay program, for instance, one principal expressed this
point clearly, concerning a lack of understanding from central administrators: "Our children are from poor homes and they have difficulty
with the language and learning to read. We're happy if we get them to
read anything. The district wants us to show nine months growth each
year (on standardized tests). They must be dreaming. At our school, we
concentrate on the (input) kinds of merit pay." A third source of difficulty
for management is the isolation of teachers from one another and authority. That is, most elementary classes are still taught in separate classrooms in several, sometimes many, schools across a district. Simple and

even bureaucratic forms of control cannot keep track of teachers sufficiently well to ensure that all teachers are working directly and efficiently
toward district goals.

Technical control is more subtle; that is, it seems natural to the definitions and physical realities of the job to be performed. In reading
programs, commercial materials, basal series, and the other myriad of
packaged sets of workbooks and worksheets, supply the means for the
technical control of reading instruction in order to render it more predictable and more productive. Since both administrators and teachers
reify reading instruction as the application of commercial reading materials, few school personnel question the legitimacy of this form of control. In these materials, administrators realize an economical, effective,
and less confrontational method to meet their concerns for instructional
accountability, and teachers find both the source and the practical tools
of reading instruction. Commercial reading materials, then, control the
program's goals, methods of instruction, main source of texts for reading,
and evaluation without noticeable objections on the part of teachers.

As I noted above, school personnel were not administrative puppets
within their respective programs; they complained loudly and responded
cleverly to what they considered to be arbitrary exercises of simple and
bureaucratic control. Yet, it is the technical, not the simple and bureaucratic control, that has the greatest repercussions for teachers. In a very
real sense, as commercial reading materials become more prominent and
persuasive in reading programs, teachers become less important in the
process of reading instruction in America. To understand this inverse
relationship—the deskilling of teachers—it is necessary to reflect back
on the control teachers exerted during instruction prior to the 1920s and
the advent of the basal series in contrast to the current conceptualization
of appropriate reading instruction.

Not to romanticize the past, it is accurate to characterize teachers in
the late 19th century into two groups: drillmasters and overseers, who
accepted reproduction of the text as the goal of reading instruction and
memorization of sets of rules and flawless oral reading as the proper
means; and interpreters of culture—later practitioners of the New Education—who attempted to demonstrate the utility of literacy by embedding their instruction in the everyday lives of their students. To be sure,
the lessons from each group were not always ideal by today's standards
and knowledge, and the first group outnumbered the second by a considerable margin. However, teachers in both groups developed daily lesson objectives, methods for instruction and practice, a pace for that
instruction and procedures for evaluation. Despite the first group's
dogged reliance on the reading textbooks and courses of study, these
documents did not include explicit descriptions of daily lessons which
drillmasters and overseers could simply apply. Moreover, for the second

group, the course of study and content of lessons were open to negotiations among school staff. In short, these lesson-planning skills and the ability to translate those self-developed plans into daily lessons for individual groups of students, were the skills of teaching reading. For better or worse, teachers controlled most of the aspects of their reading instruction.

Compare those skills with the expectations of proper reading instruction in the four districts I studied, where teachers were to apply the basal materials according to the directions in the guidebooks. One way of looking at this administrative expectation is to consider the array of offerings basal materials present to teachers. For example, basals typically include: a) anthologies of stories and essays considered appropriate for students of various reading levels, b) a scope and sequence of objectives reflecting areas that are often considered necessary for children in order to learn to read, c) directions for instruction and practice activities designed to lead students to meet the stated objectives, d) tests to determine objectively whether the goals have been met, and e) recording systems to keep track of student progress. These materials are offered by reading experts and publishers as the best methods, scientifically sound, and beyond duplication by individual teachers. That is, basal materials are thought to improve the skills of teachers as they conduct their reading instruction.

However, it seems just as reasonable—I think more reasonable—to see the opposite as true; the rise of the reading expert and publishers through the requirement of guidebook-directed instruction deskilled teachers in terms of their ability to offer thoughtful reading instruction independently. To explain this process of subtraction, it is necessary to look closely at the directive nature of the teacher's guidebook in detail. For this digression, I selected the teacher's guidebook for level F, *Moonbeams*, from the Houghton Mifflin Reading Series (Durr et al. 1983), because the series is one of the top sellers in the elementary school market. My work was greatly aided by a thirty-six page advertisement for the series at the front of the guidebook which explains the basic components of the program (Levels A through O), the scope and sequence of skills, how the program works, ancillary materials, about the authors, the authors' philosophy (on one half page), and a table of contents for this particular guidebook.

In its preliminary discussion of the series, the publisher suggests that the program includes a complete listing of skills and the appropriate sequence for instruction, helpful teaching scripts for each skill, and a simple three-step format of read, teach, reteach. "When it comes to offering teachers guidance, Houghton Mifflin proves that giving you *more* can help you work *less*!" (pp. 1–8). And more is what teachers get. Besides a scope and sequence of skills listed in three ways and scripts for each lesson which I will address in a moment, the publisher offers stories for both instructional and recreational reading, charts listing examples so that teachers won't have to think of their own, workbooks, worksheets, "bonus" worksheets for practice, two forms of lesson tests, two forms of chapter tests (published in workbook or worksheet style for teachers' convenience), placement tests, vocabulary tests, floppy disks for scoring all the tests, record cards for keeping track of students' test scores, administrator's guidebooks to help them manage the program more effectively, specially written monographs to offer research support for the program's suggestions, and letters and activities for teachers to send home to students' parents. That is, the goals, directions, practice, assessment, record keeping, and communication with parents are all prepared and packaged for teachers to use.

When presented with all these materials, the Houghton Mifflin three-step procedure for instruction may not seem so simple after all. But the publisher offers a key to help teachers use the guidebook efficiently: "Regular type is used for statements and questions that you direct to students. Ellipses (. . .) following the questions and directive statements indicate that you should give students time to think and time to follow your directions before you continue. Boldface type indicates material addressed solely to you. Boldface italic type with parentheses indicates expected student responses" (pp. 1–36). The publishers make good on their offer of help. The first directive on page one in boldface type tells teachers: "Distribute copies of *Moonbeams*. You may wish to allow time for children to look through their new books" (p. 1). This is followed by a script for both teacher and students to follow as they look at the cover, title page, and table of contents for *Moonbeams*. Now you may wonder if anyone really follows these directions. Since Houghton Mifflin conducts extensive market research, publishes revisions every five to seven years, and is among the six top-selling basal series in a billion dollar industry, it seems reasonable to conclude that this level of specificity is appreciated.

Unit 1 of *Moonbeams* covers ten pages in the student's anthology, four pages in the workbook, six pages of the example charts, a set of assessment forms, all in order to read a story, learn to categorize, practice short and long *a*, and review sound associations for *c*. The directions to teachers are equally didactic as the directive to pass out the books. Teachers are told which vocabulary to teach, what concepts their students need to have in mind while reading, how to look at the pictures to motivate students to want to read, how much students should read before interruption, which questions to ask during interruptions and after completion (correct answers for all questions are listed in boldface italics), when and how to use oral reading during the interruptions. After teachers and students have completed all of these directives they have finished only the first section of Unit 1—read.

The second section, teaching reading skills, provides no explanation concerning why categorization is important for the students to learn at this time, rather it simply starts with a script for a teacher monologue followed by a series of questions and answers designed to lead students to supply class labels for sets of two or three words. No attempt is made to connect this skill to the story for the unit or the students' everyday lives. Teachers are told to conclude this lesson by stating, "Today we talked about how we can group things together because they are alike in some way," (p. 15), to assign page 1 in the workbook and later to assess students' understanding of the examples with either assessment form A or B. The two forms of assessment are needed in case some students fail to reach criterion on their first test and must be retaught (the third section of the scripted lesson) and tested again. Similar directions are presented for the other activities included in Unit 1. For example:

> Print the following words on the board:
> plane   spoon   sweater   flat
> *Say:* Let's play a game of word riddles. Here are four words you know when you hear someone say them. But you may not recognize them when you see them like this. If you use what you know about the sounds of letters as I tell you something about each word, you should be able to tell me what the word is.
> *Point to plane.* This word names something that can fly.
> What is the word? . . . (plane)
> How did you know it wasn't plan? . . . (no sense)
> How did you know it wasn't helicopter? . . . (wrong sounds). (p. 17)

For this, teachers went to a university for four years and took one or more courses on how to teach reading. I have digressed at length here to give some concrete indication of the extent of the deskilling of teachers in this form of technical control. Since most teachers cannot tell the various basal series apart shortly after months of careful study (Farr, Tulley, and Powell 1987), I think I am on safe ground with this one example.

What is left of the teaching skills which teachers possessed before the rise of reading experts and publishers and the advent of guidebook-directed instruction? Goals, instruction, examples, practice, and assessment which were once in the repertoires of classroom teachers when they conducted reading instruction are now considered to be in the domain of others. Although each of the components of this technical

control was originally introduced as an improvement over teachers' subjective practices, the expectation that teachers follow these guidebooks
closely has stripped teachers of the skills of their craft. And of late, some
teacher education experts have acknowledged teachers' fate in this process.

> Teacher education programs are often designed as if teachers were
> responsible for establishing appropriate educational objectives for
> their students, preparing appropriate curriculum materials, con-
> ducting and evaluating the outcomes of instruction, and making
> whatever adjustments should prove necessary in these activities.
> Teachers may have done all of these things in the distant past, but
> at present, most of these functions are performed by school boards,
> school administrators, and commercial publishers. (Brophy 1982:
> 11)

WHERE HAVE THE SKILLS GONE?

If teachers have lost control of the skills of planning and implementing
reading on a daily basis in their classrooms, then some other group or
groups must have absorbed and now exercise these skills. In his remarks
concerning teacher education, Jere Brophy (1982) mentions school administrators and basal publishers as the most obvious winners in this
contest over the control of reading instruction. Although those groups
have indeed benefited from teachers' loss of skills, Brophy neglects an
important and increasingly active group—the state. In Southern, South-
western, and most Western states, the most apparent connection between
government and reading instruction is the state level committee which
selects a subset among all basal series on the market from which local
districts must choose if they wish state funding for textbook purchase
(Tulley 1983). In the twenty-two states with such an adoption policy,
the skills of goal setting, instructional design, and materials selection are
partially usurped by the state committee—a small number of officials
from the state education departments, reading experts from local universities, school administrators, teachers, and interested, appointed
members of the public.

While this policy has obvious effects on the reading instruction in
adoption states, it also influences the reading programs in nonadoption
states through a phenomenon called the "California" or "Texas" effect.
These states, and large urban districts, influence the date and content
of basal revisions (Squires 1985). For example, modern basal reader
"birthday parties are devoid of ice cream and cake (California considers
them junk food), while many adventures occur with Texas backdrops
(Texas, which dominates the control of the market with its unique direct

purchase of textbooks, prefers Texas settings)" (Muther 1985: 7).[3] Perhaps of greater importance is that these states exert undue influence on basal goals and structure because publishers attempt to align their products with the curriculum outlines and instructional guidelines from Texas and California's Departments of Education (Follett 1985).[4] In this way, the centralized bureaucratic control of at least two states exert considerable effects on the technical control in elementary classrooms throughout the country.

Beyond these textbook adoption policies and their ripple effect, state legislators have recently taken a more proactive role in schools (Darling-Hammond and Wise 1985). Certainly, politicians have always been concerned about schooling. Joseph Mayer Rice considered political intervention one of the major reasons for poor, mechanical teaching in 1893. However, that previous intervention—appointing cronies instead of progressive educators—was different in scope and intent. The new state initiatives attempt to standardize the goals, monitor student progress closely, and regulate teaching methods (Wise 1979). For example, "through legislation, Florida prescribes statewide curriculum, instructing teachers what books to use, what topics to cover, and what tests to administer. . . . Florida's priorities are comparable to those of the thirty-five other states that have passed some school accountability legislation" (Bondi and Wiles 1986: 45). With the state's Educational Accountability Act of 1976, legislators set basal materials as the only legal means to provide reading instruction, making the scope and sequence of skills the state's official reading curriculum.

Government, then, has increased its control over planning and implementation of reading lessons at the expense of teachers' traditional repertoires. Whether through textbook adoption, minimum competence tests in reading, or teacher performance evaluation, legislated learning makes teachers more accountable to the state than ever before (Frymier 1985). In most states in the Union, state officials now exercise the skills of goal setting, pacing instruction at a general level, instructional design in some detail, and assessing students' progress closely, while teachers have become legally dependent on commercial reading materials.

Three groups of writers contribute to the production of a basal series which provide the goals, means, and assessment for everyday reading instruction in most classrooms across the country. The most visible group in this process is the team of basal authors, composed of prominent reading experts from universities and well-respected school personnel from areas around the country chosen to ensure representation from important regions from a marketing standpoint. While it seems reasonable to believe that the authors write most of the goals and lessons included in the teacher's guidebook, according to Kenneth Goodman, former basal author (Goodman, Shannon, Freeman, and Murphy 1988) and George Graham, author of the only in-house study of basal publishing (Graham 1978), nothing could be further from the truth. Rather, the authors act primarily as consultants, directing the efforts of others within a limited authority. According to Graham, a revision of a basal series is "a company product being shaped, not an individual's ideas being transformed" (p. 95). That is, basal publishing is a lucrative and conservative business, wherein marketing analysts, who conduct continuous research on their current and potential customers, have "more influence over these specifications than most of the authors" (Goodman, Shannon, Freeman, and Murphy 1988: 31). Authors' primary responsibility is to plan with senior editorial staff, to evaluate the subsequent attempts by junior editors to realize those plans, and to write scholarly inserts for teacher's guidebooks and in-service monographs.

Basal editors, sometimes former teachers, come with various titles and job descriptions: trainee, assistant, associate, editor, supervising editor, executive editor, and editor in chief. Graham (1978) suggests that lower level "editors do not have much influence over the structure of the reading program, but it is their language that guides teachers through the lessons" (p. 125). Typically, the components of the basals are written by different teams of editors—one group handling teacher's guidebooks for a particular grade level, another writing the practice materials, a third producing the tests, and so forth, each working within strict specifications from publishers and authors. The supervising editor has the responsibility of pulling the components together into a coherent series within the revision time lines set to correspond most likely with California's or Texas's textbook adoption dates.

The third group in the production of basals are contract workers who supply stories, artwork, practice activities, and sometimes tests on a demand basis. Professional children's book authors and illustrators who are willing to sell their work to publishers to be modified for inclusion in the anthologies, and commercial artists who design the covers and inserts for the rest of the materials, all fall into this category. In some publishing houses, much of the repetitive production of workbooks and worksheets are contracted to external independent companies which specialize in the production of practice activities for the many companies competing for the elementary school market. At times, even graduate students of the authors consent to supply part of lessons on a limited basis, hoping to catch on with a basal publisher (Goodman, Shannon, Freeman, and Murphy 1988).

Although at first glance it may have seemed obvious that employees of basal publishers have increased their skills to plan and write reading lessons at the expense of classroom teachers, a closer look suggests that the production of basal materials is such a large undertaking that it too has been rationalized according to bureaucratic and simple control. That is, the process of planning and writing lessons has been divided into a great number of finite jobs, which junior editors repeat for the numerous levels of the program. At a very general level, authors and senior editors plan the goals and lesson formats within the parameters set by the market, but they do little of the actual writing of lessons or goals. Although the finished product includes long-term and daily goals, lessons, and assessment, in fact, it is really only the publishing companies, the corporate enterprises and not individual employees, which have absorbed the majority of teachers' skills.

In virtually all school districts including those in adoption states, a textbook selection committee convenes periodically to choose one, or less often more than one, set of basal materials to be used in district elementary schools for the following several years. As it turns out, this is the most important decision made concerning the reading program because "selection of a basal reader is tantamount to selecting the reading curriculum" (Farr, Tulley, and Powell 1987: 268). Despite the importance of the committee's decision, most studies of the reading textbook selection process are not very generous in their descriptions of committee operations, (See Farr, Tully and Powell 1987 for a review of this research.) They suggest that little time is devoted to the actual examination of basal materials, that committee members work from checklists which emphasize the presence of factors rather than an evaluation of their quality, and that committee members are often unduly influenced by publishing company representatives. The result, by all accounts, is a basal program selected more for its surface appearance than its underlying philosophy or instructional design.[5]

Regardless of how the basal is selected, once it is in place, administrators' attention is fixed on the management of the program, as my four and other studies have demonstrated (Cuban, 1984b; Duffy, Roehler, and Wesselman 1985). Administrators seem content to let the basal publishers choose the goals, methods, and assessment for reading instruction, focusing their efforts on managing teachers' use of the chosen materials in order to render it more effective and efficient in raising students' test scores. And, it is these management skills that administrators hope teachers will incorporate in their instruction.

THE RESKILLING OF TEACHERS

Although the technical control of reading programs based on the use of basal materials deskills teachers by supplying the goals, means, and evaluation of their reading instruction and bureaucratic control from state officials and local school administrators limits teachers' choices among sets of these materials, these practices also engender new skills which teachers need in order to run the technology of reading instruction. That is, deskilling is accompanied by reskilling as the management skills required to raise test scores by leading students through the basal materials are substituted for the abilities to plan and implement independent reading lessons on a daily basis. This managerial role reduces both the quantity and quality of the skills required to perform the teachers' duties during reading lessons and, thus, decreases the impact of teachers' work on students learning to read. Certainly, someone must manage the technology, but it is the technology that is seen as the teaching agent in the production of literate students.

As I mentioned in chapter 3, this redefinition of what it means to be an effective teacher of reading has taken place over the last five or six decades. However, at present the process seems almost complete as most reading experts confine their arguments to which are the best ways to use the teacher's guidebook and other basal materials in order to produce high student test scores in reading. Called by several names, including direct instruction (Becker 1977) , process/product research (Hoffman 1986), teacher effectiveness procedures (Rupley, Wise, and Logan 1986), the goals and means are always the same. The question is not why or whether to use basal materials during lessons, rather it is how to improve teachers' productivity during their use. Perhaps the two best sources for information on the new skills of teaching reading are *Becoming a Nation of Readers: The Report of the Commission on Reading* (Anderson 1984) and the *Handbook of Reading Research* (Pearson 1984), two widely quoted and influential texts.

Under the direction of the Commission on Reading, *Becoming a Nation of Readers*, a project sponsored by the National Academy of Eduction and the National Institute of Education, attempts to summarize the state of the art in reading research and to deduce instructional principles from their summary. Heralded as a document akin to the surgeon-general's reports, the Commission concludes their diagnosis of what ails American reading instruction with the statement, "America will become a nation of readers when verified practices of the best teachers can be introduced throughout the country" (p. 120). Behind this statement are the goals, means, and skills of new effective reading instruction, offered with the official approval of the United States government.

The Commission bases its remarks on an implied equation for becoming a nation of readers—that improved scores on standardized achievement tests equals better readers.[6] Most of their recommendations are tied to this metaphor for industrial production because they define the verification process for determining who are the "best teachers" as the practice of comparing teachers according to their students' test scores. In a manner reminiscent of Bobbitt's and Spaulding's three-step adaptation of scientific management, these achievement scores drive the new skills of reading instruction. Much of the body of *Becoming a Nation of*

Readers is devoted to discussions of basal materials and their use. Despite the occasional rebuke concerning the formulae publishers use to modify basal stories, the means which the best teachers use is clear—they use basal materials in their pursuit of higher test scores.[7]

At times the Commission seems to apologize for the attention it devotes to commercial materials: "In most classrooms, the instruction will be driven by a basal reading program. For this reason, the importance of those programs cannot be underestimated" (p. 74). Here the Commission suggests that it only discusses basal materials because teachers rely on them, but their firm commitment to these materials is found in their discussion of "whole language" approaches, an alternative, nonbasal method of teaching reading which requires teachers to plan and implement their own reading lessons. First, the Commission acknowledges that the whole language method has been used successfully in New Zealand, and that "in the hands of very skillful (American) teachers, the results can be excellent" (p. 45). However, citing the First Grade Studies (Bond and Dykstra 1967) as evidence, they argue "but average results are indifferent when compared to approaches typical in American classrooms" (p. 45). Since the Commission had already acknowledged that most American teachers use basal materials, it leaves little doubt that it recommends the guidebook-directed instruction over the alternative.

But there is more here. First, it leaves unexamined altogether why New Zealand—the most literate country in the world, having the highest achievement test scores in international comparisons—is able to achieve this success and legitimacy with its public without guidebook-directed instruction. Second, why the average New Zealand teacher seems to be the match of the very best American teachers? And third, in these remarks, the Commission begins to equivocate on what it means by the "best teachers." By its test score definition, New Zealand teachers with their traditional skills of planning and implementing lessons must be the best in the world since their students' scores are highest. But the Commission does not suggest that American teachers emulate their New Zealand counterparts.

Obviously, there is another agenda here, and it begins to become clear when the Commission explains its statement, "an indispensible conclusion of research is that the quality of teaching makes a considerable difference in children's learning. . . . In addition, teachers influence children's learning in the following ways: managing the classroom environment, pacing and content coverage, and grouping for instruction" (p. 85). The manner in which teachers manipulate these influential factors comprises the new skills of reading instruction which teachers need employ if they are to be successful in raising students' achievement scores.

The Commission turns to the *Handbook of Reading Research* for a

detailed explanation of these new skills. In Chapter 23, "Classroom Instruction in Reading," Barak Rosenshine and Robert Stevens (1984) sort
these new skills into three categories: general instructional procedures,
specific instructional practices, and indexes of effective instruction. General instructional procedures begin with teacher-directed initial instruction in which teachers present the topic, control the practice, set turn
taking routines, and determine the acceptability of student responses.
In fact, the highest correlation between teacher direction and student
achievement scores comes when "teachers control and students follow
prescribed lessons" (p. 747). During their lessons, teachers are encouraged to "maintain a business-like, but cordial atmosphere, present clear,
concise goals for students, to lapse into few digressions and to use students' input wisely" (p. 757)—because programs with the highest academic focus also have the highest achievement scores and highest scores
on standardized self-esteem tests.

Specific instructional procedures are to be incorporated in a demon-
strate-practice-feedback instructional cycle. During the demonstration
portion of the lesson, teachers teach students what, when, where, how,
and why to use the skill listed as next in the basal scope and sequence.
Practice should be frequent, teacher led, and rapid paced. Questions
asked during practice should be factual, encourage choral response from
the group, and be carefully sequenced to lead students successfully to
the goal without diversion.[8] Correct responses from students warrant an
acknowledgment or an immediate translation to the next question, in-
correct questions require feedback in the form of a hint or an easier
question.

Overall during the instructional cycle, teachers should communicate
to students that they are aware of what is going on in all areas of the
classroom ("withitness"), should be able to deal with two or more activities simultaneously ("overlapping"), end one and start another activity
without interruption ("smoothness"), maintain a fast pace ("momen-
tum"), be aware of all students' progress during teacher-led practice
("accountability"), and attempt to keep all students participating during
practice ("alerting"). Following the lessons cycle, teachers should monitor students' independent practice actively by walking about the classroom asking students questions about their work.

Rosenshine and Stevens offer three indicators of effective reading
instruction leading toward high achievement scores. Teachers who move
their students through the basal lessons quickly and complete more of
the scope and sequence of skills are more likely to produce students with
higher test scores. The best method in order to improve this content
coverage is through increasing students' engagement in their lessons.
The more time on task, the more content covered; the more content
covered, the higher students' achievement scores. Of course, teachers

should remain sensitive to students' success in these efforts; students should answer teacher questions and complete practice activities with 80 percent accuracy or they are moving too quickly. Teachers can assure this high level of success by pursuing objectives through small steps, asking frequent "low level" questions, and assigning primary grade students to basal materials below their tested level.

Wayne Otto, Anne Wolf, and Roger Eldridge (1984) begin Chapter 24 of the *Handbook*, "Managing Instruction," by admitting their skepticism concerning the use of achievement test scores as the main criterion for judging the effectiveness of curricular, organization, or instructional components of the reading program. They hypothesize that this global measure of student progress is not sufficiently sensitive to detect subtle but important effects and test scores have "washed out" the results of many promising investigations concerning the effects of general plans for program curriculum and organization (homo- or heterogeneous grouping, basal or individualized curriculum organization, open or traditional philosophies and physical arrangements, and so forth).

What Otto, Wolf, and Eldridge do find clear results for are the "classroom behaviors" which Rosenshine and Stevens summarized in the preceding chapter of the *Handbook*, and they briefly reiterate the findings of some of the same studies. They conclude: "Despite the general inconclusive results of the context-product studies, evidence is accumulating from more recent classroom based studies that effective instruction is associated with certain management decisions" (pp. 819–20).

As the titles of Chapters 23 and 24 of the *Handbook* denote, there is some ambivalence concerning the reskilling of teachers of reading. Rosenshine and Stevens call the new skills "instruction," while Otto, Wolf, and Eldridge call them "management." In recent parlance concerning reading programs, the two terms have become almost synonymous. Note that all of the new skills of teaching reading (or any other subject for that matter) are expressed in behavioral terms. Teachers are to control, monitor, and routinize their own and students' activities during reading lessons. Conspicuous by its absence from these *Handbook* chapters and from *Becoming a Nation of Readers* is a discussion of teachers' knowledge of the content of reading instruction, the reading process, their students, and the sources of instructional goals and means in elementary school reading programs. Moreover, many of the new skills mentioned are already in the domain of publishers of basal materials (e.g., objectives, incremental instruction, rule-based skills, and frequency of practice) and administrators (e.g., student assignment to reading groups, pace of content coverage, and academic focus). Teachers are left only with the precision with which they present the basal lessons and the monitoring of students' behaviors and responses in and outside reading group. While these tasks are by no means simple, they are a far cry from the planning and implementation skills which teachers possessed before the rise of reading experts, basal publishers, and expectations for guidebook-directed instruction.

These new skills of reading instruction, originally deduced from independent lessons of teachers whose instruction yielded high test scores, come back to haunt all teachers in the form of administrators' checklists used for teacher's performance evaluation. (See the exchange among Gibboney; Hunter; Robbins and Wolfe; Stallings; L. Anderson; and Freer and Dawson concerning the Hunter model of performance evaluation in *Educational Leadership*, February 1987.) That is, these new skills become the criteria against which teachers' reading instruction is matched, giving administrators three ways of tightening the coupling between teacher and student performance during reading instruction—achievement test scores, basal criterion-referenced test scores, and "reskilled" observational schedules.

While the technical control of teachers during reading instruction through the required use of teacher's guidebooks and basal materials in order to raise student test scores—with its deskilling and reskilling of teachers—should not be overstated, teachers are not factory workers and students' reading is not easily understood as a commodity, the technical control's effect on elementary school teachers should not be underestimated either. Depending on the type of basal chosen and administrative perspective, teachers relinquish some or most of their control over reading lessons and their work. With their role reduced to that of assistant to the basal, teachers may see little incentive to improve their knowledge of reading instruction, their students, or appropriate literature as they first acquiesce to and then project the logic of technical control and reskilling. With this in mind, the teachers' apparently irrational thirst for basal-based solutions to problems during their reading instruction appears all too rational, and as a result, reading instruction becomes a managerial concern, not an educative one both for teachers, and, ultimately, for students.

7

Reading Instruction
and Students' Independence

□ The technical control of teachers during their reading instruction through the required use of teacher's guidebooks and other basal components demands a new form of professionalism among the staff of reading programs. No longer are professionals supposed to seek individual autonomy over the decisions and actions that affect and compose their work. Rather, new professionals seek better, more efficient ways to manage people in order to fulfill their responsibilities within the educational bureaucracy (Apple 1982). Accepting basal goals and means for instruction, teachers confine their activities to managing students through the materials by applying guidebook directives for smooth running lessons designed to ensure that students pass the program's tests. Principals, in turn, manage teachers in their efforts, congratulating and cajoling teachers when necessary—in many instances monitoring teachers' products closely—to promote effective school reading programs. Central administrators attempt to coordinate these separate elements into a district program which produces results worthy of public support. All have considerable amounts of responsibility and each has a role to play, but none makes substantial decisions about reading instruction once a basal series is selected as the means of technical control. That is, American reading programs have professionalism without the traditional professional activity of teaching reading.

Teachers' exchange of traditional skills for the new ones of reading instruction does result often in higher student test scores, and teachers are saved the time-consuming tasks of developing the goals and methods of instruction and collecting the materials required to implement those lessons. On the other hand, the exchange also means a considerable loss of control over their work. Not only do teachers lose control over the methods and goals, they also forfeit subjectivity within their teaching, knowledge about scientific investigations of reading and instruction, the respect due professionals, authority over classroom activities, and the history of teaching reading. For teachers, it is a bad transaction; for students, it may be even worse.

Just as with teachers, students forego much of their control over their work—learning to read—in typical reading lessons. Basal series prescribe the goals of their learning; they direct the acceptable activities in which students must engage; and they provide the content that students will read. Moreover, students are expected to attend to task religiously, to participate in every lesson, and to be successful (Otto, Wolf, and Eldridge 1984: 814). Perhaps, the only aspect that distinguishes teachers' and students' fate in this process is the fact that teachers can seek other employment, while students are compelled by law to continue in this work.

With all these constraints, students become individuals within the system only according to the rate at which they progress through the specified curriculum. Since every student must master the same objectives and information through basal use, the rate of presentation is the only variable through which teachers can tailor their instruction to meet the needs of the individual students. However, with the increasing state and administrative expectations for students' competence at specified grade levels, this method of individualization becomes questionable, at best. Taking the logic to its extreme, students would not be seen as individuals at all as they move as a monolith from illiteracy to verified competence during whole class instruction. But the logic is difficult to realize. First, few people think of children as qualitatively similar raw materials that can be manipulated as they see fit. That is, school personnel's feelings get in the way of technical control. Although this is good news for children in general because teachers and administrators offer students technical control with a heart, it also brings the prejudices of upper- and middle-class America to bear on lower-class and minority students.

THE TECHNICAL CONTROL OF STUDENTS

What does teacher reliance on teacher's guidebooks mean for students who must participate in reading lessons? Most reading instruction in the United States includes two types of activities—group lessons and individual seatwork (Anderson, Mason, and Shirley 1984). During group lessons, one of seven activities is probably taking place: students are (1) listening or reading a story from a basal anthology, (2) answering questions about that story, (3) listening to teachers present information about a reading skill, (4) practicing that skill with the teacher, (5) completing a criterion-referenced test, (6) listening to directions on how to complete assignments to be finished during seatwork, or (7) correcting worksheets or workbooks. Seatwork occupies twice as much student time as the group lessons, and typically workbooks and worksheets are predominant during this independent activity.

Reading Stories and Answering Questions

Consider a small group of students and a teacher sitting in a circle reading the same story—first silently, then aloud. Although this may seem like a simple undertaking, there is more to the activities than meets the eye. The story which the group is reading is one of the several selections included in a basal anthology. Despite recent publishers' claims that these books include a variety of types of writing, over two-thirds of the pages in grades one to six basal readers are devoted to stories and poetry (Flood and Lapp 1987). Some of the stories have the same title as children's classics or recent winners of children's literature awards. However, that is often where the similarity between basal stories and regular children's literature ends. Most basal stories are devised or adapted by editors to meet legislative criteria concerning readability formulas (mathematical adaptations which usually result in stories with short sentences composed of words with few syllables) and adoption committee concerns for what is good for children (restrict conflict, sex, and popular culture) (Goodman, Shannon, Freeman, and Murphy 1988). As a result, basal stories lack natural language and are difficult to comprehend (Anderson 1985), suggesting that anthologies may be produced more for opportunities to practice word recognition than to understand one's life better or to find pleasure in reading.

Sanitized in order to meet market demands, basal stories often present an adult version of what children's lives should be like (Freebody and Baker 1985). Girls are often sweet, demure, and bookish; boys are gregarious, active, and funny. Like Disney movies, the characters contribute unrealistically to events in the world, relegating the actual concerns of children to the unimportant. At once, the stories are found to be glib, sexist, and demeaning. Bruno Bettelheim and Karen Zelan (1981) suggest that these stories stifle children's imagination and mediate against children's attachment to reading. Rather than removing the conflict and realism from fiction, Bettelheim and Zelan argue that these aspects of stories serve as one of the most potent means by which children can resolve the problems that exist in their daily lives. Without this possible release from the pressure of these problems, children find little of interest in or little need for reading.[1]

Beyond the stories, or perhaps because of them, the interaction between teachers and students during story reading is ritualized by guidebook directives. Before reading, teachers introduce the story by providing an overview, asking questions about the title or opening illustration, or developing the suggested vocabulary for the story. Most often stories are divided into short (one- or two-page) segments, at which points students stop to answer questions about what they have just read. More questions follow students' completion of the story, and after this final question period, individual students are asked to read portions of the text aloud while their peers listen and follow along. At times, not all of these components are offered, but most often teachers and students follow this prescribed procedure on a weekly basis throughout and across school years.

From a student perspective, there is much to learn in this ritual, perhaps not exactly what the publishers and teachers hoped, however. First, students are unable to choose the stories they wish to read and the order in which they will read them. Should a basal anthology contain a story that is relevant to a day's activity, it cannot be read out of suggested order because that would demonstrate arbitrary sequence of the directives in the teacher's guidebook. Second, for many students their sense of story is challenged by the segmentation of silent reading. Rarely do story parts correspond to page layout, and often students are asked to stop in the middle of an episode, reducing their ability to follow the story's plot. Third, the talk about these stories is unidirectional. Although many children ask questions about stories as they read or are read to at home (Yaden 1984), Rose Marie Weber (1985) found that not a single student asked a question about a basal story in over sixty lessons she analyzed, while students were expected to answer as many as forty during a single lesson.[2] These questions, most often verbatim reading or paraphrases of the questions listed in the basal, are primarily text-based with one acceptable answer listed in the teacher's guidebook. Fourth, students read orally for no other purpose than to receive feedback from their teacher. Fluency is rarely attended to (Allington 1985), and few students attend at all after they have completed their turn. Finally, the entire activity is disconnected from students' lives and even from other parts of the reading lesson. This sense of abstraction prevents some students from seeing the relevance of reading outside of reading group (Johns and Ellis 1976). If John Dewey was correct and "children learn what they do," then during these story-reading rituals, students learn that reading is the attempt to memorize text which someone else selects so that you can reproduce factual information when questioned and the passage's phonetics when asked to read orally—all under the watchful eye of the teacher/monitor.

Skill Instruction and Practice

Although basal anthologies are the most colorful and prominent components of the basal series, it is the scope and sequence of skills listed in the teacher's guidebook that is the backbone of the technical control of students learning to read, and these skills are realized in the skill instruction portion of group lessons. Depending on the publisher, the skills instruction during group lessons precedes or follows the story reading. Most often its position is of little consequence because the stories are rarely connected to the skill sequence. Skill instruction consists of guidebook examples designed to tell students about decoding and comprehension rules and then to provide practice so that students can learn to use the skills in order to become independent readers at some later date. For example, a group of students might be taught the letter *b* and its sound so that they can use this knowledge to decode words the teacher presents, which in turn will eventually enable students to read the *b* words in simple stories with controlled vocabulary, and finally—when the guidebook allows—students will be free to use this skill as they please.

For students, skill instruction means that the language that they learned and use ordinarily to communicate their ideas to others in all circumstances, is fragmented into isolated bits in order for them to learn to read at school. Rather than dealing with the meaning of language and how literacy can inform and improve their lives, students are asked to consider first letters, then word parts, words, phrases, and sets of unrelated sentences in order to develop independence in reading. Moreover, the interaction between teachers and students is carefully orchestrated during skill instruction because publishers provide the goals, sequence, directions, examples, and answers. Students learn to react to guidebook directives rather than to act on and further their own knowledge.

Since Dolores Durkin (1978–79) found that teachers spend less than 5 percent of group lessons directly teaching students decoding and comprehension skills, the skill portion of group lessons has become the focus of much attention. In a later study, Durkin (1981) found that guidebook directions mentioned what a skill was, but they simply left students to their own devices during seatwork to intuit why they should learn the skill and when and how to use it. The many recommendations on how to reskill teachers so that they can improve their instruction bodes ill for students because advocates of the new procedures seek to extend the separation of learning from independent control of reading by specifying when and how students will use these skills. Although within the logic of technical control this extension makes perfect sense, from a student perspective it separates the act of learning from the knowledge students produce, reducing the likelihood that they will understand or make use of the knowledge beyond the controlled lesson. Perhaps three examples will illustrate my point that things get worse for students under direct instruction.

Gerald Duffy and Laura Roehler (1982a; 1982b; 1982c) require that all steps within a lesson must be known before the lesson begins. Consequently, teachers must extend the basal plans beyond the initial presentation portion (the what) to provide explicit information on how students can incorporate the lesson objective into their repertoire of reading skills (rather than allowing students to discover its use during seatwork). In fact, Duffy and Roehler maintain that lessons must include step-by-step explanations of why, how, and when students should use a skill in order to be considered instruction at all. As a result, students are asked to suspend control over their answers and knowledge until the teacher allows them to use the guidebook's skill in the teacher's prescribed way. Students not only lose control over the topic of the lesson, but also the context of subsequent use of the skill. Duffy and Roehler insist that this formula will work for decoding, comprehension, and even skills dealing with students' attitudes toward reading (Roehler and Duffy 1982).

Ann Brown, Joseph Campione, and James Day (1981) provide a more restrictive version of teacher-directed instruction. They divide knowledge about reading into two types: basic knowledge which is considered vital to students' academic survival and esoteric knowledge which is assumed a luxury that those who are able will learn after they master the basics. Accordingly, teachers are to devote primary interest to basic knowledge, raising students' competence to minimum standards. "If adequate performance depends on the application of a set of rules, and rules can be specified exactly, then it should be possible to design lessons that introduce the uninitiated to these possibilities" (p.18). The key words here are "adequate performance," "set of rules," and "rules specified exactly." Beyond the specification of correct answers required in the first version of directed instruction, in this version, students' range of appropriate knowledge concerning reading is restricted to basic skills, defined as a set of rules on which they must be tested for competence. Who will specify the rules? Rather than allowing students to develop their own rules through reading and discussion with peers and teachers, Brown, Campione, and Day further the technical control. "The more detailed understanding the teacher has of effective rules for reading and studying, the more readily those rules can be trained" (p.19). And where will teachers find details concerning the rules? In the teacher's guidebook.

A third alternative of directed instruction takes technical control to its logical conclusion by incorporating hand signals for student response, tightly sequenced scripts, massed practice in choral chant, and modified alphabet for easy access to the skill (Becker and Carnine 1980). When first introduced in the late 1960s, advocates' calls for scripted lessons, a focus on basic skills, and biweekly monitoring of student test scores were met with scorn from many reading experts. Now these previously deplorable elements are incorporated into most basal programs. What separates the University of Oregon's Direct Instruction Model, the most widely celebrated exponent of this alternative, from other versions is its unapologetic advocacy of the need for total control over teachers and students during reading instruction—teachers read from scripts and students respond only when signaled.

In a curious turn of logic, these new ways of reskilling teachers are proposed in the name of students' independence when reading. Yet in each, students are asked to forego control over their learning in order to receive the teacher's gift of literacy. Can students learn to be free by participating in tightly sequenced lessons which define how, why, and when they should use a particular skill? In other words, is it freedom in reading when a student learns to use someone else's rule of decoding or comprehending in a specified way?

Tests, Assignments, and Corrections

Formal testing is a ubiquitous occurrence in American reading programs. Excluding the placement tests—used primarily for initial identification of the appropriate basal level for an individual student in order to begin instruction—first grade students might complete between 200 and 1500 test items during the year depending on which basal series their district selected (Goodman, Shannon, Freeman, and Murphy 1988). Basal tests are designed and used to determine whether or not students have mastered the skills and vocabulary suggested in the guidebooks; and, therefore, basal tests are keyed directly to the scope and sequence of decoding and comprehension skills. The criterion for passing these tests is usually set at 80 percent correct; however, because of the high number of skills that must be tested, some skills are tested with only three or four items reducing passing criterion to 67 or 75 percent. Nearly all items are written in a multiple-choice format for ease in scoring.

Because of the importance placed on these tests by teachers and administrators, the basal tests have received considerable attention. First among the concerns expressed is the idea that these tests fragment reading into isolated skills, assessing at best, skill knowledge, not reading, and at worst, familiarity with one set of commercial materials (Kavale 1979). Because typically only 20 percent of the book tests deal with comprehension of passages (Goodman, Shannon, Freeman, and Murphy 1988), students are rarely asked to read more than a couple of sentences during testing. Most often their attention must focus on decoding and individual word meaning—selecting the appropriate word part or word to fit a narrow context. Other critics question the arbitrary selection of too few test items to gain reliability of information concerning students' abilities to perform even this narrow definition of reading (Johnson and Pearson 1975). All told, basal tests give more the illusion of assessment of a student's reading ability than they supply sufficient information necessary to make weighty decisions concerning students' futures.

"Taking a test" during reading group entails isolating students from one another to ensure privacy and honesty. Although the tests hold little mystery for the students because the vocabulary and item formats are the same as the exercises that students have encountered in basal stories and practice materials, during the tests reading becomes an individual and solitary activity, without questions or conversation.[3] Since much depends on students' scores—for both students and teachers—there is a certain amount of anxiety among group members as each struggles to perform his or her duty. Once the tests are completed, students rarely see them again, although the results will determine whether students enter the reteaching phase of a particular skill or set of skills, whether they will progress to the next book, and sometimes whether they will graduate to the next grade.

The final two activities which occupy time during group lessons are directions for how to complete seatwork assignments and correcting those assignments after their completion. According to Dolores Durkin (1978–79), these activities often are designed to provide students with opportunities to practice independently the skills learned during reading group, and correcting them during group affords teachers the opportunity to provide immediate assistance to students who may need further help (Osborn 1984). However, there is another more practical reason to take time during reading group to present and monitor students' seatwork. Since two-thirds of students' time during reading lessons is spent in independent practice at their seats while another group of students occupies the teacher's attention, there must be sufficient amounts of work to keep students busy for between forty-five minutes to an hour each day. Moreover, students must be sufficiently aware of how to complete the assignments or they will fail to gain adequate practice, or perhaps worst yet, become disruptive during another group's lesson. The importance of seatwork in both pedagogical and management terms may be reflected in the time teachers devote to explaining and correcting it. However, for students it means sitting and listening to the teacher rush through explanations of typically five or six different activities.

Seatwork

Nearly 70 percent of students' time during reading lessons is spent working independently on seatwork—workbooks, worksheets, and boardwork (Fisher et al. 1978). Most often workbook and worksheets are assigned according to the directions in teacher's guidebooks, and students work page by page until the workbook or box of dittos for a particular level is completed, only to start afresh on remedial worksheets or the next level the following day depending on how they fare on the criterion-referenced book test. Boardwork is usually assigned to an entire class and is often unrelated to the rest of the reading program. These activities are routine for students, occurring five days a week during each week of a school year for every year of their elementary school career. Describing the fate of students concerning seatwork, Linda Anderson (1984) states: "In addition to death and taxes, we might include seatwork in elementary classrooms as a certainty in life" (p.93).

According to Anderson (1984), in one of the few studies concerning seatwork during reading lessons, this inevitability of school life presents a formidable challenge for students. In many instances, most students recognize neither the purpose nor the payoff from completing seatwork assignments. They do their seatwork "just to get it done" because it is how they do their work and "looking busy" is what is most important during seatwork.[4] Anderson offers three types of evidence to substantiate her conclusion. Students often check with one another about their relative state of completion ("How are you doing?" "How far are you?"); they make marks on pages without reading directions and rarely review a page before simply turning the page and starting on the next; and they express relief when finished ("There! I didn't understand that, but I got it done").

Upon closer inspection, Anderson found that these remarks and behaviors were not always equally distributed across students from different ability groups within observed classrooms. That is, students in lower groups were more often confused and were attempting to look busy in order to avoid drawing attention to themselves. These students demonstrated remarkable coping strategies which enabled them to complete their assignments with moderate success, but without practicing the intended skill (e.g., asking the teacher or another student to read whatever text was required to complete the task, marking answers without reading the instructions or items, using a process of elimination to obtain correct answers, and going to the box where completed seatwork is kept and looking at other students' answers). Although these coping strategies were effective, they subverted any pedagogical benefit seatwork might offer. Moreover, the entire process presents students in low achievement groups with a different message about learning and reading than teachers intend.

Within the aforementioned limitations of basal lessons, students in higher achievement groups receive a more useful message from their seatwork. While the seatwork did not always make sense even to them (Anderson 1984), higher group students were successful often enough during seatwork and reading lessons to know that both are supposed to make sense, and, therefore, they should try to reduce ambiguity before proceeding. This self-monitoring, truly literate act is quite different from the coping strategies their lower group counterparts used during seat-work. Unfortunately, this variation in the implicit message is not confined only to seatwork portions of reading lessons.

UNEQUAL TREATMENT OF ABILITY GROUPS

Several researchers have recently examined the differential treatment of ability groups during reading instruction.[5] Richard Allington (1983) con-cludes from his investigations that good and poor reading groups differ in reading competence as much from differences in instruction as they do from variation in individual aptitudes. These differences take several forms: teacher interruption behaviors, the amount of students' reading during reading lessons, the content of those lessons, and the difficulty of the reading materials used during reading lessons.

Teachers interrupt students in lower ability groups during oral reading between two and five times more frequently than they do students in higher ability groups, regardless of the type of mistake that was made (Allington 1980; Hoffman et al. 1984; Pflum et al. 1980). Teachers give students in low groups less time to correct themselves and are likely to pronounce any troublesome word immediately to keep the lesson moving. These frequent interruptions contribute to general hesitancy of lower group students during oral reading, to their frequent appeals for assis-tance from teachers, and to their reluctance or inability to monitor their own reading.

With both students and teachers interrupting, students in low reading groups have few opportunities for sustained reading (Allington 1977). In fact, students in higher ability groups read about three times as many words per day during reading group as lower group readers do. Allington (1983) explained this discrepancy by identifying that 70 percent of the high groups' reading is done silently, while lower group students read orally 70 percent of the time. Because oral reading is slower paced and requires more management, lower group students are denied access to the same number of words as higher group students. Moreover, these differences may actually be greater for individuals than Allington reports because during group silent reading everyone must read, but during group oral reading only one student is reading while the others may be listening. This finding led Allington (1977) to ask: "If they don't read much, how they ever gonna get good?"

During oral reading, teachers are likely to direct the lower groups' attention to the phonic characteristics of isolated words and how they are pronounced, whereas their comments to high group students deal more often with the semantic and syntactic context which surrounds the troublesome word (Allington 1980; Alpert 1974; Collins and Haviland

1979; Gambrell, Wilson, and Ganett 1981). For instance, Linda Gambrell and her co-authors found that fourth grade students in low groups: a) worked on phonics in isolation twice as often as students in high groups, b) spent half as much time on reading in context, and c) engaged in nonreading activities during half of their reading lessons compared to only a third for high groups. These differences were exaggerated for students in low groups who found the assigned reading materials difficult. These students spent twice again as much time on isolated phonics instruction, half again as much time reading, and 61 percent of their time on nonreading activities.

The relative difficulty of the assigned reading materials also provides evidence of unequal treatment of reading groups (Clay 1972; Gambrell, Wilson, and Gannett 1981; Hoffman et al. 1984). Students in high groups are often asked to read texts which are easy for them—in which they misread about one in one hundred words—however, students in low groups are often placed in difficult materials in which they misread over 15 percent of the words. This difficulty inhibits low group readers' use of context, forces them to read word by word, and makes them rely on the phonic characteristics of unknown words. Their frequent mistakes trigger student and teacher interruptions, and the unfortunate cycle begins anew.

Overall, these studies suggest a clear discrepancy between the messages sent to students in high and low ability reading groups. Within the limited strictures of the basal lessons, high group students are told and shown that reading is supposed to make sense, that getting the author's message is the purpose of reading, that self-monitoring of this comprehension is the goal, and that reading is a useful process outside the reading group at which all students can be successful. Lower group students are sent a very different message, one which suggests that reading need not make sense, that accurate pronunciation is of prime importance when reading, that reading is a school function at which some students are likely to be unsuccessful, and that teachers will monitor their performance closely. In fact, several researchers note that teachers use more language of control while working with lower reading groups than they use when directing high group lessons (Eder 1981; Brophy and Good 1986; Rist 1970). Jere Brophy and Thomas Good (1986) suggest that in order to be at all successful, lower group reading lessons must be more teacher-centered, more tightly controlled, and more focused on literal interpretations of the text. What is left unclear in these studies is just who are members of these ability groups.

MEMBERSHIP IN LOW ABILITY GROUPS

Students' initial placement into a reading group occurs during kindergarten or at the beginning of first grade. Typically, two sources of information are used to make this decision: students' standardized achievement test scores and/or teacher's judgment. Whether schools rely on one type of information or both, the results are usually the same—lower-class children are more likely to be assigned to lower reading groups than middle- or upper-class children. Donna Eder (1981) comments on the consequences of this unfortunate procedure.

> Because students are exposed to different learning contexts when they are assigned to ability groups, their behavior is likely to be differentially influenced in line with their group assignments. (Since) little movement across groups has been found either during the academic year or between years, it is important that those assignments be accurate. However, since most students are assigned to ability groups within the first few weeks of first grade, it is highly unlikely that accurate assessments of student aptitudes have been made. The lack of accurate measures of academic aptitude in early grades is particularly important since it increases the likelihood of ethnic and class bias in ability group assignment. (p.160)

When students' test scores are available, teachers rely heavily on them when forming reading groups (Borko, Shavelson, and Stern 1981). In fact during experimental studies, teachers often overlooked other relevant information and made their grouping decisions on test scores alone (Russo 1978)—rank ordering the scores and then segmenting them into high, middle, and low ability groups. However, according to the Committee on Ability Testing for the National Academy of Sciences, achievement test scores are correlated highly and positively with social class status (Wigdor and Garner 1982). That is, upper-class students typically score higher (one standard deviation in some instances) than lower-class students. And although there have been flare-ups of controversy every decade on this subject, the bias in favor of children from middle- and upper-class homes has been recognized since the beginning of the educational testing movement during the early decades of the twentieth century (Linn 1982). Thus, when scores are used to sort students, lower-class students are more likely to be assigned to lower reading groups, remedial reading programs, and special education classes than their middle- and upper-class counterparts (Fotheringham and Creal 1980; Rowan and Miracle 1983).

This relationship between test scores and social class holds across racial groups also, although minorities are usually the lowest of the lowly. For example, Low and Clement (1982) found that although "Black and Hispanic students scored significantly lower than their white peers in lower, middle, and upper classes, lower-class children in general scored significantly below middle- and upper-class children on standardized tests of reading comprehension."[6] Achievement tests, then, seem based on experiences (rather than cognitive abilities) to which children from different classes do not have equal access. Tests seem as much an indicator of family background as they are a projective device concerning students' true potential for learning to read. That these early tests have been found to be correlated with later academic success can be interpreted as confirmation that groups are treated differently during instruction after group assignment, which suggests a larger school bias against children from economically poorer homes.

Quite often standardized test scores are not immediately available to primary teachers when they are faced with decisions on grouping for instruction. Group assignments in these instances are made on the basis of teacher observation and subsequent evaluation of students' potential for learning to read (Salomon-Cox 1980). The outcome under these circumstances is the same as when test scores are used—lower-class children end up in the lower ability groups (Hamilton 1983). At first glance this may seem reasonable since teacher judgment confirms the test scores, but a closer look suggests that anything but individual student aptitude is taken into consideration during these decisions. What is most often found is that differences in dress, deportment, manners, language, and language use are interpreted as intellectual deficits. Perhaps three extended examples will make my point clearer.

One of the most well-known, but controversial, observational studies of reading groups is Ray Rist's (1970; 1973) investigation of the reading instruction received by black children in one St. Louis class during kindergarten, first, and half of second grade. Rist found that in the absence of test information, the kindergarten teacher worked from her own implicit "ideal type" characterization of fast learners when she made decisions about reading groups during the first few weeks of the school year. This ideal type was based on social rather than academic information. Children were assigned to the "fast learners" table if they "appeared clean and interested, sought interaction, spoke with less dialect, were at ease with adults, displayed leadership within the class, and came from homes which displayed various status criteria valued in the middle class" (1970: 444). Children who did not meet these implicit standards were placed at different tables away from the teacher's immediate visual field during whole class instruction.

For students at table 1 (the fast learners), "the classroom experience was one where the teacher displayed interest in them, spent a large proportion of teaching time with them, directed little control-oriented behavior towards them, held them as models for the remainder of the class and continually reinforced statements that they were special students" (1970: 447). "Slower students [tables 2 and 3] suffered a higher degree of control-oriented behavior, a lack of verbal interaction with the teacher, a disproportionately small amount of teacher's time, and ridicule"

(1970: 445). Because of the differential treatment, students fulfilled the kindergarten teacher's assessment of their potential by year's end. Table 1 students were well on their way to success in reading, and most table 2 and 3 students were barely beyond their entry point, and several students had withdrawn from participation in class altogether.

The first and second grade teacher maintained initial group placement because it seemed warranted based on past academic performance. This "caste system" within the class was broken only in the second half of second grade (after completion of the study) when two table 1 students were demoted to table 2 because neither "could keep a clean desk" and table 1s were "a very clean group." Two table 2 members replaced the fallen table 1s because they were "extremely neat with their desk and floor."

This may seem like an extreme example—perhaps it is—however, several researchers note a similar independent effect of family social background on ability group assignment across grade levels (Alexander and McDill 1976; Michaels 1981; Rosenbaum 1976) and others find a permanence of ability groups within and across grades once original groups are formed (McDermott 1976; Pikulski and Kirsch 1979). Moreover, the tendency toward self-fulfilling prophecy is discussed by many (Brophy 1979; Eder 1981; Good 1981; Seaver 1973). Merton (1957) explains why these prophecies are so resistant to change.

> The self-fulfilling prophecy is, in the beginning, a "false" definition of a situation evoking a new behavior which makes the originally false conception come "true." The specious validity of the self-fulfilling prophecies perpetuates a reign of error. For the prophet will cite the actual course of events as proof that he was right from the very beginning. Such are the perversities of social logic. (p. 423)

In an account of a three-year study of the school experience of black children from a low income urban area, Perry Gilmore (1985) extends Rist's evidence of social factors as the basic determiners of group placement by suggesting that student attitude as expressed in their outward behavior becomes a contributing factor in whether or not students gain access to literacy instruction. To illustrate his point, Gilmore examined the group placement and subsequent treatment of students who regularly engaged in two key behavioral events—"stylized sulking" and "doin' steps" —which teachers considered indicative of students' bad attitudes toward authority and schooling. Above all, "it was clear to staff and parents as well as students, that in cases of tracking and/or selection for honors or special academic preference, attitude outweighed academic achievement or IQ test performance" (p. 112).[7]

According to Gilmore, teachers interpreted stylized sulking, a pouting, defiant posturing struck when students clashed with teachers, and "doin' steps," rhythmic dancing full of "taboo breaking and sexual innuendo," as black behaviors. Students who engaged in these activities were considered menacing or even lewd, and they were denied the quality literacy instruction which was provided to students "who demonstrated alignment with, if not allegiance to, the school ethos" (p. 113). Although teachers' bias in favor of well-behaved students was not as blatant as Rist had observed, Gilmore suggests that teachers had much lower expectations for "Black" students and were less willing to give them opportunities to prove their linguistic competence because it was usually embedded in a "street" context.[8]

Shirley Brice Heath (1983) expands our frame of reference still further in her account of a ten-year study of the working class and townspeople in one North Carolina community. After a detailed description of the language and language use in black working-class (Trackton), white working-class (Roadville), and racially mixed middle-class sections of town, Heath explains that teachers' expectations concerning appropriate school knowledge, language, and behavior could only be matched by middle-class children. Accordingly, most working-class students, both black and white, were assigned to lower reading groups because they seemed unable to adjust to school use of time, space, talk, and materials, even though Trackton and Roadville children responded to schools in very different ways. Heath explains this phenomenon as a mismatch between school and home cultures for working-class children, which cannot be overcome if schools remain rigid in their expectations and treatment of lower-class children.

School is a place ruled by time schedules and space restrictions. There is a time and a place to sit, a time and a place for reading work, and a time and a place for play. Town and Roadville homes, which run by similar rules, prepared children well for these time and space expectations. Children from both groups expect adults to make and enforce such rules. However, Trackton homes were seldom so structured and, consequently, demands for Trackton children to conform to time and space constraints at school were often met with confusion and resistance. For example, Trackton children, who played outside most of the time, were perplexed by teachers' categories of inside things and outside things, and they often brought toys and books to inappropriate places. Similarly, they were puzzled by teachers' time schedules which did not seem to be tied to any task directly. Sometimes children sat for long periods of time after finishing a task because the period was not over, and other times they were interrupted during enjoyable activities because "time is up." Teachers frequently interpreted this confusion as a lack of intellect and resistance as a demonstration of poor upbringing.

Roadville and Trackton children's language use caused teachers con-

siderable concern. Beyond dialect differences, the grammatical and prag-
matic functions of language differed among the three groups and often
resulted in teachers taking offense at students' statements or actions
when none was intended. For example, both Roadville and Trackton
children had difficulty deciphering indirect questions and commands
such as "Is that where the scissors belong?" and rarely complied with
such teacher requests. For lack of similar home experience, Trackton
children were struck mute by direct questions for which both asker and
answerer knew the answer. In Trackton, questions were asked only for
legitimate informational purposes and not to test the obvious. Roadville
children, who were used to adults setting the rules for talk between
adults and children, often felt betrayed when teachers interrupted children's conversations and arguments because children talk among themselves was outside adult "territory."

Basal materials and teachers' equivocation concerning the meaning
of the term "story" distinguished middle class from working-class children also. Stories in common school and basal parlance refers to any
written text beyond a sentence in length, either fiction or nonfiction. Yet
in Roadville, telling a story meant a close, factual account of some actual
event that was used to correct past behavior and to present a moral to
guide future behavior. With this background, Roadville students excelled
in factual retellings, but were confused by the apparent lack of purpose
in the stories they were asked to retell, and they failed often in activities
which required them to use their imaginations to produce fantasies.
Trackton children were familiar with stories which combined fact and
fiction, told in a style that could hold an audience's attention as the story
teller entertained. They had little experience with straightforward, factual
accounts and often found these activities boring.[9]

Taken together these studies suggest that whether schools rely on test
data or teacher judgment, lower-class students wind up at the bottom of
the heap. Wilkins (1976) argues that the process is actually middle-class
school personnel perhaps unconsciously demonstrating a general societal
philosophy which holds that citizens are personally responsible for their
position in society—that lower-class people possess intellectual and character flaws which account for their lack of previous success and inhibit
their prospects for the future, while middle- and upper-class people are
successful because they are resourceful and industrious. In response to
such claims, school officials offer their commitment to one scope and
sequence of goals for all students, compensatory and district remedial
programs, and the students' academic records as evidence that their
initial assessment of students was proper and of their commitment to
low-achieving students.

What they fail to acknowledge is the fact that the manner in which
these goals are pursued differs across social classes: 1) teachers attempt

greater control of lower-class children; 2) the number of skills addressed differs considerably according to class—lower-class students' attention is directed toward decoding and middle- and upper-class students are expected to consider the text message; and 3) academic decisions are often made based on social criterion. As a result, reading instruction silently, but surely, contributes to the maintenance of present social class stratification in American society. During reading instruction, it is clear that the rich get richer, while the poor get poorer.

Summary

American reading programs are organized to produce students with verifiable levels of reading competence in order to assuage the concerns of the public, who expect graduates to be productive citizens, and business, which needs workers who can follow written directions and executives who can understand and produce production reports accurately. Just as with most modern social institutions, schools adopt business and scientific practices to render reading instruction predictable across classrooms and schools through the standard use of technology. Toward that end, the process of reading instruction is redefined from the development of goals and means on a daily basis to assist students learning to comprehend written messages to the management of students as they work their way through a basal series according to the directives in a teacher's guidebook. To aid schools in this process, state legislatures and departments of education have passed laws and developed policies of testing students' competence at regular intervals to ensure that schools are accountable for the funds they receive. "By one criterion of literacy, that of simply recognizing the words of a text or answering a multiple choice test on what it is about, the United States has been reasonably effective" (Purves 1984: 3).

Several variations of this reorganization exist—simple required use of basal materials, mastery learning, merit pay, and school effectiveness—but the underlying logic which enables these programs to function appears to be the same. The entire process seems based on school personnel's reification of reading instruction as the application of commercially produced basal reading materials. This reduction of all possible alternatives to this one concrete set of materials enables the technical control of teachers' and students' actions through the directions and material included in the program. Foremost among these opportunities for control may be the direct connection between the criterion-referenced tests and the skills, vocabulary, and procedures of the basal series, which enable administrators to monitor teachers' and students' actions as if by remote control. The combination of the attempts to rationalize reading programs and the reification of reading instruction alienates teachers—at least objectively—from their work. This in turn furthers the opportunities and improves the environment for control because teachers begin to consider it appropriate to withhold their subjectivity from their work and to rely on materials to solve their problems and on tests to evaluate their students' and their own success.

Ultimately, the biggest losers are the students who are processed through these reorganized programs. All students are subject to the strictures of the basal programs which emphasize decoding over comprehension, divide literacy into discrete skill components, and provide stories written to be easily decoded and not to offend any interest groups rather than to engage students enthusiastically in the process. Furthermore, basals reduce consideration of text to the reproduction of explicit content through a series of specified questions and prescribed answers. After participating only a short time in such instruction, students learn that reading means not to question the authority of teacher or text. For lower-class children, the outlook is even more dismal since they are often denied full access to even this limited type of literacy because teachers, basals, and tests are products of mainstream culture which seem unable to accommodate diversity in language, appearance, or behavior.

Virtually no one, including the teacher, is offered a literacy which asks readers to go beyond the word and literal translation of text to tackle the sense, feeling, truth, and intention of an author through the words he or she used in a text. Moreover, no one is asked to develop his or her ability to express understanding of a text—what it does and might mean in one's life. In short, no one is asked to be truly literate by any criterion beyond a standardized test.

This summary is written in perhaps an exaggerated style to demonstrate in the strongest language possible the consequences of current reading programs on the work and lives of teachers and students. If over 90 percent of reading instruction is delivered according to guidebook directions and through the completion of basal materials, my analysis is relevant, if not totally descriptive of, 90 percent of the elementary school teachers and students in America. Of course, there are sensitive and effective teachers (inside and outside of schools) who help a few students to become truly literate, but these successes come in spite of the technical control of reading lessons, not because of it. However, this bleak picture need not lead to the pessimism which suggests that reading instruction in schools is hopeless (e.g., Kozol 1985) or the cynicism which suggests that more enlightened control of teachers and students is the answer (e.g., Resnick and Resnick 1985). There are seams within the logic, organization, and outcomes of these reorganized reading programs which allow, and even invite, those interested in change to organize their efforts in order to reverse the current patterns of American reading programs.

□PART III□

*Resistance to the Management
of Reading Instruction*

Reaction and Resistance
to Managed Reading Programs

□ American reading programs are organized to reduce the contribution of teachers and students to reading instruction in order to render it more productive and its outcome more predictable. This may sound odd to those who believe that hard work and personal involvement are the keys to success in any endeavor. But in fact, that is the intention and result of the rationalization of reading programs in which quotas for student competence and basal technology are substituted for teachers' and students' subjectivity. From outside the classroom context, in the central offices of school districts, in the state and federal education departments, and in state legislatures, this line of reasoning has a curious attraction for policymakers. "Were not business and scientific principles the reasons for America's great success in economic affairs? Then, why won't these same principles produce effective reading programs?" But inside American classrooms, the rationalization of reading instruction has a destructive impact on teachers, students, and literacy as it reduces each to the status of objects to be manipulated in efforts to find the right formula for higher test scores and greater confidence among the taxpaying public.

Max Weber (1964) called the rationalization of everyday life and social institutions an "iron cage" from which there was no escape except to return to preindustrial society and to give up its considerable material benefits. In short, the unequal distribution of power and wealth and hierarchical social relations at work and in leisure are simply facts of modern life. Recently, several educational critics have adapted Weber's gloomy conclusion for the context of education, suggesting that American schooling cannot be equitable and just toward teachers and students because it is a tightly designed, rationalized institution which functions to reproduce contemporary social structure (Bourdieu and Passeron 1977; Bowles and Gintis 1976; Jencks 1972). According to these critics, there must be a prerequisite change in American social structure for there to be a change in American schools.

Contemporary reading instruction has also been painted in such black and white tones, implying that without rationalized programs and the technology of reading instruction, Americans would be unable to keep pace with the rapidly increasing demands on literacy in modern life (Carroll and Chall 1975; Rosenshine 1981). Titles like *Becoming Readers in a Complex Society* (Purves and Niles 1984), *A Nation at Risk* (1983), and *Becoming a Nation of Readers* (Anderson 1985) add a sense of patriotic drama and tie progress in reading instruction directly to economic issues. The message is clear, though, and remarkably similar to Weber's; either Americans accept the rationalization of reading programs (and try to make the best of it) or they sink to the status of a third world country.

Although my analysis of elementary school reading instruction may appear equally bleak (if all society is rationalized and appears unchangeable, how can reading instruction be any different), I do not accept Weberian pessimism which leaves participants in reading instruction impotent in developing a truly literate culture. There are a sufficient number of contradictions and seams within current American reading programs to allow a different view of literacy to develop in schools and for a correction of the subject/object inversion wherein teachers, students, and literacy become objects and basal publishers, reading experts, and teacher's guidebooks become subjects during reading lessons. While I do not wish to imply that a change in reading instruction will by itself lead to direct changes in the rationalization of other aspects of life or American social structure, within the proper context, American schools could develop citizens who can, in Paulo Freire's words, "read the word and the world." And there are students, parents, teachers, and teacher educators who share this belief.

Simply because students and teachers are managed within rationalized reading programs does not mean that they totally acquiesce to the basal directives—nor does it mean that the rationalized programs run like clockwork. Participants' interest in controlling their work and the problems in managed instruction provide room to maneuver for those who seek change in the current conditions of reading programs. For example, neither students nor teachers are particularly well prepared for a rationalized system. Students, especially lower-class and minority children, do not fit easily into the structure and routines of rationalized lessons. Often, teachers see their work as really prescientific—as a craft improved through experience rather than by formal experimentation—and child-centered rather than business-oriented. Literacy, itself, enables students and teachers to read and follow directions, but also enables them to pursue counterarguments if they so desire. Finally, the logic of rationalization seems vulnerable in elementary schools. Advocates have been unable to make good on their promises to produce a large number of verifiably, highly literate graduates, and the pursuit of this goal across schools and within classrooms is often interpreted as oppressive and divisive by some participants in reading instruction.

Response to rationalized reading programs has come in four forms. First, there are those who agree with Weber, more or less implicitly, and see managed instruction as the means to keep pace with modern society and willingly participate in managed reading lessons. Second, there are participants who seek personal relief from what they consider the excesses of rationalization or who seek to reduce the pressures that it causes. These individuals hope to give rationalization a humane face while its body continues its standardization of literacy and instruction for the sake of efficiency and productivity. A third group distinguishes itself from the second with a questioning of the philosophical and pedagogical assumptions of rationalized reading. These latter two groups seek ways to counteract the force and influence of the rationalized programs; however, their reactions often fail to transcend the immediacy of their own circumstances in order to analyze and act upon the underlying social and political foundations of their plight.

The fourth group finds the present conditions of reading instruction intolerable, and it recognizes that the consequent pressure and stress that participants feel are not an isolated, personal experience, but a result of the conditions of their work. Those categorized in this fourth group seek to understand these conditions, to analyze how they connect to the larger social structure, and to act to change their circumstances. The reactions of the second and third groups and the resistance of the fourth present hope for the future of American reading programs.

REACTIONS TO MANAGED INSTRUCTION

Students

Student reactions to a steady diet of guidebook-directed instruction are often exerted in constructive ways which further their literacy and their understanding of their lives. Any observer in elementary classrooms will notice some students sneaking a look at a library book or a popular magazine when they are supposed to be finishing their seatwork and others talking to their classmates about some fact of life they deem more important than the task at hand. At times though, the reactions are destructive—refusal to participate or acting out—which leads frequently to students' isolation from other students and separation from any sort of text. Some students seem to do little more during reading instruction than engage in a series of ploys to avoid management. Most teachers have stories to tell about students who reacted to the control of basal instruction in this way.

During a recent observational study (Shannon, in press), I visited twenty classrooms to watch teachers' and students' behaviors during reading instruction when student/teacher ratios were reduced below twenty to one. In eighteen of the classrooms, teachers and students participated in guidebook-directed lessons with teachers following the directives closely, conducting group lessons, and monitoring seatwork, while students attended group lessons, completed seatwork, and reacted to the order imposed by the basal. In each classroom, there were at least a few students demonstrating constructive and destructive reactions to lesson content, instructional routines, and teacher comments. In fact, only two of the eighteen group lessons that were observed closely were free from student disruptions. These two lessons were teacher-directed games for vocabulary practice in which students were allowed to talk quietly while they waited for their turn.

In the other sixteen lessons, reactions ranged from forgetting necessary equipment (e.g., pencils, books, workbooks) and returning to retrieve them from desks to repeated requests to visit the washroom or drinking fountain to nearly unison chants of "I don't get it." Each reaction disturbed the flow of events in the scripted lesson and caused minor irritation for the teachers. Some of the more imaginative reactions during seatwork included dropping a box of one hundred twenty-eight crayons on the floor and taking twenty-three minutes to pick them up, turning a student desk away from the teacher's line of vision and coloring the worksheet illustrations, and handing in untouched seatwork to the "completed box" and playing until the teacher asked to see the assignment during the group lesson. Beyond these overt responses of contempt for managed lessons were more subtle reactions which frequently caught my eye.

For example, in eleven group lessons one student insisted on telling the events of his or her last night's or weekend's experience regardless of the teacher's attempts to press on with the lesson. These storytelling reactions began almost immediately upon the teacher's request for the group lesson to start. "Teacher, do you know what I did last night?" Without exception, teachers listened to these stories for a minute or two and then attempted to begin the lesson. Invariably, whether the lesson objective was vocabulary, phonics, or story reading, something in the lesson reminded the student of the previous evening or weekend and the story would start again. In several of the groups, other students asked the storyteller questions while the teacher tried to quell the interruption. In one classroom, the student competition became too great and the teacher sent the group back to its seats to finish its assignments without benefit of appropriate instruction.

To be sure, in the two classrooms I observed in which reading instruction did not revolve around a teacher's guidebook and basal materials, students were not always engaged in the group story writing about a previous trip to the museum lesson or book reading, writing, and analysis lessons, but students' "off task" behaviors were not directed toward subversion of these lessons either. With very few exceptions (e.g., nonparticipation), the teachers in these two classrooms considered students' digressions from their assignments to be an essential part of their making sense of the activities. During one observation, one of these teachers became a bit self-conscious about my writing continuously in my notebook while watching a group of students talk freely when they were supposed to be finishing a story silently at their desks. Perhaps because she thought I would disapprove of the student "misbehavior" she asked them to include me in their discussion of whether or not it was lying when the tailor said, "I killed seven with one blow."

Others have reported similar student reactions to guidebook-directed instruction (Bissex 1980; Bussis 1982; Smith 1986). They suggest that otherwise bright white middle- and upper-class children as well as poor and minority students work carelessly, making progress in fits and starts, and pretending confusion when none really exists—all apparently to insert their personal voice into the din of the technological instruction. Like the factory worker who drops his or her wrench into the machinery in order to stop the production line, many students seem intent on disrupting the management of their literate thoughts and actions. Some students choose to react in this way often.[1] Students do gain space and time for themselves through these acts and they do learn to "read" the world of classroom reading instruction, at least well enough to plan, execute, and get away with these practices. Their reactions, however, do little to further their literacy in constructive ways and seldom lead them to analyze their circumstances sufficiently well to understand why their reading instruction is so mechanically organized.

Parents

Although schools legitimize themselves by garnering the support of the taxpaying public, few schools actively solicit the public's involvement in schools beyond the fund-raising activities of parent/teacher associations (Epstein 1986). This separation of home and school is understandable within the bureaucratic logic which suggests that schools and families have different roles to play in the organization and reproduction of society.

Accordingly, schools can achieve their goals most effectively and efficiently if left alone to exert their professional judgment concerning children's education without parental interference (Parsons 1959; Weber 1964). In reading programs, this interference manifests itself when parents complain about group placement, attempt to teach erroneous phonic rules (e.g., "when two vowels go walking"), or violate the scope and sequence of goals listed in the teacher's guidebook. In short, many school personnel question parents' competence to teach their children to read and prefer that they would leave it to the experts.

Yet some parents have not accepted this limited role which excludes them from active participation in the education of their children. For example, in the midst of the merit pay reading program that I investigated, parents of children attending a magnet school for physical education insisted that a literature-based language arts program be initiated to supplement the guidebook-directed classroom reading instruction. As a result of the parents' organization and continued pressure, a teacher was hired, given a budget, and allocated separate space to conduct small group lessons in writing and story analysis using books from the classroom and school libraries and students' own writing. Each student at the school—lower-class, minority, foreign language, handicapped, as well as white middle- and upper-class—participated in the program, although children labelled gifted received twice as much time as other students (and thus some white middle- and upper-class children received somewhat preferential treatment). Parents provided support for the program through budget supplements raised in typical ways, by serving as aides during some lessons, and through vigorous campaigns to preserve the program during district budget cuts. These parents' reactions to the rationalization of the formal reading program was to move literacy outside the parameters of formal reading instruction and thus outside the parameters of rationalization.

More permanent coalitions of parents can be found in Washington D.C., Chicago, Seattle, and New Jersey, where grass-roots parent groups evolved into permanent organizations which support local parent initiatives to improve public schools (Bastian et al. 1986). Although most of the organizations began in response to cutbacks in funding for public schools, each has established research and policy branches which propose as well as react to school policy and actions in their region. Chicago's Designs for Change program can serve as an example because it has enjoyed the most noticeable success.

Designs for Change began in 1977 as an advocacy group for black and Hispanic students who were considered to be over-represented in the percentages of students who failed to make adequate progress in learning to read or graduate from high school. In a 241-page report on the relationship between student classification and their access to reading instruction. Designs for Change researchers (1981) identified the programmatic racism in the process used to refer students to special education programs, where they were denied their right to learn to read. Their follow-up study, *Caught in the Web* (1982) and a class action lawsuit led directly to the retesting and reclassification of 10,000 black students in the Chicago public school system. In *The Bottom Line* (1985), they challenged the effectiveness of the mainstream reading program—the Chicago Mastery Learning Reading Program—demonstrating that only a small percentage of the students who did manage to graduate could read at or above grade level. Designs for Change's analysis of the problem placed blame on the CMLR program, which prompted the new superintendent of Chicago Public Schools to replace CMLR (unfortunately) with a guidebook-directed program.

Within these reactions to rationalized schooling, parents seek to bridge the traditional gap between professional and lay logic concerning the goals and methods of ideal schooling. In these instances, parents and their surrogates sought to modify the control of the technology of reading instruction and group placement in order to brighten the prospects of students learning to be literate. Certainly, not all parental reactions toward current reading instruction favor less management of students' and teachers' thoughts and actions (e.g., the Reading Reform Foundation of Scottsdale, Arizona), but there are some signs that parents believe that reading is more than skill mastery, that tests cannot measure students' intellect, and that more business and more science are not the only solutions to the problems of developing a literate citizenry.

Teachers

In each school district I studied in attempting to discover why teachers rely on commercial reading materials and school personnel believe that these materials can teach reading, teachers reacted to the various forms of rationalization of their reading programs. As I have mentioned previously, teachers in the first study challenged administrators' insistence that the basal scope and sequence could not be altered despite widespread failure of students to master reading skills in the prescribed order. These teachers carried their concern to an author of the basal program, who agreed with the teachers' position that the objectives in question should be moved to a later basal level.

This teacher response may seem like a minor incident out of the context of the Right to Read district, but the story of these third grade teachers was related to me in no fewer than half of the interviews with teachers, during all of the interviews with reading teachers, and one interview with a principal. Although no one mentioned names and the reading teachers and principal assured me that there were no reprisals for the embarrassment that these teachers caused the central administrators, the classroom teachers were not so sure that the outspoken teachers would escape without some form of reprimand. Each of the teachers who mentioned the incident expressed a similar concern about the scope and sequence of skills at their levels, but confided that they simply told students how to answer the three or four items on the criterion-referenced test which were to assess those objectives.

My other studies also include examples of teachers' reaction to managed instruction. Chicago teachers reduced the number of essential skills from the Chicago Mastery Learning Reading program (and the corresponding paperwork) through the collective bargaining process of contract negotiations (Schimdt 1982). Despite the humorous side of conceding salary consideration in order to reduce essential skills, the example demonstrates the lengths to which teachers will go to relieve the pressures of management. In the merit pay program, teachers' reaction to quotas for student competence was destructive for themselves and their students. Because most teachers found reading instruction under the merit pay program less fulfilling, they became somewhat cynical about bonuses for more productive reading instruction—several mentioned that they were insulted by the implications that they were not providing their best instruction without such incentive—and as a result they withdrew their interest from this aspect of their work.

Teachers in the fourth study rejected most of the assumptions of rationalized instruction—the separation of planning from instruction, the centralization of decision making, and the primacy of test scores. Although they did accept basal use, these teachers sought to re-emphasize their subjectivity in order to know their students better and to form cordial relationships so that they could share the joys, not just the skills of reading; to decide which reading skills were worth pursuing for their students, and to judge students' reading competence for themselves. These teachers resented administrators' attempts to bring change to the reading program, calling them intrusions into "their territory," and fought administrators' plans for increased observation beyond the number specified in their union contract.

Project SOARR (Strategic On-going Application of Reading Research) presents another variation of teachers' reaction to managed instruction, one that is much more formal and carefully organized than the previous examples. Teachers from the Plymouth and Canton school districts designed Project SOARR as a course of study to prepare themselves and other teachers to understand and to participate actively in the implementation of the state's new definition of reading (see Wixson and Peters 1984). Funded for two years by the Michigan Department of Education (1985–87), each of six sessions included a series of ten lectures from reading experts on relevant research which would help teachers use basal materials more effectively in pursuit of the state's new goals.

The teachers who organized SOARR soon realized that the teachers participating in the sessions would benefit from more time to discuss the content of the lectures and accompanying readings, and by the second session they reduced the lecture time and introduced weekly discussion groups. At the end of the second session, many of these groups agreed to meet on their own during the regular school year. During these independent group meetings, teachers have begun to discuss changes in district policy to realign the district reading programs with their new understanding of reading and instruction. This series of reactions demonstrates a growing confidence among these teachers that they should understand, not just accept, state policy, that they need not rely so heavily on reading experts to inform their position, and that through discussion they can make, not just follow, district policy.

In Albuquerque, New Mexico, Carol Red and Ellen Shainline (1987), two school district reading consultants, found teachers eager to rely more on themselves and their students during language arts instruction and less on guidebook directions and tests. Through a series of journal entries from teachers who were attempting to make such changes, Red and Shainline demonstrate teachers' abilities to identify the contradictions in the rhetoric of current programs, to withstand the pressures against change, and to implement self-designed and self-directed lessons on a regular basis, after opportunities to discuss their work in formal in-service sessions.

> (Teacher T.R.) The district is putting on the pressure to raise those test scores—to isolate skills, to drill our children, to prepare them for standardized tests—and then turns around and puts out curriculum guides and implements programs that promote "holistic education."

> (Teacher C.H.) Well, I am learning that with writing they are assimilating the skills. . . . But, can those children isolate the skills on a test? Probably not. So I still feel pressure to practice isolated skills so they can recognize them. . . . I really want to do all those super writing and reading activities. But, I can't do everything. I just get my plan figured out and then start revising.

> (Teacher A.W.) I purchased various materials on the recommendation of successful teachers and found that their success factor for me was zilch! Which is why as a resource teacher I make it up as I go along, using lots of poetry and incidental things. I haven't related to a packaged program yet.

Students, parents, and teachers in the previous examples all seemed eager to get some relief from what they considered the excesses of rationalization—to make it a little more human, a little more tolerant of individuality, or a bit more effective. However, after a moment's respite, each seemed willing to return to the conditions of an improved, but still rationalized, reading program. Left unexamined and untouched in these reactions is the assumption that knowledge is a thing separate from the process of knowing—that knowledge can be produced outside the context of classrooms and then simply implanted in students' minds in some way. Despite basal publishers' and reading experts' rhetoric to the contrary, this separation of knowledge from knowing is central to the rationalization of reading programs wherein basal publishers in New York, Chicago, or Boston determine what knowledge is worth knowing, and then, teachers around the United States transfer this knowledge from basals to their students. If this were not true, then teacher's guidebooks and basal materials would not exist, and reading experts would not allow their names to appear on products which by necessity separate knowledge from knowing.

Some "reactors" to rationalized reading programs do not accept this assumption of separation. Rather, they argue that knowledge and knowing are dialectically related and inseparable—that knowledge is nothing more than the product of individuals involved in the social process of coming to know something. Thus, these teachers and teacher educators take reaction to managed instruction a step further than the simple search for relief, and they reject current reading programs because of the confusion of teachers teaching with students learning. Advocates of this dialectical position maintain that knowledge is not a gift from others, but a gift to one's self, the result of curiosity, action, uncertainty, judgment, and conversation as the next four examples demonstrate.

The final teacher-example comes from Winnipeg, Manitoba, Canada, and may be the most successful reaction to managed instruction. There in 1972, seven classroom teachers formed a study group, CEL (Child-centered, Experienced-based Learning), which met initially only to clarify their own concerns about guidebook-directed instruction and the authority of standardized tests and in order to design instructional methods based on children's language and teacher's judgment. By the late 1970s, members of the group (then thirty teachers) were presenting in-service programs for teachers all over Canada and parts of the United States carrying their "wholistic message." In 1986, over twenty-five hundred teachers and administrators attended CEL's fifth convention, and the group's book, *Reading, Writing, and Caring* (Cochrane et al. 1984) is a required textbook in thirty colleges of education (Smith 1986). At each opportunity, members of CEL challenge the advocates of rationalized reading instruction on philosophical and psychological grounds based on their experience in their classrooms.

Teacher Educators

Perhaps the most well-known proponents of constructive reaction to managed reading lessons are Kenneth Goodman, Donald Graves, and Frank Smith, whose work is largely responsible for the reawakening of the New Education in reading instruction in the United States during the past two decades. Through their efforts and those of their students and associates, they have forged a counterculture of sorts among teachers and some administrators who feel ill at ease with their present circumstances and hope to better themselves and their students. At the center of this uneasiness is the notion that rationalized reading programs cannot deliver on their promise of literate citizenry because they rest on the false separation of knowledge and knowing, which ultimately prevents students from taking control of their literacy in order to make sense of text the same way that they make sense out of other experience. As a result, students become proficient at reading skills but not at reading. And even advocates' own criterion for success—test scores—demonstrate that Goodman, Graves, and Smith are correct on this point. "By the criterion of comprehending the sense, feeling, tone, and intention of a text, and expressing this understanding of the text, the United States educational system has been less effective than that of some other countries, such as New Zealand" (Purves 1984: 3), which practice reading instruction consonant with the suggestions of Goodman, Graves, and Smith.

Kenneth Goodman's psycholinguistic, transactional, whole language theory of reading is in itself a reaction to the mechanical assumptions of current reading programs (Goodman 1984). His view challenges the putative unidirectional flow of meaning from text to reader assumed by basal publishers and the interactional, purely psychological assumptions currently popular among reading experts. Rather, Goodman argues from a dialectical standpoint that both the author and reader are transformed during the act of reading. The writer has another interpretation of the text he or she produced and the reader has a reorganization of previous knowledge, and therefore, new knowledge is produced during reading and later upon reflection. This is a far cry from the scripted question and answer sessions which pass for comprehension during guidebook-directed instruction. But Goodman's challenge to rationalized reading programs has not always been so indirect. In "Basal Readers: A Call for Action," Goodman (1986) lists shortcomings of the basal and states "publishers, editors, authors, teachers, administrators, superintendents, teacher educators, and parents must join in either replacing or turning around the basals and eliminating the growing gap between the basals and the best knowledge about helping pupils become literate" (p.363).

Donald Graves approaches reading instruction through children's natural interest in expressing their ideas and curiosity about the ideas of others. He explains that his renewed interest in the relationship between reading and writing comes nearly a decade after he became disillusioned with the pessimism of clinical approaches to reading instruction which seemed to blame students for their problems and focus on what they could not do well (Graves 1984). During the interim, Graves designed and participated in research concerning elementary grade students' development of writing strategies and in projects to help teachers in New England to become more sensitive to students' attempts to make themselves understood. The method he used most frequently in these projects was to engage teachers in the writing process and discussions concerning their writing and that of other teachers, while they attempted to bring their classroom instruction in line with what they were learning about the writing and learning processes. Appropriating these methods to help teachers recognize the connection between the processes of reading and writing, Graves challenges the rationalized logic of managing teachers or students during reading lessons and the orthodoxies of basal materials, grammar texts, and standardized tests (Graves and Stuart 1985).

Insult to Intelligence, Frank Smith's (1986) book, details the mismatch between a psycholinguistic view of literacy and the current goals, instruction, and materials of schools in the United States. Written "as ammunition" for parents to use when attempting to change the mechanical status quo, Smith offers commentary on testing, grouping for instruction, computers, and the basic mistrust of teachers and students in the "education industry." He finds the logic of rationalized reading programs to be in fact irrational.

> The common belief that experts can be constructed from instructional blueprints might have remained a minor educational oddity, had it not been piggy-backed onto two other myths. The first . . . holds that instruction in all subjects will succeed if it is delivered to students in the same systematic way. . . . The second fantasy . . . is that people outside the classroom can make better instructional decisions than teachers who actually know and see the students involved. (p. 85)

The reactions of teacher educators, teachers, parents, and perhaps even students have produced some successes in bringing about change in rationalized programs. Beyond the changes of individual teachers in isolated classrooms, Chicago abandoned its mastery learning program; Portland, Oregon, adopted a Canadian basal series which requires much less control over teachers and students; and the Des Moines, Iowa, school districts have elected not to adopt a basal series in the late 1980s. Furthermore, California's Department of Public Instruction (1987) has just released an English-Language Arts Model Curriculum Guide which emphasizes children's literature, children's writing, and teacher judgment as the basis for sound reading instruction. Each of these acts is a step back from rationalized reading programs and management of instruction through basal technology and, therefore, should be cause for celebration. However, in most of the United States as I documented earlier, the legislatures' and administrators' urge to manipulate and manage reading programs on the one hand and teachers' reification of reading instruction as the application of basal materials on the other are gaining considerable strength under the banner of higher standards, accountability, and economic progress. And this fact may explain why some teacher educators' reactions have beome more strident of late.[2]

RESISTANCE TO MANAGED INSTRUCTION

Why have these and other reactions failed to stem the tide of rationalized reading programs in the United States? I believe it is because the participants in these reactions failed to connect literacy instruction with the concrete relations of the institutional roles of schooling and of society in general. The reactions, when they go beyond the immediate relief of the pressures of management, remain largely at an idealist level, suggesting that all that is necessary to bring about change in America's reading programs is to change the individual minds of teachers. There is a naivete in these reactions concerning the power relations in schools and society and an uncritical optimism that allows individuals to feel better about themselves, but fails to develop a collective activism sufficient to alter the current circumstances of reading programs.

Perhaps the clearest example of the failure to see politics as relevant to reading instruction is Frank Smith's (1986) discussion of "the revolution that died in schools" in which he relates how Noam Chomsky's theories of language and language learning were poorly translated, even coopted, by basal publishers and reading experts. In his discussion, Smith presents an interesting analysis of Chomsky's review of B.F. Skinner's behaviorist *Verbal Behavior*, detailing Chomsky's rejection of the notion that outside reinforcement develops and controls students' capacities to use language. However, Smith does not mention Chomsky's parallel theories about political life (Chomsky 1979, 1981) in which he argues that dominant classes attempt to control the thoughts and actions of Americans. I don't think that this is an oversight on Smith's part; it is indicative that even progressive participants in reading instruction do not acknowledge the political realities in American society and their manifestations in schools.

Without this political awareness, there is little hope of defeating—not just finding relief from—rationalized reading instruction. The participants in reading instruction must come to understand that the relations in reading programs are a microcosm of the relations of American society as I tried to explain in my analyses of teachers' and students' work during reading lessons. With this awareness, participants' reactions become constructive resistance to the management of teachers' and students' lives within and without reading lessons as the following examples demonstrate.

SUBS

Substitutes United for Better Schools (SUBS) is a Chicago union for substitute teachers formed in the middle 1970s to increase the bargaining power of teachers in a system that for one reason or another relies heavily upon adjunct teachers. Among many functions and services, SUBS publishes a monthly journal, *Substance*, which combines news of school policy and events with analyses of their impact on the lives of Chicago teachers, students, and parents. It often reports on women's and minority issues from a position of advocacy, and its staff has gained a reputation as effective investigative journalists. For example, in the early 1980s shortly after President Reagan offered Marva Collins, the private school headmaster and teacher, the position of secretary of education because of her success with students that public schools "could not or would not help," *Substance* published a detailed inquiry into the policies and reported successes of Collins' school and revealed that both had been exaggerated considerably and that the request that Collins serve as secretary was more a political slap at Chicago and other city schools throughout the United States than a reasoned choice.

From the very beginning of the Chicago Mastery Learning Reading Program, *Substance* published critical analyses challenging CMLR on moral, economic, social, and pedagogical grounds. It is interesting to compare the Designs for Change's reaction and SUBS' resistance to this program. Although Designs for Change waited until 1985 to challenge the program on the grounds that it reneged on its promise to produce large numbers of students with high test scores, SUBS characterized CMLR's topics for stories and practice examples as racist and sexist from its inception, commented almost monthly on CMLR's attempt to deskill Chicago elementary and later secondary teachers, and examined the enormous expense of the project. To document their articles in *Substance*, SUBS members attended every open schoolboard meeting, scrutinized every policy document and expense sheet, and attempted to interview Chicago school officials whenever appropriate and possible. At the same time they were criticizing the assumptions and reality of CMLR, *Substance* offered a series of articles on alternative organization and ways to conduct literacy instruction, ones based largely on the idealism of Goodman, Graves, and Smith. What sets SUBS apart from reactions to rationalized instruction is the efforts to analyze its business and political aspects as well as its psychological and pedagogical roots and the attempt to foster teachers' and parents' critical literacy through *Substance*. What sets SUBS apart from most teachers' unions is its actions to involve members in the development of school policy and curricular matters as well as collective bargaining for better wages and working conditions in general.[3]

Highlander Folk School

In *Illiterate America*, Jonathan Kozol (1985) examines the human costs of adult illiteracy and outlines a program to recover the estimated 60,000,000 illiterates in the United States. During his discussion of programs, he makes fleeting reference to the Highlander Folk School as a model for rural programs.

> Here in a single center, art and music, oral testimony and folk history are skillfully combined with literacy work, as well as with its practical correlative in voter education, to create a total climate of empowerment and of collective self-respect which has been admired, but too seldom given the attention it deserves, for something over fifty years. (p. 121)

Perhaps an example from the history of the school (Adams and Horton 1975) will give an indication of the school's resistance to rationalized instruction. Although the example considers adult education, it has implications for elementary grade instruction as well, as demonstrated remarkably well in the second half of Shirley Brice Heath's (1983) *Ways With Words*.

In 1954, well before the civil rights movement, when literacy tests prevented many black and poor Southerners from voting, Myles Horton, the founder and leader of the Highlander School, was asked by a local bus driver/teacher from Johns Island, South Carolina to help establish an adult education program that would, in the words of the local inhabitants, "help them become better citizens." During the six months following the request, Horton travelled from the Highlander School in Tennessee to Johns Island to interview locals in order to determine why the government-funded state-run school had not produced a single reader. Horton found that the state's program was run as a formal school, using a skill-based basal program meant for children with reading content irrelevant for even South Carolina children.

To develop a program that would help these citizens help themselves, Horton encouraged the bus driver/teacher to move the school away from an institutional setting, to use local literate people who spoke the same dialect as the illiterates to serve as teachers, and to make "the work of learning to read adult work and work that was part of the islanders' own lives"(p. 115). During the literacy lessons, teachers were to challenge the adults/students concerning the stereotypes ascribed to Blacks and to help them overcome their own feelings of inadequacy developed from years of discrimination. The successes of the school were measured in three ways: its enrollment increased three-fold in its first six months of operation, its graduates were able to read the parts of the United States Constitution required in order to register to vote,[4] and other "citizenship schools" patterned after the Johns Island school were established in other poor black communities.

This is one of many examples of how members of the Highland Folk School helped poor and working-class people resist not only the rationalization of education, but also resist the rationalization of work through classes for union organizers and rationalization of life through their classes in hill traditions and folkways. In every case, the project was designed with the direct assistance of those who sought help in order that they might begin to realize their ability to make changes in their lives. The Highlander School's efforts to help individuals not only understand and celebrate their histories, but to increase their political and economic power through collective educational efforts sets the school apart from other "hill" programs like Elliot Wigginton's *Foxfire.*[5]

The Boston Women's Teachers Group

Sara Freedman, Jane Jackson, and Katherine Boles (1983) describe an ongoing Women's Teachers Group project to help teachers recognize the institutional constraints on their work in elementary schools. Basing their original analyses on interviews with twenty-five practicing teachers from urban and suburban school districts over a two-year period, they conclude that four institutional contradictions are the basis for most teacher stress in schools, although school officials and educational experts have previously tried to explain teacher "burnout" as an individual phenomenon. Freedman, Jackson, and Boles, all members of the Teachers Group, offer several quotes from the interviews to substantiate their points; I have included an example for each to give a flavor of these teachers' concerns.

Contradiction #1: Teachers are supposed to prepare students for adulthood, but teachers are not treated as adults themselves.

> When our principal is talking to a first, or second, or third grade teacher . . . I find that she's repeating directions one, two, or three times, almost as you would to a first, second, or third grader. When you get higher up—fourth, fifth, and sixth—the directions are not repeated as much, but they're done more like an outline form as you would give to kids who are a little bit older. (Teacher AA, p. 3)

Contradiction #2: Teachers are to develop the entire child but their actions are directed only toward cognitive aspects of schooling and students.

In my school, it's a luxury to think about those things—interpersonal relationships, how to encourage spontaneity—we have to teach the basic skills for life. Basic skills, that's the most important thing I teach them. Reading and math because those are the tools to succeed in life, you know, to help you live. (H. p. 7)

Contradiction #3: Teachers are to provide equal opportunity for students but they are required to use materials and tests that are racially and class biased.

If there's a kid in the classroom that a teacher is having a problem with, and it looks like there might be something the matter, they go through the core examination process, and they discover that he does have a problem. He has an auditory figure ground problem. So automatically he's going to get picked up by the person in charge of auditory figure ground problems. So now we've created a label for a kid and a person to deal with that label. There's a pattern and the pattern is they're minority kids, they are ESL kids, they are the kids who walk to the beat of a different drummer. (W. p. 7)

Contradiction #4: Teachers are to develop citizens ready to participate actively in a democracy, but there is little democracy in schools.

We can't use any supplementary materials until we've finished all the textbook work. . . . I can show you the memo. "Teachers are reminded that only materials found in the adopted textbooks can be duplicated. Supplementary materials are not to be stenciled and duplicated. It is the feeling of the administration that materials in the textbooks are adequate and must be completed before other materials are to be introduced in the curiculum." Even the kids who are repeating go back through the same materials. . . . Last week I was teaching a reading lesson and the story was about Galileo. Now I have a wonderful ditto about Galileo and telescopes. But it's from the science unit, so I couldn't use it. The administrator's aide controls the ditto machine and files all the dittos that you run off. If we have any supplementary dittos, they have to be cleared first. (E. p.8)

Because "teachers are never urged to look beyond the classroom to search for similarities and differences between themselves and others" (p. 20) and because "teachers must recognize how the structure of schools controls their work and deeply affects their relationships with their fellow teachers, their students, and their students' families" (p. 21), the Boston Women's Teachers Group developed a thirty-minute slide-tape presentation entitled "The Other End of the Corridor" to help teachers understand their work more fully. The presentation includes scenes of typical classroom and school experiences (e.g., teachers with students and basals for group lessons, teachers speaking with administrators, students working on seatwork) which serve as focal points for discussions of teachers' lives at school. Accompanying the slides are relevant quotes from the original teacher interviews which typically "prompt strong reactions from teachers." Beyond the initial presentation, the Women's Teachers group offers four- to six-week workshops designed to create support groups for fostering and maintaining analyses of the structure of schooling in general and a school in particular and to promote teachers' action to change their circumstances, because "understanding their situation is only the first step toward changing it" (p. 22). This explicit attempt to connect the analyses of feelings of stress with the structural constraints of schooling separates the resistance of the Boston Women's Teachers Group from the discussion group reaction of SOARR or even CEL.[6]

In summary, these few acts of resistance demonstrate that participants in reading instruction can successfully challenge managed instruction. They show that rationalized reading programs do not represent an "iron cage" which denies students, teachers, and parents their voices in the determination of present and future reading lessons. This resistance offers hope through collective efforts to defeat the assumptions and concrete relations that keep the participants in reading instruction alienated from their work and one another, even though they interact daily. Acts of resistance also present a challenge to those interested in change—just how can the many and varied reactions of students, parents, teachers, and teacher educators be raised to acts at a level of resistance in which the participants no longer see themselves as objects to be manipulated, relegated to reactive responses, but rather in which they become subjects in the development of a new literate culture?

9

The Possibility of Constructive Change in American Reading Programs

☐ In order to defeat the rationalization of reading programs, teachers and students must understand how that rationalization came to exist, how it controls their lives at school, and how and why it is now maintained. Moreover, they must realize that current organizations of reading programs are historical constructs—the results of past negotiations of rules and meanings among unequal participants in reading programs—and therefore, that these organizations can be changed. In this book, I attempted to provide a basis for developing such understandings. That is, I told the story of how and why teachers' and students' subjectivities have been devalued in favor of the technology of reading instruction in order to prepare verifiably literate students who can perform the varied tasks of the American economy from laborer to business executive. For those interested in redirecting reading programs from their current course, this story and the pedagogical elements from the last three examples offered at the end of chapter 8 suggest ways in which you might help yourself and others to resist and hopefully defeat the rationalization of reading programs.[1]

SUBS, the Highland Folk School, and the Boston Women's Teachers Group based their projects on three fundamental points. First, they shared a common goal to increase participants' understanding and control over their lives and work. Second, each facet of their endeavors was directed toward this real, but unpredictable goal, extending the definition of traditional literacy, the decoding of words to reproduce the meaning

132

of text, to critical literacy, a tool for understanding one's own history and culture and their connection to current social structure on the one hand and an activism against external control on the other. As such, this literacy is not only a means to better the conditions of lower-class and minority groups, but also a means by which members of middle and upper classes can respond to the encroachment of rationalization in their lives. Third, each project recognized that the production of this new critical understanding of reality and any constructive movement toward change were social processes in which participants reject the passive and alienative roles assigned them in order to come to know and to act together.

Although they worked in different contexts at different speeds, using different techniques, participants in SUBS, the Highlander Folk School, and the Boston Women's Teachers Group projects, pursued these points in similar ways. (1) Each project began with discussions of concrete examples from participants' experience, trying to come to grips with what it meant to be a Chicago teacher working under the constraints of the CMLR program, a Johns Island black in the Jim Crow South, or a Boston elementary school teacher in the 1980s. (2) During these discussions with the help of a "teacher," each group attempted to situate its experience within the larger social and historical context in order to identify the objective reasons for their present conditions and subjectivities. (3) These discussions included moral, political, and social questions about the strengths and contradictions in participants' thoughts, beliefs, and behaviors as well as those of their situation and the social structure. (4) Finally, each project encouraged participants to act on their new understandings in efforts to take more responsibility in and control of their lives. This activism had unpredictable and often incomplete consequences—for example, the substitution of one rationalized reading program for another in the Chicago School District.

But it is not the immediate results or the specific techniques of these projects that are important—if it were a question of technique then the defeat of rationalization could proceed according to a formula. What is important in these projects is the way in which each worked toward establishing a different relationship among people, knowledge, and society, one in which knowledge and society serve to increase individual and collective freedom. Although the basic points and the pedagogical elements from the examples do not provide a blueprint for change—in fact we must go well beyond these isolated examples to build state and national networks eventually—they do provide a framework for discussion concerning the process of constructive change in reading programs. A first step in that process is the development of critical literacy among participants in reading instruction, a rigorous and difficult undertaking, one that has many false starts and blind alleys in the best of conditions.

And American schools do not provide the best of conditions. The development of critical literacy requires discipline and active participation from both teachers and students, things that neither group has practiced frequently during the recent past. But the payoff for this first step and the overall struggle against rationalization is great—teachers and students increase control over their lives in reading programs and perhaps in everyday life—and therefore, it seems well worth the effort.

WORKING WITH AND FOR TEACHERS

Elementary school teachers are the key to critical literacy and the defeat of rationalization at school. Without their resistance, there is little hope for change in reading programs. Typically, teachers are characterized as a fairly conservative lot, opting for tradition over innovation, apparently coopting progressive methods and movements alike. There is a certain pessimism among reading experts concerning elementary school teachers' potential for change, leading many to the cynicism of making the best of managed instruction when they acknowledge privately that there is little benefit for teachers or students in such activity. I think these pessimists and cynics fail to consider why teachers appear at once to be conservative, apathetic, yet confident during reading lessons. That is, they neglect the objective conditions—the connections between teachers' experience and subjectivity and current social structure. As I argued previously, teachers internalize the alienative and reified assumptions of rationalized reading programs and act according to their prescribed roles, although many feel uneasy and unfulfilled in that role. However, with an understanding of these connections elementary teachers' reactions to the current organization of reading programs could become active resistance, a force too great to control bureaucratically or even technically.

The process of making these connections requires that teachers engage in discussions to reconsider the historical and philosophical foundations of reading programs through the analysis and reanalysis of their daily work experience. The purpose of these initial discussions is to create a sense of self and institutional doubt that will enable teachers to see that reading programs need not be organized as they are currently in the United States and that these programs do not serve either teachers' or students' needs. They impose information rather than help to develop knowledge, and they control teachers' and students' literate thoughts and actions rather than foster independence.

This doubt and purpose must also inform the "teachers of teachers" in this process. And let me be clear that anyone—teachers, administrators, parents, teacher educators—who has experienced this type of discussion and practices critical literacy can act as "teacher" in these activities. Typically at universities or in teacher in-service programs, presenters tell or show elementary school teachers the correct way in which to interpret their work based on scientific generalization from experiments conducted outside the teachers' actual practice. In Paulo Freire's (1970) words, these presenters attempt to bank preconceived knowledge in teachers' empty heads. This scientific certainty leads to a hierarchy of authority and knowledge in which the science of the presenters is considered superior and more useful than the practice and interpretations of teachers. But in fact, teachers' heads aren't empty and their experiences differ across classrooms, schools, and states, rendering scientific generalizations statistically significant but practically useless. Moreover, knowledge cannot be separated from the act of coming to know, in which teachers create new understandings from their analysis and discussion of their unique, but shared situations. In short, traditional practices of colleges of education and in-service programs are not conducive to the development of critical literacy or change in reading programs; in fact, they usually socialize teachers toward a confident dependence on basal publishers and reading experts.

Here again, I think the examples of resistance are illustrative of a better way. Rather than seeing themselves as explainers of the correct interpretation of teachers' lives, project leaders sought to develop a forum in which participants could discuss and re-examine their daily experience among people who share that experience. Far from a passive role, these project leaders questioned participants' interpretations in order to cast doubt on the pat answers we all so comfortably rely on during our work. When participants seemed stuck on a particular point, project leaders seemed quick to provide the missing link, not in an attempt to relegate other participants to second-class status, but to contribute to the discussion in their own way—acknowledging their experience and analytical skills. If participants became passive, preferring to listen to someone tell them what to do or how to think rather than to engage in the rigorous practice of active discussion, project leaders would help these participants discover what and how objective conditions mediated against their demonstration of independence in learning. While not equal, project leaders and other participants were together in coming to know what it means to be critically literate.

Although local issues may serve as starting points for these discussions, the history of American reading programs and deskilling of teachers suggest that there are general topics from teachers' everyday experience that must be dealt with if teachers are to understand and later transcend the rationalization, reification, and alienation that pervades their work. For example, teachers' theoretical and practical definitions of literacy, instruction, and learning must be made explicit. The role of basal materials, particularly teacher's guidebooks and criterion-referenced tests, warrant systematic treatment. The use of these objects for grouping, grading, and classroom routines should be examined for their intellectual and emotional effects on students and teachers. Finally, the bureaucratic and professional relationships among school personnel and other participants in reading programs must be analyzed. Each of these general concerns has a surface, descriptive level in teachers' work and a deeper set of connections with the larger social structure in the United States. During discussions, teachers will shift freely across levels and among pedagogical elements from the examples—from descriptions to making connections to identifying contradictions to making plans for constructive change and back to any previous element. Rather than a hierarchy or a sequence, the topics and elements are simply moments in the teachers' growing ability to critically read the word and their world.

Element 1: Teachers Coming to Know Their Own Experience

To understand their work, their experience, and their school culture, teachers must look again at the everyday events of their lessons. Not through the rationalized subjectivity that suggests that basal reading materials, tests, and bureaucratic structure are necessary to keep pace with modern demands on literacy, but through discussion of these objects to determine what they mean for teachers' and students' thoughts, feelings, and actions. Since teachers can only create new knowledge based on their current understanding, they must be subjects in the educative process and the discussions must be based on teachers' lived experience.

Although I have no simple, packaged methods concerning how to conduct these discussions of teachers' concrete experience, there are several methods that have been used successfully in specific situations in the United States. The Boston Women's Teachers Group has adapted Paulo Freire's (1971) problem-posing, dialogistic methods to fit their purposes. Members use slides of teachers and students busy working to serve as one source of stimuli for conversation. The scenes are not setups in any way, rather they capture teachers engaging in daily practices such as explaining worksheets to students, addressing a reading group, administering tests. According to published accounts, these slides lead teachers to first describe their work, and then, to analyze it as they slip between personal narratives and pertinent generalizations. To push these discussions when necessary, representatives of the Boston Women's Teachers Group play tapes of their original interviews with teachers who analyze particular events in insightful or controversial ways. Rather than silencing participants, as well these tapes might if offered as the correct analysis, these taped statements stimulate stronger reactions and often lead teachers to new levels of analysis as they provide a different perspective on the topic at hand.

Shirley Brice Heath's (1983) "teachers as ethnographers" offers useful means for helping teachers come to grips with their practice and its effects. Teachers enrolled in her classes observed and recorded their own and their students' use of time, space, and language in order to make sense of their situations at home and at school. During discussions of their data, teachers began to realize how their standard practices and materials prevented as many as two-thirds of their students from active participation in their reading instruction. By systematically analyzing their own behavior, teachers were able to identify the particular routines in their instruction that proved problematic for different groups of their students, and through open discussion of their problems, these teachers were able to devise hypotheses for more helpful instruction which they could later test in actual practice in their classrooms. This type of "reflection in action" (Schon 1983) led to wholesale, but short-lived changes in teachers' work and their attitudes toward their students.[2]

Another form for beginning these discussions comes from Donald Graves' and Jane Hansen's work with teachers in New England. Here, the basis for the teachers' discussions is their own writing and reading—their intentions for, and their interpretations of, their literate work and that of other teachers. These analyses move teachers' definitions of literacy from the intimidating number of objectives listed in teacher's guidebooks for reading and language arts instruction, and focuses their attention on the use of language for real and practical purposes. During their discussions with other teachers, comparisons between their work and the reading and writing instruction in their classrooms leads many teachers to reconsider the pedagogical foundations of their work and to recognize the constructive essence of self and institutional doubt so necessary to critical literacy.

Element 2: Teachers Making Connections Between Their Experience and Current Social Structure

Chapters 2 and 3 present my account of how American social structure and reading lessons offered in American schools are connected. There are direct links between: the need for predictability in the economy and the demands for rationalization of reading programs, the scientific efforts to control the physical environment and the science of management during reading instruction, and the advocacy of technology over workers in industry and the ascent of basal materials and tests over teachers during reading lessons. These connections between society and teachers' work shape the roles, routines, and subjectivities that comprise American reading programs. However, because of the dense tangle of modern social relations and a lack of opportunity for analysis, teachers often fail to recognize these connections, although they live with their effects on a daily basis. By bringing the connections to a level of consciousness, teachers can begin to see what it will take to change their current circumstances and who are their allies in these efforts.

There are, of course, blockbuster social issues which are thoroughly documented in reading programs. From time to time, basal materials have been found to be racist, sexist, and age-biased. Similarly, tests are acknowledged to sort students along lines of social class and race, helping perpetuate self-fulfilling prophecies and current social structure. And many teachers complain about mandates and policy statements from state and local officials, who have little to do with actual reading instruction. Although these points provide excellent sources for lengthy discussion, they do little to directly help teachers recognize what rationalization is and how it is maintained. To develop these understandings, the discussion must move from earlier concrete descriptions of teachers' work to a more abstract level of analysis in which teachers treat their work as an object to see who is actually served by teachers' standard use of basal materials and testing. This step can be a source of problems because over-zealous leaders may attempt to force these abstractions too soon, causing teachers to doubt their capabilities for such analyses, or complacent leaders, who find it sufficient for teachers to concentrate solely on reforming their personal practice, may never attempt to make the connections at all. The difficulty in this step, of course, is being sufficiently sensitive to what teachers are saying to know when to capitalize on a particular moment when teachers are ready to make use of such analyses.

I have used an adaptation of Ira Shor's (1977, 1980) "critical teaching" to begin this process and to help teachers see the ideological underpinnings of the use of the most ubiquitous part of current reading programs—the worksheet. I begin by describing in detail a worksheet which I distribute—its smell, its clarity, its literal objective, and the like. Next, I discuss the worksheet's immediate social context. How is it typically used? By whom? For what purpose? Why does it appear in consumable form? Discussions usually proceed smoothly up to this point. Teachers seem eager to comment on specific incidents from their experience about worksheets. Some teachers defend the practice of using worksheets, if not the objects themselves; others begin to make connections between reading lessons and publishers' stake in perpetuating the status quo.

The next series of questions asks teachers to consider their personal histories with worksheets. How have you used worksheets in the past? Has your use of worksheets changed over time? How did you use them today? What determines how, when, and which worksheet you use? How do your students react to worksheets? This series of questions brings the discussion closer to home and encourages comparison of teachers' theories in their heads and their theories in practice. Quite honestly, this part of the discussion can be painful for some teachers as they begin to recognize contradictions in their thoughts and actions for the first time or they begin to realize how little control they have over their lessons. Often the most vocal teachers when talk was at a general level become silent during this part of discussions.

Finally, teachers are asked to consider the history of worksheets and their future. When did worksheets first appear? What did they replace? Why did they appear? How have they changed? Who brought them into existence? How have they affected the routines of reading lessons? And what would reading lessons be like without them? Young teachers often find this line of analysis difficult because they have very little sense of the history of reading instruction; many have virtually no experience as a student or as a teacher of reading instruction without worksheets, and they listen in awe to older teachers explain how they taught without them.

I have yet to work with a group that didn't have someone who compares worksheets to some other form of remote control of another object, someone else who exclaimed that basal materials are a closed system developed and maintained for publishers' profit, and someone else who argues that teachers now possess fewer skills for teaching reading after many more years of education than they did in the past. I do not mean to suggest that everyone in these groups came to such realizations, but I have been told by many participants that they had never looked at their work in this way before and that handing out the next worksheet would be much more difficult than it was the day before we had the discussion. In short, my experience has been that teachers are quite capable of critical thought about their work, able to trace the connections of objects and routines to their societal roots in the social structure, and eager to hypothesize about a future in which they have greater control over their instruction. Moreover, they seem to realize quickly that other teachers are their allies in their struggles to resist the management of their instruction.

Element 3: Teachers Believing That It Doesn't Have To Be This Way

During discussions concerning their concrete experience and its connections to the larger social structure, teachers recognize that there are aspects of reading programs and their own lessons that can withstand their critical examinations, but that there are others that they now consider useless, even injurious, to themselves and their students. Identification of these strengths and contradictions begins during the first discussion and continues regularly throughout subsequent meetings. Teachers begin to realize that the contradictions suggest a need for personal, programmatic, and institutional change, but without a complementary view that change is indeed possible, it is likely that these new ideas of hope will soon become sources of frustration and subvert any possibility of movement toward constructive change. To avoid this pitfall, some discussion should center on the unique historical construction of the current organization of American reading programs.

Two approaches to help teachers realize the relativity of the organizations of reading programs are to analyze expert opinion in reading methods textbooks and to investigate reading programs in other countries. For example, if methods textbooks are treated as historical documents and their cursory explanations of alternative organizations to guidebook-directed instruction are analyzed closely, teachers find that language experience, themed approaches, and individualized reading were and are really elements of an alternative social movement, not merely auxiliary methods, a movement based on counter-definitions of literacy, learning, and science and whose advocates fought (and still struggle in places) for different goals and for control over reading programs in the United States. Moreover, when teachers examine experts' opinion in these books, they frequently mention how during reading education courses at universities, reading experts fiercely protected their own academic freedom to determine course topics and argued for more control over their working conditions, while they actively promoted, passively accepted, or said nothing about basal publishers setting the goals, means, materials, and evaluation of elementary school teachers' work. Finally, teachers seem startled to discover that few reading programs in other countries share the rationalized organizations of American programs. Even within heavily bureaucratic systems, there appears to be very little of the technical control through teacher's guidebooks and corresponding testing systems which manage American teachers' work.

Examined in the light of these studies, teachers begin to see reading programs as contested matters that are decided through social negotiations rather than as objective necessities which are ideally suited to our times. Other jurisdictions in the past and present organized reading programs quite differently than current American programs in order to reach the similar goal of preparing their students to be productive citizens in the relative complexity of contemporary times. During discussions of these matters, teachers begin to talk about the need for action in local programs in order to negotiate on a more equal basis with the united front presented by basal publishers, reading experts, and administrators. Teachers not only recognize the need for change, but they begin to believe that change is possible, paraphrasing Herbert Kohl's (1980) statement about school and society by asking "what small power can I use in working with others to change reading programs in order to make them more democratic in process and outcome?"

Element 4: Teachers Act on Their New Knowledge

Constructive movements toward change in reading programs must be collective efforts, and they must be local. Analyses of failed movements of the past suggest that too great an emphasis on individual change without collective support often proves fatal to the movement. Although individual teachers can shut their classroom doors and pretend that school policy and the world do not really affect their work and even make substantial changes for themselves and their students, theirs is a selfish act, regardless of how benevolent and effective it may appear. It is a chance to feel superior to one's peers while actually helping to perpetuate the status quo by keeping teachers isolated from one another in competition. At best, these teachers face the pressures of secrecy and the dilemma of what to do for their students at year's end when they must pass on to a less "enlightened" teacher. At worst, they face the pressures of rationalization alone, and when they fail, they serve as an example that lasting change in reading programs is really impossible. A more constructive approach is for teachers to seek their individuality in reading programs through a collective of teachers willing to tackle the fundamental issues of their work and work conditions. These collectives can supply the support necessary for teachers to take the individual risks involved in making reading instruction more democratic and provide the framework for the resistance to the rationalization of reading programs.

Because communities present unique challenges to literacy and schools, the organization of reading programs must be a local endeavor. There is little need for centralized administrations on a state or national level—such organizations cannot address the real needs of local communities and they must in the end impair teachers' abilities to meet those needs. Even at a local level within school districts, distinct communities require special attention from teachers which standard districtwide policies preclude. In the same way, movements for change in reading programs only make sense at a local level. But rationalization of reading programs is not solely a local issue, state and federal education agencies are exerting ever-increasing pressure to maintain and even to extend the rationalization of reading programs and the management of teachers' instruction. In order to combat these efforts, local collectives need to form state and national networks, which allow local collectives to use many voices to speak as one in negotiations with government officials and representatives. Here, professional organizations such as the International Reading Association and the National Council of Teachers of English could provide a vital service for their members by providing collectives with the time, the space, and perhaps even the funds to talk with one another concerning their successes and failures at the local level and allowing them the opportunity to forge state and national plans of resistance. Additionally, this diversion of time and space during state and national conventions would balance the professional organizations' current one-sided support of basal programs and the status quo in school reading programs.

The outcomes of these discussions at local, state, or national levels cannot be predicted with any certainty. Even some of the examples that I have presented have enjoyed mixed success and have not resulted in lasting change at local levels. However, what sets these new discussions apart from many of the previous movements is that this time teachers would supplement the moral indignation and pedagogical concerns of the past responses with a sophisticated critical literacy which would bring political, economic, and social analyses to bear on the current logic and organizations of reading programs. This form of literacy enables teachers to identify and to expose the contradictions within rationalized programs, provides them with the moral conviction to acknowledge the flaws within their own positions and actions, and offers teachers the civic courage to stand up for their own and their students' rights.

WORKING WITH AND FOR STUDENTS

But is critical literacy possible in elementary schools? Can young children learn to read the word and the world simultaneously? The answer is most certainly, yes, they can. In fact, students bring an undeveloped form of this literacy with them when they first enter school (Harste, Burke, and Woodward 1984; Teale and Sulzby 1986; Wells 1987). As children learn to make sense of their world, to read it if you will, they develop more or less knowledge about the written word and its role in that world. For example, Heath (1983) reports remarkable sensitivity among children of different ages, social classes, and racial backgrounds to the implicit and explicit signs of behavior, attitude, and intentions of the people of their community and an equal ability to understand how oral stories and written language were used in their singular contexts. Moreover, Heath found that when allowed, these children could and wanted to talk about their world and language and how they made sense of them.

From this viewpoint, reading of the word is a natural development of children's reading the world, a talent on which rationalized reading programs fail to capitalize in their attempts to standardize experience and to ignore students' subjectivities for the sake of efficient, predictable outcomes. As I mentioned in previous chapters, there has long been a minority of teachers and teacher educators who have attempted to embed their literacy lessons with students' experience—"interpretors of culture" in the nineteenth century (Rice 1893), New Educators at the turn of the twentieth century (Dewey and Dewey 1915), and more recently practitioners whose work can be categorized under the rubric "whole language teaching" (Goodman 1986; Hansen, Newkirk, and Graves 1985).

The more successful of these movements recognized the importance of students' experience and choice, the necessity of children acting on their environments through play and writing, and the requirement that teachers renounce authoritarian control without relinquishing authority. They fostered students' creativity through open-ended projects based on students' expressed interest, developed a sense of solidarity among students by allowing them to work collectively and cooperatively toward a common goal, and promoted a healthy sense of self and institutional doubt through constructive criticism of their own and other students' literate work and behavior. Each of these successes demonstrates that elementary students can develop a personal voice in order to make better sense of and to analyze their concrete experience.

There is also evidence that students can make connections between their immediate experience, their language, and larger social structure and issues, if given the opportunity. Sara Zimet (1983) reports on attempts to help students as young as six years old to answer questions about social stereotypes—girls as docile, minorities as lazy, and handicapped as helpless—after reading from basal readers. Nine and ten year olds were capable of charting characteristics of protagonists in basal anthologies in order to determine similarities between story characters and themselves. Moreover, these students were later able to locate stories with more realistic and relevant characters in local libraries and bookstores. Heath (1983) provides examples of lower-track fifth grade students who were able to study local agriculture to investigate scientific concepts and small-scale farming as a viable occupation and second grade students who used ethnographic techniques to study language differences and their effects on inhabitants of their local communities. "The stress (in these activities) was on students making linkages between how they learn information in their daily lives and ways they could talk about these ways of knowing on a 'meta level' " (p. 337). Finally, Alex McLeod (1986) offers the essays of lower-class middle school students as evidence that students can discuss and write passionately and cogently about racism, war, and imperialism. These examples suggest that when whole language methods for developing personal voice through literacy are combined with the other three elements—making connections, identifying contradictions, and acting on that new knowledge—students can develop critical literacy with the support of a critically literate teacher.

There is no single or simple formula for students' development of critical literacy, but ironically, rationalized reading programs provide an ideal context for students' critical literacy because they need search no further to find a comprehensive attempt at the technical control of their lives. In its routines, materials, and content, managed instruction reduces and confines students' literate thoughts and behaviors to rote memorization of rules for decoding, comprehending, and studying sanitized texts within the humanistic but insincere rhetoric of personal fulfillment, self-betterment, and citizenship. Students' reactions to this mechanical instruction, which I have described earlier, might be turned into resistance against rationalized reading programs by allowing them to analyze carefully and to discuss thoroughly the various components of rationalized programs and the implicit intentions of basal publishers using the very language, thought, and analytical skills that such programs do not develop. That is, rationalized reading programs can become the curriculum of critical reading instruction in order to enable students to understand their past experiences at school in hope that they will later transcend these experiences.

One place to begin might be a comparison between how students and adults use literacy in their daily lives and the practices promoted during regular reading lessons. Collecting data for these comparisons requires students to use both oral and written language for the practical purpose of investigating the true relevance of reading instruction. The regular objects of reading lessons must also be examined from many angles and discussed in detail. For example, a group of students might consider the language used in rationalized programs through a comparison of the adapted texts that they find in basal anthologies with the original stories found in their school and community libraries. This close analysis of text will reveal publishers' reckless editing and oversimplification, while students increase their decoding skills, their vocabularies, and their knowledge of how real authors use language. Another group might consider content of these stories to examine what they have to say about how people should live their lives. This group will find a bias toward individualism and competition at the expense of cooperation and collective action toward shared goals (Shannon 1986a), while they exercise their capacities to comprehend the world through the literature they explore. Another group might examine the teacher's guidebook to gain some perspective on who controls reading lessons. And still another group might look at the criterion-referenced tests and the logic of standardized testing after reading Miriam Cohen's *The First Grade Takes a Test*, a book that displays test writers' and test advocates' disregard for students' knowledge and experience and the intellectual and emotional effects of school meritocracies built on the use of such instruments.

Each of these examples and any other systematic investigation of basal materials and the current organizations of reading programs will reveal the deliberate intent to reduce students' literacy to accurate decoding and reproductions of the meaning of meaningless texts. A steady diet of such fare is not only an insult to students' intelligence, as Frank Smith (1986) suggests, it lulls students into a false sense of what literacy is and what it could be for them. It robs students of their abilities to deal with difficult texts and difficult ideas that are required for them to become independent participants in reading programs, their education, and everyday life. Through discussions of these objects, routines, and intentions, students' reactions—both the passive acceptance of managed instruction and outright rejection of it—are channeled into a recognition of the need for resistance to these, not so subtle, attempts to control their lives.

Just as with teachers, this new knowledge will turn to despair unless students find support for their critical literacy from other students and teachers and some reason to believe that change is possible in rationalized reading programs. Of course, students would not even be entertaining such thoughts in any systematic way unless some change had already taken place in at least one classroom. However, the goal is not for individual change *per se*, it should be toward the defeat of rationalized reading programs in America. Accordingly, students must realize the historical relativity of reading programs. However, rather than examining methods textbooks as teachers might, students could look to family members and community members who can describe how they were taught reading at school. Young parents and siblings have approximately a 90 percent chance of having experienced guidebook directed instruction; grandparents might predate the widespread standardized norm- and criterion-referenced testing; great grandparents may have used textbooks instead of basals. By conducting these interviews, students can piece together the history of reading instruction and discover that reading programs were organized and realized in quite different ways across America during this century. Discussions of these insights should lead students to see that variation and change are indeed possible, particularly at local levels.

In order to communicate their new knowledge with other students, teachers, and parents, students might find it useful to contribute their stories, essays, and reports to classroom, school, and community libraries and to recommend books which more closely approximate and more realistically portray their lives and cultures. If necessary, students could establish counter-libraries, should school personnel reject their work and suggestions. There is currently clear precedence for students' right to publish and distribute such information at school (Hentoff 1980). Beyond the attempt to have their voices heard, these libraries could serve as centers for support among students, teachers, and even parents in which they can read and discuss the strengths and contradictions of modern life and organize themselves to resist the rationalization of reading programs in order to reverse the subject/object inversion in managed reading lessons. That is, they might work collectively to ensure that students and teachers become and remain the subjects of reading lessons and that texts remain their objects.

Summary

Although the odds are clearly stacked against teachers and students in American reading programs, some successfully overcome the internalized logic and the external pressure to express their dissatisfaction with their present circumstances. Most often these responses come in the form of reactions to managed instruction in which individuals, and less frequently groups, attempt to take "time out" from the standardized routine of guidebook-directed instruction, only to later rejoin the mechanical procedure with a sense of resignation. Others object to the underlying epistemology of the current organizations of reading programs—the separation of knowledge from the act of knowing, of teaching from learning, and of planning from implementation—which precludes both teachers and students from learning to be literate during reading lessons. This latter group suggests and practices reading lessons that do enable students to come to understand their lives better through learning to be literate.

But these reactions fail ultimately, I argue, because they see rationalization as largely a subjective problem—one that can be solved simply by changing individual teachers' minds—while ignoring the objective reality of the connections between the rationalization of reading programs on the one hand with the rationalization of industry, social institutions, and everyday life on the other. By neglecting these connections, teachers' and students' reactions of any type may bring individual changes but they cannot bring collective, long-lasting relief from managed instruction; and, therefore, they cannot help teachers and students control their literacy and their literate work. There are currently a few groups which combine the epistological rejection of the separation of knowledge and knowing with the political awareness that rationalization is not solely a subjective matter. These groups struggle against the subjective and objective barriers to teachers' and students' control of reading lessons by exposing and exploiting the contradictions of rationalized thought and classroom reality.

These few examples of resistance to the current organization of American reading programs reveal that the "iron cage" of rationalization does not preclude constructive change through the development and use of critical literacy. Helping both teachers and students to develop their abilities to read their own histories and culture, to see their connections with the large social structure, and to act according to this new knowledge against external control will not only arrest the spread of rationalization of reading programs on a local level but can also lead to its defeat across the United States. It will not be easy—basal publishers, business, government, and school administrators will not give up their power over reading instruction without a struggle—but there are sufficient numbers of contradictions and the possible rewards are so great to allow and encourage collectives of teachers and students to organize, to combine their efforts with critically literate parents and teacher educators, and to resist the management of their literacy, their work, and their lives.

The identification of the need and opportunities for change completes my attempt to use the methods of critical research to understand how reading programs are the result of social negotiation conducted not among equals, how these programs are connected to the larger social structure, and how they work to form subservient subjectivities among participants in reading instruction. My intention in this work was to convey a sense of possibility for change and to propose some ideas about what it might entail for teachers and students to gain their rightful place in reading programs. The book is a representation of the small power I can use in working with others in a movement that I hope will eventually lead to the defeat of the rationalization of reading programs in American schools. It is a product of my emerging understanding of what it means to be critically literate which I hope will assist others in like development. And, just as rationalization does not affect teachers and students through managed reading lessons alone, critical literacy cannot be limited to the consideration of reading programs alone. Perhaps, the defeat of rationalization of American reading programs will be a first step in a better life for teachers and students outside of schools as well.

Notes

INTRODUCTION

1. This stereotype of American reading instruction is based on a number of sources: Richard Anderson, *Becoming a Nation of Readers* (1985); Mary Austin and Coleman Morrison, *The First R* (1963); Dolores Durkin, "What Classroom Observation Reveals About Reading Comprehension" (1978–79); and my "Class Size, Reading Instruction, and Commercial Reading Materials"(in press). Although the characterization may not represent anyone's classroom exactly, it is at least close to the description most often offered for reading instruction in primary grades.

2. Several histories of basal reading materials are available. Most notable, and least critical, is Nila Banton Smith, *American Reading Instruction* (1965; 1st pub. 1934); H. Robinson has just provided a third edition with new introductory and concluding chapters. For more critical analyses see Mitford Mathew, *Teaching to Read* (1966); Richard Venezky, "A History of the American Reading Textbook" (1987); and Kenneth Goodman, Patrick Shannon, Yvonne Freeman, and Sharon Murphy, *A Report Card on Basal Readers* (1988).

3. Although there are subdisciplines in anthropology and archeology which concern themselves with interpretations of present and past cultures through the analysis of artifacts, these types of symbolic research have made little headway in educational research. See, for example, Walter Precourt, "Ethnohistorical Analysis of an Appalachian Settlement School" (1982). Virtually no such studies have been published on American reading instruction.

148

4. There are some fine theoretical treatments of literacy instruction from a critical perspective: Paulo Freire, *Pedagogy of the Oppressed* (1970); Henry Giroux, *Theory and Resistance in Education* (1983); Jonathan Kozol, *Illiterate America* (1985); and Ira Shor, *Critical Teaching and Everyday Life* (1980). Unfortunately these arguments have not penetrated reading research journals and are treated as unscientific, biased opinions by the reading research community.

CHAPTER 1

1. Dick, Jane, and Sally were recurring characters in the Scott, Foresman and Company basal reading series which was originated by William S. Gray. During its heyday, it's estimated that Scott, Foresman controlled 85 percent of the elementary school market for reading textbooks, and all competing companies had their own version of Dick and Jane. To demonstrate Dick and Jane's importance to Scott, Foresman, there is a monument to these characters on the front lawn of the company's headquarters in Glenview, Ill.

2. Kenneth Lockridge (1974) disputes Cremin's response to the American wilderness hypothesis by arguing that most New England colonists were already prone toward literacy and schooling before they came to the United States because they practiced some form of Protestantism which required them to know the word of God as written in the *Bible*.

3. Cohen suggests that educational legislation did not apply equally to all Americans, particularly not for girls, Indians, and blacks. In seventeenth-century New England, these groups were often taught to read and write, although few went beyond petty schools to grammar schools. A 1710 version of the 1642 apprenticeship law stipulated that "females [should be taught] to read as they may be capable," and no mention was made of teaching them to write. In Southern colonies, the situation was quite different. Most legislation which allowed girls to participate in schooling was forty to fifty years behind that for boys, and after 1650, there was little interest in trying to civilize Indians by teaching them to read the *Bible*. Several laws were passed restricting literacy instruction for slaves. For example in 1740, it was illegal to teach a slave to write, punishable by a 100 pound fine.

4. Merle Curti (1935) argues that the separation of petty schools from grammar schools in 1647 is the first indication that schooling in America was not going to be democratic because it served to perpetuate the class structure of European society. Upon completing petty school, most children were placed in apprenticeships, while only the boys from wealthy homes went on to the grammar schools. Curti maintains that even the reading and writing instruction favored the wealthy since they attended private schools with relatively highly educated masters, while poorer children received less adequate instruction at dame schools.

5. Joel Spring (1986) presents an interesting discussion of the early challenges to the close association of church and schooling in the United

States and England. He suggests that the impetus for *Cato's Letters* was Robert Molesworth's *An Account of Denmark as it was in the Year, 1692* (reprinted in 1976), in which Molesworth argues that literacy and education designed to promote submission to authority was the direct cause of the authoritarian government in Denmark. Molesworth questioned both church *and* government sponsorship of schooling.

6. American publishers took advantage of the War of Independence to break English copyrights on popular English books, enabling them to be sold at less than a third of the previous price. This opportunism furthered American's interest in literacy and libraries (Huck 1976).

7. Mosier provides an early (the book was first published in 1947) study of the hidden curriculum in schools with a thesis that the contents of the *McGuffey Reader* profoundly affected the American public, popularizing previously unacceptable social and moral ideas which furthered the cause of industrialists and the wealthy.

8. Lelia Patridge (1889) estimates that 30,000 people from most states and several European countries came to observe the Quincy system before 1880. Some Quincy teachers reported that at times the observers outnumbered the students in their classrooms.

9. Although Rice was generous in his praise for all the schools in this third category, he saved his superlatives for Francis Parker and his colleagues: "Of all the schools that I have seen, I know of none that shows so clearly what is implied by an educational ideal as the Cook County Normal School" (pp. 209–10).

CHAPTER 2

1. Of course, many people did not enjoy any form of prosperity, particularly immigrants and minorities, but my point here is to give some texture to the rising expectations of many Americans during this period when Horatio Alger stories were so popular and when the accumulation of wealth seemed to be the main attraction of the American dream.

2. Callahan suggests that the public comparison of business and schooling was extremely effective in bringing about changes in public education because of what he calls "the vulnerability thesis," which suggests that school administrators are eager to please because their jobs depend on the good will of a relatively few powerful people in a community. Since power in most communities typically resides with business interests, it is not surprising that superintendents quickly attempted to implement their perspective.

3. Charles Judd, dean of the University of Chicago's School of Education and editor of the *Elementary School Journal*, set aside space in several issues of the 1919 volume in order to discuss the lag between educational science and textbook design and content. Included among these essays is a publisher's response to criticism in which he argues that publishers are responsible only to the marketplace and do not attempt to lead teach-

ers in any direction—if scientific textbooks are sought, there first must be an established market for them. However, as early as 1902, John Dewey accused publishers of manipulating school curricula through their publishing and advertising practices.

4. Several decades later in *Sources of Science of Education*, Dewey (1928) argued against the adaptation of procedures from physical science popular at the turn of the century. First, Dewey agreed with William James who doubted if a science of pedagogy patterned after physical science was possible because there was a qualitative difference between physical and social phenomena. Second, Dewey thought that teachers— not educational experts—should use the scientific method to better their instructional practice on a continuous basis while they worked. In fact, Dewey considered educational science a dialectical process in which, "any portion of ascertained knowledge that enters into the heart, head, and hands of educators, and which by entering in, renders the performance of educational functions enlightened. . . . But there is no way to discover what is more truely enlightened except by the continuation of the educational act itself. The discovery is never made, it is always in the making" (pp. 76–77).

5. The law of identical elements and the interest in the science of pedagogy led Thorndyke and his students to design tests for arithmetic (1908), handwriting (1910), spelling (1913), drawing (1913), reading (1914), and language ability (1916).

6. According to Horn, these summarizations of scientific information on specific elementary school subjects had not been done previously. However, it started a trend in the *Elementary School Journal* which began to publish such reports on a regular basis beginning with its 1918 volume. For reading, William S. Gray increased his summary of 35 studies of reading and instruction which was included in the fourth Committee report to a book length document in 1925 describing 436 such studies.

7. A comparison of Gray's "Principles" with two other documents may give some indication of the conservative nature of his recommendations. First, consider Emma Davis's "Fourth Grade Reading Directions for Teachers in Cleveland, Ohio" which was included in the *5th NSSE Yearbook* (Davis 1906). Davis outlines briefly two types of recommended reading instruction, which she calls intensive study and extensive reading. Without benefit of scientific investigation, Davis's prescriptions for teachers closely resemble Gray's, although she may overemphasize oral reading. She suggests that teachers feature content over elocution, word study with phonics for primary and syllabication and structural analysis for intermediate, initial silent reading for independent practice, testing for comprehension, and simple texts for rate training, all of which were later recommended by Gray. In this context, Gray's summary of science seems only to confirm logical opinion available ten years prior to the Committee's fourth report.

A second source of comparison is John and Evelyn Dewey's *Schools of Tomorrow* (1915) which describes contemporary practices in schools attempting to design reading instruction according to principles of the New Education. For example, at the elementary school on the University of Missouri campus in Columbia, "the pupils learn to read and write and figure only as they felt the need of it to enlarge their work . . . about trees, plants, and animals . . . or in the study of their own food, shelter, and clothing" (p. 44–45). "The hour devoted to stories is no more a reading and writing lesson than all the rest of the day's work. . . . During this period, the teacher and the children tell stories to each other; not stories they have studied from their primers, but stories that they already know, that they have listened to, or read because they enjoyed them. . . . Soon they want to learn a new group of stories, and then quite naturally; they go to the school library, pick out a storybook and read. It has been found that the first grade pupils read from twelve to thirty books during the year; the second grade pupils from twenty-five to fifty. In this way, they learn to read . . . "(p. 49).

8. Venezky argues that Nila Banton Smith's history of basals fails to identify the beginning of teacher's guidebooks in the 19th century. He writes, "separate teacher's manuals did not become commonplace until the 1920s, but the pattern for such texts was established in the late 1880s and early 1890s with the publication of Ballard's *Synthetic Method* and Ward's *Rational Method in Reading*" (p. 253). However, as I will argue shortly, these guidebooks were not based on scientific evidence and therefore only offered a simple form of control (Apple 1982), someone else's opinion, which teachers could easily ignore. My point is that the guidebooks of the 1920s and thereafter provided a scientific context for a technical control in which teachers would *choose* to follow the direction of someone else. As an aside, the Spaulding which Venezky mentions as an author of the Aldine series which offered a 219–page guidebook in 1907 is the same Frank Spaulding who later became a leading advocate of scientific management and a member of the Committee on the Economy of Time in Education.

9. As early as 1925, Lehah Crabbs developed an equation for determining teachers' efficiency of instruction through their students' scores on standardized tests. Since the tests were designed to examine students' knowledge of what was taught (following the law of identical elements), and test designers' definition of what was taught was the information that was included in students' textbooks, this method of supervision through test scores applied pressure on teachers to follow the basal guidebooks closely during reading instruction.

CHAPTER 3

1. After the *60th NSSE Yearbook*, the twelve-year cycle was discontinued, with the last report on elementary reading instruction appearing in 1968. The most recent *NSSE Yearbook* concerning reading instruction (Purves 1984) presents a discussion of secondary school and adult reading instruction and materials.

2. *Language Arts* was originally published as *The Elementary English Review* (1924–47) and later as *Elementary English* (1947–75). For a more detailed account of the articles concerning basal materials in these journals, see my "A Retrospective Look at Teachers' Reliance on Commercial Materials" published in *Language Arts* (1983) on the eve of its 60th anniversary.

3. Since the editorship of *Language Arts* changed from Julie Jensen to David Dillon, there has been a marked change in the tone of the editorials and articles. Generally, Dillon and the contributors have taken a more critical stance concerning traditional guidebook-directed reading instruction. Since 1984 the three typical patterns which were consistently present in nearly every volume of *Language Arts* are no longer present. In fact, it is difficult to find any mention of basal materials at all, with the notable exception of Kenneth Goodman's "Basal Readers: A Call for Action" (1986) in which he sharply criticizes the use of basal readers during elementary school instruction and suggests alternative methods to be more appropriate and effective.

4. It's interesting to note that this emphasis on teachers' use of basal materials has perhaps unintentionally strengthened the publishers' and advocates' opinion by suggesting that if only teachers would learn to use the basal technology properly all students would learn to read. This attempt to split the materials from their use seems to be acceptable to the reading research community since very few critics have been successful in arguing that the logic of the basals—their design and directions—provides the rationale for teachers' questionable use of the materials. If this were not true, there would be much greater variability in the ways that teachers use these materials and conduct their instruction than there appears to be.

5. According to Bob Jerrolds (1977), the International Reading Association began in 1957 upon the merger of the International Council for the Improvement of Reading Instruction (the group which began with six members in 1947) and the National Association of Remedial Teachers. In each of the eleven chapters in his rather saccharine history of the organization, Jerrolds reports on the financial difficulties of the organization lending further support to my hypothesis concerning the vulnerability of the organization to the publishers' capital in order to conduct regular business.

6. The percentages reported concerning students' achievement as being one or more years behind grade level favor upper classes over lower classes by 3 percent in first grade and by 50 percent by sixth grade. Percentages reported for students being one or more grades ahead of grade level favored upper classes by a steady 50 to 60 percent across the elementary grades. Barton and Wilder conclude that guidebook-directed instruction simply confirms home-related advantages for upper classes, doing virtually nothing to correct the differences for lower-class children.

7. Although this may seem like an extreme example, most state legislatures have recently taken a more active role in elementary education

(Darling-Hammond and Wise 1985). For example, Florida's Educational Accountability Act of 1976 requires tests for minimum competence in reading and designates basal publishers as responsible for proper instruction toward that minimum competence. Florida requires basal publishers to supply "written proof of the use of the learner verification and revision of the materials . . . themselves, revision of the teachers' materials, and revision of the teachers' skill through retraining . . ." (Wise 1979: 22–23). Florida has thus legislated basic skills as the goal of reading instruction, basal materials as the means of reading instruction, and minimum competency tests and basal publishers as the arbiters of program effectiveness.

8. There is some economic justification for basal publishers' resistance to experts' recommendations for changes in basal format based solely on research findings. For example, in the late 1960s and early 1970s, Scott, Foresman experienced a 65 percent drop in sales when it published a basal series with significantly reduced directions in teacher's guidebooks, fewer workbooks, and dramatically altered beginning anthologies.

9. Durkin (1987) demonstrates how teacher's guidebooks adopted only the spirit of the 1960s by featuring the terminology of phonics while maintaining the status quo concerning "decoding" instruction, the spirit of the 1970s by creating basal management systems, and the spirit of the 1980s by highlighting the correlations between the basal goals and those of standardized reading achievement tests. She concludes that while the marketing strategies and terminology changed frequently over time for new customers, the programs remained essentially the same to keep previous customers satisfied.

CHAPTER 4

1. In chapter 7, I will demonstrate that teachers who group by ability for reading instruction do in fact differentiate among students by providing different content, using different methods, and holding different expectations for success. However, the entire range of teachers' efforts are provided in the teacher's guidebook.

2. More information, including methodological details and statistical support, can be found in "The Use of Commercial Reading Materials in American Elementary Schools" published in the *Reading Research Quarterly*, 1983.

3. Previously serving small towns and rural communities, the school district had experienced rapid growth in the past ten years, including extensive building, promoting of administrators, and hiring of new faculty. According to the previous supervisor of elementary curricula, the growth provided an excuse to reorganize a "mediocre" reading program, replacing it with a mastery learning orientation which regained public support for the district.

4. The teachers also noted that they had to use the basal materials in order to prepare their students for the book and chapter tests because

often the vocabulary, procedures, and even the skills were idiosyncratic to one set of basals. One teacher who had experienced repeated failure in trying to teach her fourth grade students a certain skill offered the following anecdote: "I took several tests home and asked my husband to take them. He's a vice president of his company and has a degree in engineering. I can vouch for his ability to read. Anyway, there were at least three tests on which he failed to reach mastery because he couldn't pass the sub-tests. The funny part is that our fourth grade son who goes to school in this district. . . . Well, the funny part is that my son could pass all the tests."

5. Several reading and classroom teachers confided that the former supervisor of elementary education and the present reading coordinator were authors of the basal series used in the district. Since the reading coordinator directed the textbook selection committee (but abstained from the final committee decision), these teachers questioned the objectivity of the selection process. One teacher stated: "We pick another series and she [the reading coordinator] loses money . . . you tell me how open the process is."

6. Other methods of the not-so-covert pressure to maintain at least a standard pace for reading instruction within a school were to form support groups only for "slow" teachers, circulating "good news" information sheets when classes passed reading tests, or posting scores on teachers' doors.

7. Reading teachers proved to be a difficult group to classify. They agreed moderately with all four hypotheses equally across various types of measures. Their only distinctive feature besides their job description was that they had taken at least three times as many graduate level reading courses as the other two groups. Reading teachers formed two groups; one which closely approximated the responses of administrators, the other the classroom teachers' responses. Since reading teachers in this district were both teachers and administrators, it may be that they were unable to reconcile the different responsibilities and saw themselves as either administrators or teachers with no common ground.

8. Most reading researchers seek answers to all questions concerning reading instruction within the teacher/student dyad, using some type of behavior or attitudinal index to measure the phenomenon in question in order to explain it. Even when they call for consideration of the outer context (e.g., Duffy 1982), this consideration is always limited to some immediate, readily apparent effect on teacher/student interaction. This "insiders" position restricts the scope of questions reading researchers will consider and moreover confines the answers they will accept to those which quantitatively explain observable behavior or student products. In this way, reading research becomes a conservative, even destructive force in reading programs, shoring up the problem spots of the status quo because the researcher cannot contemplate and act toward constructive change.

9. In the only detailed study of basal publishing operations, George Gra-

ham (1978) discusses the steps for the development of basal series in two major publishing houses. The process begins with a product plan and market analysis. At this point, authors are considered only in terms of whose name would lend greatest credibility to the series to help sales. Next the publishers estimate the cost, price, and profits of attempting such a product. Cost is manipulated by alternatives in printing, artwork, and inhouse versus contracted labor expenses. Price is set by the market. Profits are calculated by the market share that is considered soft or already controlled by the publisher in previous editions. Third, the publisher develops a marketing strategy—what are the favored parts of already successful programs? which of those parts are most profitable (e.g., consumable products that are resold yearly)? and which markets are available at the end of the production timeline? Only at this late point when content becomes somewhat of a concern are authors considered. Graham states "on arriving at the publishing house for the study, the first question . . . was 'how do you select your senior authors for the series?' The liaison laughed and said, 'That is a very premature question, if you are really interested in what makes this business tick. Author selection is one of the least important parts of putting together a series' " (p. 93).

CHAPTER 5

1. In 1985, the Chicago School District officially stopped using the Chicago Mastery Learning Reading Program (CMLR) as the only acceptable procedure for teaching students to read. The expense of the program and the lack of results after ten years of development and implementation were cited as the reasons for the abandonment of the program after millions of dollars had been invested. However, CMLR materials are still available commercially because the district sold the publishing rights in 1982.

2. For a comparison of the Chicago program and the Right to Read district, see my "Mastery Learning in Reading and the Control of Teachers and Students" published in *Language Arts* in 1984.

3. George Schmidt, a Chicago substitute teacher and editor of *Substance*, the official journal of the Substitutes United for Better Schools organization, won the International Reading Association's journalism award for his articles on the impact of the CMLR program on Chicago teachers and students.

4. For more information and statistical data to substantiate my remarks, see my "Teachers' and Administrators' Thoughts on Changes in Reading Instruction within a Merit Pay Program Based on Test Scores" published in the *Reading Research Quarterly* in 1986.

5. The superintendent of schools for this district, who is generally considered to be the originator of the merit pay program, has since left the school district to work for the publishers of the basal materials used in the district.

6. See my "Conflict or Consensus: Views of Reading Curricula and In-

struction Within One Instructional Setting" published in *Reading Research and Instruction* in 1986 for more information and the statistical data from this study.

7. Again, reading teachers proved to be difficult to characterize as a group. Just as in the study of the reading program from the Right to Read school district, reading teachers split into two groups. Eleven reading teachers, who took more than four graduate level reading classes provided information closely aligned with classroom teachers, and seven, who took two or fewer such classes, offered responses similar to those of administrators. If this factor can serve as evidence of whether reading teachers considered themselves to be teachers or administrators, then this data lends support to my hypothesis of reading teachers' thoughts and actions from the first study.

CHAPTER 6

1. During interviews, the central administrators and principals from the merit pay school district made several remarks concerning the difficulty of setting quotas for standardized achievement test scores for individual schools. The primary reasons for those problems, all agreed, were the economic class and racial background of the families served by the local schools. Principals from schools "in better neighborhoods" complained that parents had unrealistic expectations for their children and that because their students "topped out" the tests in the early grades they did not show much growth across the elementary grades, excluding their teachers from getting merit pay. Principals from schools in poorer sections of town wondered aloud about the validity of such tests as measures of their students' knowledge and reported that their parents were "happy with our reading program regardless of mediocre scores." There is much evidence available which suggests that this phenomenon is not limited to this school district (Heath 1983; Jencks 1972).

2. Of course, there are many programs which attempt to alter the raw materials of schooling—the students—before they enter schools. Perhaps the most ambitious attempt was project Head Start initiated during the Great Society era of the middle 1960s. This experimental federal project funded alternative preschool programs charged to improve "at risk" students' chances for success at school. Although several programs with differing sets of goals were funded, the evaluation of each project was based solely on its ability to raise the children's scores on standardized readiness tests in language, reading, and math (House 1978; Rivilin 1971). Programs which exerted greater control over teachers' and students' actions during formal lessons in these subjects showed the greatest increase in academic test scores and continued to be funded.

3. Mike Bowler won the International Reading Association's Print Media Award in 1977 for a series of articles in the *Baltimore Sun* entitled "The Selling of the 3Rs." In a condensed version published in the 1978 volume of the *Reading Teacher*, Bowler explains the soap opera-like quality of

state adoption procedures in Texas, complete with $30,000,000 lawsuits, searching for God within the textbook pages, and tearful testimony about the effects of "cusswords" (slang) on the minds of young Texans.

4. At present, this must cause basal publishers to become somewhat perplexed. Texas rivals Florida for the most legislation attempting to control nearly every facet of reading instruction. The state curriculum guides are skills-based and closely tied to mastery learning. Joseph Hannon, former superintendent of the Chicago Public Schools when the mastery learning reading program was developed, is now a high-ranking official in the Texas State Education Department. California, on the other hand, has just drafted a course of study document for reading instruction to be based primarily on children's literature. At this writing it has not been put into effect, and it will be interesting to see how basal publishers reconcile the new California and Texas effects.

5. Attempts to improve the objectivity of textbook selection committees have met with mixed success (Dole, Rogers, and Osborn 1987). For example, the Center for the Study of Reading has developed a series of booklets to inform committees concerning new developments in reading research which have certain applications to classroom instruction. In four pilot studies of these booklets, committee members greeted the intervention with a variety of responses from enthusiasm to guarded concern. The researchers report that some committee members were unable to use the booklets effectively and others were sad that they had used the booklets at all: "It's disappointing to do all this work and then find that there are not really any good programs out there" and "How do I tell other teachers this?"

6. For example, instruction should proceed in small steps followed by easy practice because "available evidence does suggest that high levels of success are associated with large year to year gains in reading" (p. 88). Or teachers should react to students' mistakes in a certain way because "teachers who deal with oral reading errors in [this] manner . . . produce larger than average gains in reading achievement" (p. 53).

7. This equation ultimately causes the Commission on Reading problems. After advocating one instructional method over others because it has greater influence on test scores, the Commission acknowledges that "the strength of a standardized test is not that it can provide deep assessment of reading proficiency but rather that it can provide fairly reliable, partial assessment cheaply and quickly (p. 98). . . . A more valid assessment . . . could be obtained by ascertaining whether students can and will . . . read aloud . . . with acceptable fluency; write satisfactory summaries . . . ; explain plots and motivations of characters . . . ; [and] read extensively . . . " (p. 99). The irony of these statements is lost on the Commission as they do not mention the contradiction they created between their proposed means and ends for reading instruction. What prevents schools from using the latter "more valid" forms of assessment is that they rely on teachers' subjective opinions of acceptable fluency, satisfactory summaries, and so forth, and it is teachers' subjectivity that school administrators, reading experts, and basal publishers are trying to minimize during reading instruction.

8. High level cognitive questions are to be discouraged during reading lessons for two reasons. First, they are not correlated with high achievement test scores. Since comprehension questions on achievement tests are usually written in a multiple choice format concerning topics mentioned briefly in less than 300 words and are machine scored, this is not a surprising finding. However, Rosenshine and Stevens offer a second reason for not asking these questions—there are no generic rules students can use to answer them. Worse yet, according to Rosenshine and Stevens, the answers may require personal opinion to answer them and, therefore, do not really test students' comprehension of a passage.

CHAPTER 7

1. Although Bettelheim and Zelan's thesis met with initial resistance from reading experts—most claimed that Bettelheim and Zelan examined obsolete editions—many researchers now recognize that student motivation is a key element in students learning to and continuing to read. Suggesting that students must have both the "skill and the will," reading experts now seek methods to directly instruct students in how to enjoy reading. It seems that even students' pleasure cannot escape technical control.

2. Weber challenges the recent enthusiasm for reciprocal teaching wherein students and teachers exchange places and roles in order to facilitate students' understanding of particular text and the process of closely reading texts. What Weber finds problematic is the control over the student/teachers once the exchange has been made. Students are not allowed to follow their own judgment concerning how to interrogate a text, rather they are to follow the teacher's model and control the other group members' discussion of text content. Reciprocal teaching seems intent on reproduction of technical control of reading lessons at the student level rather than on providing opportunities for students to demonstrate independence in thought and action.

3. This absence of communication among students or between teacher and student is particularly troublesome during basal tests. According to Goodman, Shannon, Freeman, and Murphy (1988), the tests are often fraught with ambiguity in text, illustration, and item answers. Students' inability to reduce this ambiguity increases the likelihood that they will fail to reach criterion even though they understand the skill sufficiently well to use it when they read. With so few items and so many ambiguous points, there is considerable opportunity for invalid and unreliable results.

4. Because teachers cannot leave group lessons to monitor students' seatwork closely, teachers' remarks to students away from reading group are exclusively directed to whether or not students appear engaged in their assigned seatwork activities (Anderson 1984). Since Anderson observed only first grade classrooms, students seem to learn quickly that their job during seatwork is to "look busy" and to "get done."

5. See Elfrieda Hiebert's "An examination of ability groupings for reading instruction" published in the *Reading Research Quarterly* in 1983 for a review of this research.

6. Harris and Amprey (1982) attribute these differences between races within a social class to the continued isolation of racial groups from one another which fosters different language patterns and experiences. Since tests are written in standard dialect concerning mainstream experiences, minority children regardless of social class will score lower than their white peers. It is important to note that the black and Hispanic upper- and middle-class students scored significantly higher than white lower-class students, suggesting that social class is a more potent factor than race in reading achievement.

7. The students in both Rist's and Gilmore's studies were of the same racial and roughly the same socioeconomic background, making it difficult for teachers to make social class distinctions among students. Teachers usually followed their first impression, often ascribing middle-class values to students and then largely creating distinctions among groups in their classes through differential feedback. Rist reports an initial wide range and overlap of aptitudes and behaviors within and among students in original group assignments and a slow process of castes being created throughout the year. Both Rist and Gilmore speculate that these differences in treatment would be exaggerated considerably in schools serving racially integrated or mixed class neighborhoods.

8. When Gilmore shared his findings with neighborhood parents, one mother commented that the teachers' assessment of "Black" students was remarkably reminiscent of typical portrayals of slaves as either "sullen" or "dancing." Gilmore wonders if teachers' attitudes toward sulking and steps are an indication of "our own brand of modern-day racism" (p. 126).

9. Several teachers from the town elementary school recognized that many lower-class students failed to make progress in the lowest group despite what teachers considered to be their best efforts to help these students. With Heath's assistance, these teachers became ethnographers in their classrooms and communities to discover the impediments to lower-class children's success. Much to their credit, many teachers acknowledged that they were partly responsible for students' failure because they were unable or unwilling to identify lower-class students' strength in, and needs for, written communication. After much hard work, these teachers learned to adapt their programs in order to give lower-class students more opportunities to demonstrate their linguistic competence and to relate reading lessons immediately to their lives in Roadville and Trackton. When Heath's study ended, most teachers from the school seemed to be making changes in their regular routines to accommodate Roadville and Trackton students' ways with words as teachers attempted to extend their competence to include the standard dialect.

CHAPTER 8

1. At times lower-class children's actions during schooling contribute to their assignments to low ability groups and thus the reproduction of social

classes. John Ogbu (1974; 1978) has shown that minority lower-class children do not expect schools to improve their social and economic lot in life and often do not invest much energy into school matters. Paul Willis's (1977) study of working-class youths in England demonstrates how lower-class students can select themselves for lower-class status by rejecting all that the school and teachers deem important. And William Labov (1972) has shown that lower-class black children often appear mute and disinterested within traditional schools. In each case, students seem to engage in destructive reactions as if they wanted to remain with their present social circumstances.

2. *Language Arts*, the elementary school journal of the National Council of Teachers of English, has led the way in attempting to connect the "whole language" work of Goodman, Graves, and Smith and the political work of Paulo Freire, Henry Giroux, and Roger Simon. Kenneth Goodman has taken a more overtly political stance in *A Report Card on Basal Readers* (Goodman, Shannon, Freeman, and Murphy 1988), but overall the followers of whole language instruction seem content to stop their analyses of current reading programs at a personal level, rarely seeing the political implications of their work.

3. For information concerning Substitutes United for Better Schools write *Substance*, 59 E. Van Buren St., Room 810 Chicago, IL 60604.

4. The bus driver/teacher who became a leader in the citizenship schools of the area described this success of the school in a different way. He suggested that the area's solid support for Lyndon Johnson in the 1964 presidential election, when the rest of South Carolina voted solidly for Barry Goldwater, can be directly attributed to large numbers of graduates of the Johns Island and other such schools.

5. For further information about the Highland Folk School write Highland Research and Education Center, Inc., New Market, Tennessee.

6. For further information concerning the Boston Women's Teachers Group write Boston Women's Teachers Group, P.O. Box 1690, Somerville, MA 02144.

CHAPTER 9

1. Three books have been extremely helpful in formulating my argument for this chapter: Henry Giroux's *Theory and Resistance in Education*, Ira Shor and Paulo Freire's *A Pedagogy for Liberation*, and Paulo Freire and Donaldo Macedo's *Literacy: Reading the Word and the World*.

2. Although many substantial changes were made in teachers' attitudes and their instructional practices while Heath worked with these teachers, her return to the area after a ten-year absence revealed that none of the teachers had continued the innovations. Rather the individual teachers found it impossible to resist the pressures from the school district to use basal reading materials and from the state to prepare students for minimum competence reading tests. State and school district initiatives had produced "a decrease in the autonomy of teachers as professionals and an increase in the bureaucratization of teaching and testing" (p. 356).

Bibliography

Adams, C. (1935). The new departure in The Common School of Quincy (1879), reprinted in the *Elementary School Journal* 35: 495–504.

Adams, F., and M. Horton. (1975). *Unearthing Seeds of Fire.* Winston-Salem, N.C. John F. Blair Publishing.

Alexander, K., and E. McDill. (1976). Selections and allocations within school. *American Sociological Review* 41: 969–80.

Allington, R. (1977). If they don't read much, how they ever gonna get good. *Journal of Reading* 21: 57–61.

———. (1980). Teacher interruption behaviors during primary grade oral reading. *Journal of Educational Psychology* 72: 371–74.

———. (1983). The reading instruction provided readers of differing reading abilities. *Elementary School Journal* 83: 548–59.

———. (1985). Fluency. *Reading Teacher* 37: 451–62.

Alpert, J. (1974). Teacher behavior across ability groups. *Journal of Educational Psychology* 66: 348–53.

Anderson, L. (1984). The environment of instruction: The function of seatwork in a commercially developed curriculum. In G. Duffy, L. Roehler, and J. Mason, eds., *Comprehension Instruction: Perspectives and Suggestions*. New York: Longman.

———. (1987). Staff development and instructional improvement: Response to Robbins and Wolfe. *Educational Leadership* 44: 64–65.

Anderson, L., et al. (1985). A qualitative study of seatwork in first grade classrooms. *Elementary School Journal* 86: 123–40.

Anderson, R. (1985). *Becoming a Nation of Readers*. Washington, D.C.: National Institute for Education.

162

Anderson, R., J. Mason, and L. Shirley. (1984). The reading group: An experimental investigation of a labyrinth. *Reading Research Quarterly* 20: 6–38.

Anderson, R., J. Osborn, and R. Tierney. (1984). *Learning to Read in American Schools: Basal Readers and Content Texts.* Hillsdale, N.J.: Lawrence Erlbaum.

Apple, M. (1982). *Education and Power.* Boston: Routledge & Kegan Paul.

Arricule, F. (1983). A case for Chicago mastery learning. *Learning* 11: 92–94.

Artley, S. (1980). Reading: Skills or competencies? *Language Arts* 57: 546–49.

Aukerman, R. (1981). *The Basal Approach to Reading.* New York: Wiley.

Austin, M., and C. Morrison. (1963). *The First R.* New York: Wiley.

Bagley, W. (1911). *Classroom Management.* New York: Macmillan.

Barnes, M.S., ed. (1911). *Autobiography of Edward Austin Sheldon.* New York: Ives-Bulter.

Barr, R. (1986a). Commentary: Studying classroom reading instruction. *Reading Research Quarterly* 21: 231–36.

———. (1986b). The influence of basal programs on instructional activities. Paper presented at the Annual Meeting of the National Reading Conference (December), Austin, Tex.

———. (1987). Classroom interaction and curriculum content. In D. Bloome, ed., *Literacy and Schooling.* New York: Ablex.

Barton, A., and D. Wilder. (1964). Research and practice in the teaching of reading. In M. Miles, ed., *Innovations in Education.* New York: Teachers College Press.

Bastian, A., et al. (1986). *Choosing Equality: The Case for Democratic Schooling.* Philadelphia: Temple University Press.

Beck, I., and M. McKeown. (1987). Getting the most from basal reading selections. *Elementary School Journal* 87: 343–56.

Becker, W. (1977). Teaching reading and language to the disadvantaged—what we have learned from field research. *Harvard Educational Review* 47: 518–43.

Becker, W., and D. Carnine. (1980). Direct Instruction. In B. Lahey and A. Kazdin, eds., *Advances in Clinical Child Psychology,* vol. 3. New York: Plenum.

Bettelheim, B., and K. Zelan. (1981). *On Learning to Read: The Child's Fascination with Meaning.* New York: Knopf.

Betts, E. (1939). A study of the vocabularies of first grade basal readers. *Elementary English Review* 16: 65–69.

Bissex, G. (1980). *GNYS AT WRK: A Child Learns to Write and Read.* Cambridge, Mass.: Harvard University Press.

Block, J., and Burns, R. (1977). Mastery learning. In L. Shulman, ed., *Review of Research in Education,* vol. 4. Itasca, Ill.: Peacock Publishers.

Bloom, B. (1976). *Human Characteristics and School Learning*. New York: McGraw-Hill.

Bloome, D. (1987). *Literacy and Schooling*. New York: Ablex.

Bobbitt, J.F. (1912). The elimination of waste in education. *Elementary School Journal* 12: 147–57.

Bond, G. (1966). First grade studies: An overview. *Elementary English* 43: 464–70.

Bond, G., and R. Dykstra. (1967). The cooperative research program in first-grade reading instruction. *Reading Research Quarterly* 2: 5–142.

Bondi, J., and S. Wiles. (1967). School reform in Florida. *Educational Leadership* 44: 45–46.

Boney, C. (1938). Basal readers. *Elementary English Review* 15: 133–37.

———. (1939). Teaching children to read as they learn to talk. *Elementary English Review* 16: 139–41, 156.

Borko, H., R. Shavelson, and P. Stern. (1981). Teachers' decisions in planning of reading instruction. *Reading Research Quarterly* 16: 449–66.

Bourdieu, P. and J. Passeron. (1977). *Reproduction in Education, Society, and Culture*. Beverly Hills, Calif.: Sage.

Bowler, M. (1978). Textbook publishers try to please all, but first they woo the heart of Texas. *Reading Teacher* 31: 514–18.

Bowles, S., and H. Gintis. (1976). *Schooling in Capitalist America*. New York: Basic.

Brophy, J. (1979). Teacher behavior and its effects. *Journal of Educational Psychology* 71: 733–50.

———. (1982). How teachers influence what is taught and learned in classrooms. *Elementary School Journal* 83: 1–13.

Brophy, J., and T. Good. (1986). Teacher behavior and student achievement. In M. Wittrock, ed., *Handbook of Research on Teaching*. New York: Macmillan.

Brown, A., D. Campione, and J. Day. (1981). Learning to learn. *Educational Researcher* 10: 14–21.

Brown, R. (1978). Response to John Bormuth. R. Beach and P.D. Pearson, eds., *Perspectives on Literacy*. Minneapolis, Minn.: University of Minnesota.

Bussis, A. (1982). 'Burn it at the casket': Research, reading instruction, and children's learning of the first R. *Phi Delta Kappan* 64: 237–41.

California Department of Public Instruction. (1987). *English Language Arts Model Curriculum Guide* (for kindergarten through grade eight). Sacramento, Calif.

Callahan, R. (1962). *Education and the Cult of Efficiency*. Chicago: University of Chicago Press.

Calloway, A.B. (1972). Programs and materials used in reading instruction: A survey. *Elementary English* 49: 578–81.

Campbell, J. (1965). *Colonel Francis W. Parker: The Children's Crusader*. New York: Teachers College Press.

Carnegie, A. (1900). Speech at the Dedication of the Cooper Union, New York City.

Carroll, J., and J. Chall. (1975). *Toward a Literate Society*. New York: McGraw-Hill.

Chall, J. (1967). *Learning to Read: The Great Debate*. New York: McGraw-Hill.

——. (1987). Introduction. *Elementary School Journal* 87: 243–45.

Chomsky, N. (1979). *Language and Responsibility*. Brighton, England: Harvester Press.

——. (1981). *Radical Priorities*. Montreal: Black Rose Books.

Clay, M. (1972). *Reading: The Complex Behavior*. New York: International Publications.

Cochrane, O., et al. (1984). *Reading, and Writing, and Caring*. New York: Richard C. Owens.

Cohen, M. (1979). *The First Grade Takes a Test*. Westport, Conn.: Greenwood.

Cohen, S. (1974). *A History of Colonial Education, 1607–1776*. New York: Wiley.

Cohen, S.A. (1981). In defense of mastery learning. *Principal* 60: 35–57.

Collins, A., and S. Haviland. (1979). *Children's Reading Problems* (Reading Education Report No. 8). Champaign, Ill.: Center for the Study of Reading.

Courtis, S.A. (1915). Standards in rates of reading. In H. Wilson, ed., *Minimum Essentials in Elementary School Subjects—Standards and Current Practices. 14th Yearbook of the National Society for the Study of Education*. Part I. Bloomington, Ill.: Public School Publishing.

Crabbs, L. (1925). *Measuring Efficiency in Supervision and Teaching* (Teachers College Contribution to Education, No. 175). New York: Teachers College, Columbia University.

Cremin, L. (1961). *The Transformation of the School: Progressivism in American Education, 1876–1957*. New York: Vintage.

——. (1970). *American Education: The Colonial Experience, 1607–1783*. New York: Harper & Row.

Cuban, L. (1984a). *How Teachers Taught 1890–1980*. New York: Longman.

——. (1984b). Transforming a frog into a prince: Effective school research, policy, and practice at the district level. *Harvard Educational Review* 54: 129–51.

Cubberly, E. (1934). *Public Education in the United States*. Boston: Houghton Mifflin.

Curti, M. (1935). *The Social Ideas of American Educators*. New York: Scribner.

Darling-Hammond, L., and A. Wise. (1985). Beyond standardized teaching: State standards and school improvement. *Elementary School Journal* 85: 315–36.

Davis, E. (1906). The teaching of English in the primary grades of the

Cleveland public schools. In G. Brown, ed., *On the Teaching of English in Elementary and High Schools. 5th Yearbook of the National Society for the Study of Education*, Part I. Bloomington, Ill.: Brown.

Dearborn, N. (1925). *The Oswego movement in American education.* Ph.D. diss. Teachers College, Columbia University.

Designs for Change. (1982). *Caught in the Web.* Chicago: Designs for Change.

———. (1985). *The Bottom Line.* Chicago: Designs for Change.

Dewey, J. (1902) *The Educational Situation.* Chicago: The University of Chicago Press.

———. (1928). *Sources of Science of Education.* New York: Liveright.

Dewey, J., and E. Dewey, (1915). *Schools of Tomorrow.* New York: E.P. Dutton.

Dolch, E.L. (1936). How much word knowledge do children bring to grade one? *Elementary English Review* 13: 177–83.

———. (1950). *Teaching Primary Reading.* Champaign, Ill.: Garrard.

Dole, J., T. Rogers, and J. Osborn. (1987). Improving the selection of basal programs: A report of the textbook adoption guidelines project. *Elementary School Journal* 87: 283–98.

Doyle, W. (1983). Academic work. *Review of Education Research* 53: 159–200.

Donovan, H. (1928). Use of research in teaching reading. *Elementary English Review* 5: 104–7.

Duffy, G. (1982). Response to Borko, Shavelson, and Stern: There's more to instructional decision-making in reading than the "empty classroom." *Reading Research Quarterly* 17: 295–300.

Duffy, G., and L. McIntyre. (1980). *A quantitative analysis of how various primary grade teachers employ the structural learning component of the direct instruction model when teaching reading* (Research Series No. 80). East Lansing, Mich.: Michigan State University, Institute for Research on Teaching.

Duffy, G., and L. Roehler. (1982a). The illusion of instruction. *Reading Research Quarterly* 17: 438–43.

———. (1982b). An analysis of the instruction in reading instructional research. In J. Niles and L. Harris, eds., *Inquiry in Reading.* Rochester, N.Y.: National Reading Conference.

———. (1982c). Direct instruction of comprehension. *Reading Horizons* 23: 35–40.

Duffy, G., L. Roehler, and P. Putnam. (1987). Putting the teacher in control: Basal reading textbooks and instructional decision-making. *Elementary School Journal* 87: 357–66.

Duffy, G., L. Roehler, and R. Wesselman. (1985). Disentangling the complexities of instructional effectiveness: A line of research on classroom reading instruction. In J. Niles and R. Lalik, eds., *Issues in Literacy: A Research Perspective.* 34th Yearbook of the National Reading Conference. Rochester, N.Y.: National Reading Conference.

Durkin, D. (1974). Some questions about questionable instructional materials. *Reading Teacher* 28: 13–18.

———. (1978–79). What classroom observation reveals about reading comprehension. *Reading Research Quarterly* 14: 481–533.

———. (1981). Reading comprehension instruction in five basal reading series. *Reading Research Quarterly* 16: 515–44.

———. (1983). Is there a match between what elementary teachers do and what basal readers manuals recommend? *Reading Teacher* 37: 734–44.

———. (1987). Influences on basal reader programs. *Elementary School Journal* 87: 331–41.

Durr, W., et al. (1983).*Teacher's guide: Moonbeams.* Boston: Houghton Mifflin.

Durrell, D. (1940). *Improving Reading Instructions.* Yonkers, N.Y.: World.

Eder, D. (1981). Ability grouping as a self-fulfilling prophecy. *Sociology of Education* 54: 151–62.

Educational Products Information Exchange (E.P.I.E.). (1977). *Report on a national survey of the nature and the quality of instructional materials most used by teachers and learners.* (Tech. Rep. No. 76). New York: EPIE Institute.

Epstein, J. (1986). Parents' reactions to teacher practices of parental involvement. *Elementary School Journal* 86: 277–94.

Farr, R., M. Tulley, and D. Powell. (1987). The evaluation and selection of basal readers. *Elementary School Journal* 87: 267–81.

Finkelstein, B. (1970). *Governing the Young: Teacher's Behaviors in American Primary Schools, 1820–1880. A Documentary History.* Ph.D. diss. Teachers College, Columbia University.

Fisher, C., et al. (1978). *Teaching and Learning in Elementary Schools. A Summary of the Beginning Teacher Evaluation Study.* San Francisco: Far West Laboratory for Educational Research and Development.

Flesch, R. (1955). *Why Johnny Can't Read and What You Can Do About It.* New York: Harper & Row.

———. (1981). *Why Johnny Still Can't Read.* New York: Harper & Row.

Flood, J., and D. Lapp. (1987). Forms of discourse in basal readers. *The Elementary School Journal* 87: 299–306.

Follett, R. (1985). The school textbook adoption process. *Book Research Quarterly* 1, 19–23.

Fotheringham, J., and D. Creal. (1980). Family socioeconomic, educational and emotional characteristics as predictors of school achievement. *Journal of Educational Research* 73: 311–17.

Frame, N. (1964). The availability of reading materials for teachers and pupils at the primary level. *Elementary English* 41: 262–68.

Freebody, P., and C. Baker. (1985). Children's first schoolbooks: Introductions to the culture of literacy. *Harvard Educational Review* 55: 381–83.

Freedman, S., J. Jackson, and K. Boles. (1983). The other end of the corridor: The effects of teaching on teachers. *Radical Teacher* 23: 2–23.

Freeman, F. (1919). Principles of method in teaching writing, as derived from scientific investigation. In E. Horn, ed., *Fourth Report of the Committee on the Economy of Time in Learning. 18th Yearbook of the National Society for the Study of Education*. Part II. Bloomington, Ill.: Public School Publishing.

Freer, M., and J. Dawson. (1987). The pudding's the proof. *Educational Leadership* 44: 67–68.

Freire, P. (1970). *Pedagogy of the Oppressed*. New York: Seabury.

———. (1971). *Education for Critical Consciousness*. New York: Seabury.

Freire, P., and D. Macedo. (1987). *Literacy: Reading the Word and the World*. South Hadley, Mass.: Bergin & Garvey.

Fry, E. (1966). Comparing the diacritical marking system, ITA, and a basal reading series. *Elementary English* 43: 607–11.

Frymier, J. (1985). Legislating centralization. *Phi Delta Kappan* 67: 646–48.

Gallant, M. (1986). *More Fun with Dick and Jane*. Don Mills, Ont.: Penguin.

Gambrell, L., R. Wilson, and W. Ganett. (1981). Classroom observations of task attending behaviors of good and poor readers. *Journal of Educational Research* 74: 400–4.

Gates, A. (1936). Needed research in elementary school reading. *Elementary English Review* 13: 306–10.

———. (1949). Character and purpose of the yearbook. In A. Gates, ed., *Reading in the Elementary School. 48th Yearbook of the National Society for the Study of Education*. Part II. Chicago: University of Chicago.

Gibboney, R. (1987). A critique of Madeline Hunter's teaching model from Dewey's perspective. *Educational Leadership* 44: 46–50.

———. (1987). The vagaries of turtle research: Gibboney replies. *Educational Leadership* 44: 54.

Gilmore, P. (1985). Gimme room: School resistance, attitude, and access to literacy. *Journal of Education* 167: 111–28.

Giroux, H. (1983). *Theory and Resistance in Education*. South Hadley, Mass.: Bergin & Garvey.

———. (1987). Introduction: Literacy and the pedagogy of political empowerment. In P. Freire and D. Macedo. *Literacy: Reading the Word and the World*. South Hadley, Mass.: Bergin & Garvey.

Good, T. (1981). Teacher expectations and student perceptions. *Educational Leadership* 38: 415–22.

Goodman, K. (1974). Effective teachers of reading know language and children. *Elementary English* 51: 823–28.

———. (1979). The know-more and the know-nothing movements in reading: A personal response. *Language Arts* 56: 657–63.

————. (1984). Unity in reading. In A. Purves and O. Niles, eds., *Becoming Readers in a Complex Society. 83rd Yearbook of the National Society for the Study of Education.* Part I. Chicago: University of Chicago Press.

————. (1984). *What's Whole in Whole Language?* Richmond Hill, Ont.: Scholastic.

————. (1986). Basal readers: A call for action. *Language Arts* 63: 358–63.

Goodman, K., P. Shannon, Y. Freeman, and S. Murphy. (1988). *A Report Card on Basal Readers.* New York: Richard C. Owen.

Graham, G. (1978). *A Present and Historical Analysis of Basal Reading Series.* Ph.D. diss. University of Virginia, Charlottesville.

Graves, D. (1984). *A Researcher Learns to Write.* Exeter, N.H.: Heinemann Educational Books.

Graves, D., and V. Stuart. (1985). *Write from the Start.* New York: Dutton.

Gray, W.S. (1915). Selected bibliography upon practical tests of reading ability. In H. Wilson, ed., *Minimum Essentials in Elementary School Subjects—Standards and Current Practices. 14th Yearbook of the National Society for the Study of Education.* Part I. Bloomington, Ill.: Public School Publishing.

————. (1917). The relation of silent reading to economy in education. In H. Wilson, ed., *Second Report of the Committee on Minimal Essentials in Elementary School Subjects. 16th Yearbook of the National Society for the Study of Education.* Part I. Bloomington, Ill.: Public School Publishing.

————. (1919). Principles of method in teaching reading, as derived from scientific investigation. In E. Horn, ed., *Report of the Committee on Economy of Time in Learning. 18th Yearbook of the National Society for the Study of Education.* Part II. Bloomington, Ill.: Public School Publishing.

————. (1925). *Summary of investigations relating to reading* (Suppl. Educational Monographs No. 28). Chicago: University of Chicago.

————. (1933). New issues in teaching reading. *Elementary English Review* 10: 162–64.

————. (1937). The nature and organization of basic instruction in reading. In W.S. Gray, ed., *The Teaching of Reading: A Second Report. 36th Yearbook of the National Society for the Study of Education.* Part I. Bloomington, Ill.: Public School Publishing.

————, ed. (1925). *Report of the National Committee on Reading. 24th Yearbook of the National Society for the Study of Education.* Part I. Bloomington, Ill.: Public School Publishing.

————, ed. (1937). *The Teaching of Reading: A Second Report. 36th Yearbook of the National Society for the Study of Education.* Part I. Bloomington, Ill.: Public School Publishing.

Green, J. (1987). In search of meaning: A sociolinguistic perspective on lesson construction and reading. In D. Bloome, ed., *Literacy and Schooling*. Norwood, N.J.: Albex.

Guthrie, J. (1981). Reading in New Zealand: Achievement and volume. *Reading Research Quarterly* 17: 6–27.

Habermas, J. (1970). *Toward a Rational Society: Student Protest, Science, and Politics*. Boston: Beacon.

Hall, G.S. (1883). *Contents of Children's Minds*. Boston: D.C. Heath.

Hamilton, S. (1983). The social side of schooling. *Elementary School Journal* 83: 313–34.

Hannon, J., and M. Katims. (1979). The Chicago plan: Mastery learning in the Chicago public schools. *Educational Leadership* 37: 120–22.

Hansen, J., T. Newkirk, and D. Graves, eds. (1985). *Breaking Ground: Teachers Relate Reading and Writing in the Elementary School*. Exeter, N.H.: Heinemann.

Harris, D., and J. Amprey. (1982). Race, social class, expectations and achievement. In G. Austin and H. Gorberf, eds., *The Rise and Fall of National Test Scores*. New York: Academic.

Harris, J., H. Donovan, and T. Alexander. (1927). *Supervision and Teaching of Reading*. Richmond, Va.: Johnson Publishing.

Harste, J., C. Burke, and V. Woodward. (1984). *Language Stories and Literacy Lessons*. Exeter, N.H.: Heinemann.

Heath, S.B. (1983). *Ways with Words*. New York: Cambridge University Press.

Heilbroner, R. (1985). *The Nature and Logic of Capitalism*. New York: Norton.

Hentoff, N. (1980). *The First Freedom: The Tumultuous History of Free Speech in America*. New York: Delacorte.

Hiebert, E. (1983). An examination of ability groupings for reading instruction. *Reading Research Quarterly* 18: 231–55.

Hildreth, G. (1949). Reading programs in the early primary period. In A. Gates, ed., *Reading in the Elementary School. 48th Yearbook of the National Society for the Study of Education*. Part II. Chicago, Ill.: University of Chicago Press.

Hill, C., and K. Methot. (1974). Making an important transition. *Elementary English* 51: 842–45.

Hoffman, J. (1986). Process-product research on effective teaching: A primer for a paradigm. In J. Hoffman, ed., *Effective Teaching of Reading: Research and Practice*. Newark, Del.: International Reading Association.

Hoffman, J., et al. (1984). Guided oral reading and miscue focused verbal feedback in second grade classrooms. *Reading Research Quarterly* 19: 367–84.

Hoffman, J., and N. Roser, eds,. (1987). The basal reader in American reading instruction. *Elementary School Journal* 87: 243–381.

Holmes, H. (1915). Time distribution by subjects and grades in representative cities. In H. Wilson, ed., *Minimum Essentials in Elementary*

School Subjects: Standards and Current Practices. 14th Yearbook of the National Society for the Study of Education. Part I. Bloomington, Ill.: Public School Publishing.

Horn, E., ed. (1919a). *Report of the Committee on Economy of Time in Learning. 18th Yearbook of the National Society for the Study of Education.* Part II. Bloomington, Ill.: Public School Publishing.

———. (1919b). Introduction. In E. Horn, ed., *Report of the Committee on Economy of Time in Learning. 18th Yearbook of the National Society for the Study of Education.* Part II. Bloomington, Ill.: Public School Publishing.

———. (1919c). Principles of method in teaching spelling, as derived from scientific investigation. In E. Horn, ed., *Report of the Committee on Economy of Time in Learning. 18th Yearbook of the National Society for the Study of Education.* Part II. Bloomington, Ill.: Public School Publishing.

Hosic, J.F. (1915). The essentials of literature. In H. Wilson, ed., *Minimum Essentials in Elementary School Subjects Standards and Current Practices. 14th Yearbook of the National Society for the Study of Education.* Part I. Bloomington, Ill.: Public School Publishing.

House, E. (1978). Evaluation as scientific management in United States school reform. *Comparative Education Review* 22: 388–401.

Housh, E. (1918). An analysis of the vocabularies of ten second-year readers. In H. Wilson, ed., *Third Report of the Committee on Economy of Time in Education. 17th Yearbook of the National Society for the Study of Education.* Part I. Bloomington, Ill.: Public School Publishing.

Howard, R. (1985). *Brave New Workplace.* New York: Viking.

Huck, C. (1976). *Children's Literature in the Elementary School,* 3rd ed. New York: Holt, Rinehart & Winston.

Huey, E.B. (1908). *The Psychology and Pedagogy of Reading.* Boston: MIT Press (Reprint published in 1968).

Hunter, M. (1987). Beyond rereading Dewey . . . What's next? A response to Gibboney. *Educational Leadership* 44: 51–53.

Huxley, A. (1963). *Literature and Science.* New York: Harper & Row.

Hyman, J., and S.A. Cohen. (1979). Learning for mastery: Ten conclusions after 15 years and 3,000 schools. *Educational Leadership* 37: 104–7.

Ignatovich, F., P. Cusick, and J. Ray. (1979). *Value/Belief Patterns of Teachers and Those Administrators Engaged in Attempts to Influence Teaching* (Research Series No. 43). East Lansing, Mich.: Institute for Research on Teaching.

Jackson, P. (1968). *Life in Classrooms.* New York: Holt, Rinehart & Winston.

Jefferson, T. (1893). A bill for the more general diffusion of knowledge. In P. Ford, ed., *The Writings of Thomas Jefferson.* New York: Putnam.

Jencks, C. (1972). *Inequality.* New York: Basic Books.

Jerrolds, B. (1977). *Reading Reflections: The History of the International Reading Association*. Newark, Del.: International Reading Association.

Johns, J., and D. Ellis. (1976). Reading: children tell it like it is. *Reading World* 16: 115–28.

Johnson, D., and P.D. Pearson. (1975). Skills management systems: A critique. *Reading Teacher* 28: 757–64.

Johnson, S. (1984). Merit pay for teachers: A poor prescription for reform. *Harvard Educational Review* 54: 175–85.

Jones, R. (1915). Standard vocabulary. In H. Wilson, ed., *Minimum Essentials in Elementary School Subjects—Standards and Current Practices. 14th Yearbook of the National Society for the Study of Education*. Part I. Bloomington, Ill.: Public School Publishing.

Judd, C. (1934). *Problems of Education in the United States*. New York: McGraw-Hill.

Katims, M. (1979). An interview. In D. Ryan and M. Schmit, eds., *Mastery Learning: Theory, Research, and Implementation*. Toronto: Ontario Ministry of Education.

Katims, M., and B.F. Jones. (1981) *Chicago Mastery Learning: Theory, Research, and Assessment in the Inner City*. A paper presented at annual meeting of the International Reading Association (May), New Orleans.

Kavale, K. (1979). Selecting and evaluating reading tests. In R. Schreiner, ed., *Reading Tests and Teachers*. Newark, Del.: International Reading Association.

Kliebard, H. (1986). *The Struggle for the American Curriculum, 1893–1958*. Boston: Routledge & Kegan Paul.

Knight, T. (1981). Mastery learning: A report from the firing line. *Educational Leadership* 39: 134–36.

Kohl, H. (1974). *Reading, How To*. New York: Bantam.

———. (1980). Can the schools build a new social order? *Journal of Education* 162: 57–66.

Kozol, J. (1985). *Illiterate America*. Garden City, N.Y.: Anchor Press.

Labov, W. (1972). *Language in the Inner City*. Philadelphia: University of Pennsylvania Press.

Lemisch, L., ed. (1961). *Benjamin Franklin: The Autobiography and Other Writings*. New York: Signet.

Levey, L, ed. (1971). *Cato's Letters: Unabridged Reproduction of the 6th Edition, 1755*. New York: DaCapo.

Levine, D. (1982). Successful approaches for improving academic achievement in inner-city elementary schools. *Phi Delta Kappan* 62: 523–26.

———. (1985). Preface. In D. Levine and Associates, eds., *Improving Student Achievement Through Mastery Learning*. San Francisco: Jossey-Bass.

Levine, D., and Associates. (1985). *Improving Student Achievement Through Mastery Learning Programs*. San Francisco: Jossey-Bass.

Levit, M. (1972). The Ideology of Accountability in Schooling. *Educational Studies* 3: 133–40.

Linn, R. (1982). Ability testing: Individual differences, predictions, and differentials predictions. In A. Wigdor and W. Garner, eds., *Ability Testing: Part II*. Washington, D.C.: National Academic Press.

Lockridge, K. (1974). *Literacy in Colonial New England*. New York: Norton.

Lortie, D. (1975). *Schoolteacher*. Chicago: University of Chicago Press.

Low, B., and P. Clement. (1982). Relationships of race and socio-economic status to classroom behavior, academic achievement, and referral for special education. *Journal of School Psychology* 20: 103–12.

Lukacs, G. (1970). *History and Class Consciousness*. Boston: MIT Press.

McDermott, R. (1976). *Kids Make Sense*. Ph.D. diss. Stanford University.

McKee, P. (1949). Reading programs in grades IV through VIII. In A. Gates, ed., *Reading in the Elementary School. 48th Yearbook of the National Society for the Study of Education*. Part II. Chicago: University of Chicago Press.

McLeod, A. (1986). Critical literacy: Taking control of our own lives. *Language Arts* 63: 37–50.

Marcuse, H. (1964). *One Dimensional Man*. Boston: Beacon.

Mason, J. (1982). *A Description of Reading Instruction*. (Ed. Rep. No. 35). Urbana, Ill.: Center for the Study of Reading.

Mathews, M. (1966). *Teaching to Read*. Chicago: University of Chicago.

Merton, R. (1957). *Social Theory and Social Structure*. Glencoe, Ill.: The Free Press.

Meyer, J., and Associates. (1978). *Environments and Organizations*. San Francisco: Jossey-Bass.

Michaels, S. (1981). Sharing time. *Language in Society* 10: 423–42.

Molesworth, R. (1976). *An Account of Denmark as It Was in the Year, 1692*. Copenhagen: Rosenkilde and Bagger.

Moore, D. (1985). Laura Zirbes and progressive reading instruction. *Elementary School Journal* 86: 663–72.

Mosenthal, P. (1987). Research views. *Reading Teacher* 40: 694–98, 810–13.

———. (in press). *Understanding Reading Research and Practice*. New York: Longman.

Mosier, R. (1965). *Making the American Mind: Social and Moral Ideas in the McGuffey Readers*. New York: Russell & Russell.

Mueller, D. (1976). Mastery learning: Partly boon, partly boondaggle. *Teachers College Record* 78: 41–52.

Munson, O., and J. Hoskinson. (1917). Library and supplementary reading books recommended for use in elementary schools. In H. Wilson, ed., *Second Report of the Committee on Minimal Essentials in Elementary School Subjects. 16th Yearbook of National Society for the Study of Education*. Bloomington, Ill.: Public School Publishing.

Murphy, G. (1960). *Massachusetts Bay Colony: The role of government in education*. Ph.D. diss. Radcliffe College.

Muther, C. (1985). What every textbook evaluator should know. *Educational Leadership* 42: 4–8.

A Nation at Risk. (1983). Washington, D.C.: National Commission on Excellence in Education.

Noble, D. (1983). *Forces of Production: A Social History of Industrial Automation.* New York: Knopf.

Notz, W. (1975). Work motivation and the negative effects of extrinsic record. *American Psychologist* 30: 884–91.

Ogbu, J. (1974). *The Next Generation.* New York: Academic.

———. (1978). *Minority Education and Castes.* New York: Academic.

Osborn, J. (1984). The purposes, uses, and content of workbooks and some guidelines for publishers. In R. Anderson, J. Osborn, and R. Tierney, eds., *Learning to Read in American Schools: Basal Readers and Content Texts.* Hillsdale, N.J.: Lawrence Erlbaum.

Otto, W., A. Wolf, and R. Eldridge. (1984). Managing instruction. In P.D. Pearson, ed., *Handbook on Reading Research.* New York: Longman.

Parsons, T. (1959). The school class as a social system: Some of its functions in American society. *Harvard Educational Review* 29: 297–318.

Patridge, L. (1889). *The "Quincy Method" Illustrated.* New York: Kellogg.

Pearson, P.D., ed. (1984). *The Handbook on Reading Research.* New York: Longman.

Pflum, S., et al. The influence of pupil behaviors and pupil status factors on teacher behaviors during oral reading lessons. *Journal of Educational Research* 74: 99–105.

Pikulski, J., and J. Kirsch. (1979). Organization for instruction. In R. Calfee and P. Drum, eds., *The Compensatory Reading Survey.* Newark, Del.: International Reading Association.

Popkewitz, T.S. (1984). *Paradigm and Ideology in Educational Research.* Philadelphia: Falmer.

Postman, N. (1979). *Teaching as a Conserving Activity.* New York: Delta Books.

Precourt, W. (1982). Ethnohistorical analysis of an Appalachian settlement school. In G. Spindler, ed., *Doing the Ethnography of Schooling.* New York: Holt, Rinehart & Winston.

Purves, A. (1984). The challenge to educators to produce literate citizens. In A. Purves and O. Niles, eds., *Becoming Readers in a Complex Society. 83rd Yearbook of the National Society for the Study of Education.* Part I. Chicago, Ill.: University of Chicago Press.

Purves, A. and O. Niles, eds. (1984). *Becoming Readers in a Complex Society. 83rd Yearbook of the National Society for the Study of Education.* Part I. Chicago: University of Chicago Press.

Red, C., and E. Shainline. (1987). Teachers reflect on change. *Educational Leadership* 44: 38–40.

Resnick, D., and L. Resnick. (1977). The nature of literacy: An historical exploration. *Harvard Educational Review* 47: 370–85.

———. (1985). Standards, curriculum, and performance: A historical and comparative perspective. *Educational Researcher* 14: 5–20.

Rice, J.M. (1893). *The Public School System of the United States.* New York: The Century Co.

———. (1914). *The Scientific Management in Education.* New York: Hinds, Noble & Eldridge.

Riis, J. (1893). *The Children of the Poor.* New York: C. Scribner.

Rist, R. (1970). Student social class and teacher expectations. *Harvard Educational Review* 40: 411–51.

———. (1973). *The Urban School: Factories for Failure.* Cambridge, Mass.: MIT Press.

Rivlin, A. (1971). *Systematic Thinking for Social Action.* Washington, D.C.: Brookings Institute.

Robb, D. (1985). Strategies for implementing successful mastery learning programs: Case studies. In D. Levine and Associates, eds., *Improving Student Achievement Through Mastery Learning.* San Francisco: Jossey-Bass.

Robbins, P., and P. Wolfe. (1987). Reflections on a Hunter-based staff development project. *Educational Leadership* 44: 56–61.

Robinson, H., ed. (1968). *Innovation and Change in Reading Instruction. 67th Yearbook of the National Society for the Study of Education.* Part II. Chicago: University of Chicago Press.

Roehler, L., and G. Duffy. (1982). Matching direct instruction to reading outcomes. *Language Arts* 59: 476–80.

Rosenbaum, S. (1976). *Making Inequality.* New York: Wiley.

Rosenshine, B. (1978). Review of teaching styles and pupil progress. *American Educational Review* 26: 519–34.

———. (1981) *Meta-analyses of process - product research.* Paper presented at the Invisible College of Researchers on Teaching (April), University of California at Los Angeles.

Rosenshine, B., and R. Stevens. (1984). Classroom instruction in reading. In P.D. Pearson, ed., *Handbook of Reading Research.* New York: Longman.

Rowan, B., and A. Miracle. (1983). Systems of ability grouping and the stratification of achievement in elementary schools. *Sociology of Education* 56: 133–44.

Rugg, H. (1941). *That Men May Understand.* New York: Harpers.

Rupley, W., B. Wise, and J. Logan. (1986). Research in effective teaching: An overview of its development. In J. Hoffman, ed., *Effective Teaching of Reading: Research and Practice.* Newark, Del.: International Reading Association.

Russo, N. (1978). *The Effects of Student Characteristics, Educational Belief, and Instructional Task on Teacher's Preinstructional Decisions in Reading and Math.* Ph.D. diss. University of California, Los Angeles.

Salmon-Cox, L. (1980). Teachers and tests: What's really happening. Paper presented at the annual meeting of the American Educational Research Association, New York.

Schmidt, G. (1982). Chicago mastery reading: A case against a skills-based reading curriculum. *Learning* 11: 36–40.

Schon, D. (1983). *The Reflective Practitioners: How Professionals Think in Action.* New York: Basic.

Seaver, W. (1973). Effects of naturally induced teachers' expectancies. *Journal of Personality and School Psychology* 28: 333–42.

Shannon, P. (1983a). The use of commercial reading materials in American elementary schools. *Reading Reseach Quarterly* 19: 68–85.

———. (1983b). The treatment of commercial reading materials in college reading methods textbooks. *Reading World* 23: 147–57.

———. (1984). Mastery learning in reading and the control of teachers and students. *Language Arts* 61: 484–93.

———. (1986a). Hidden within the pages: A study of social perspective in young children's favorite books. *Reading Teacher* 39: 656–63.

———. (1986b). Teachers' and administrators' thoughts on changes in reading instruction within a merit pay program based on test scores. *Reading Research Quarterly* 21: 20–35.

———. (1986c). Conflict or consensus: Views of reading curricula and instruction within one instructional setting. *Reading Research and Instruction* 26: 31–49.

———. (1987). Diversity within the reading research community. A paper presented at the National Reading Conference, St. Petersburg, Fla.

———. (in press). Class size, reading instruction, and commercial materials. *Reading Research and Instruction.*

Sharp, R., and A. Green. (1975). *Education and Social Control.* London: Routledge & Kegan Paul.

Sheldon, W., and D. Lashinger. (1968). A summary of research studies relating to language arts in elementary education. *Elementary English* 45: 794–817.

———. (1969). A summary of research studies relating to language arts in elementary education. *Elementary English* 46: 866–85.

———. (1971). A summary of research studies relating to language arts in elementary education. *Elementary English* 48: 243–74.

Shor, I. (1977). Learning how to learn: Conceptual teaching in a course called "Utopia". *College English* 38: 640–47.

———. (1980). *Critical Teaching and Everyday Life.* Montreal: Black Rose.

Shor, I., and P. Freire. (1986). *A Pedagogy for Liberation: Dialogues on Transforming Education.* South Hadley, Mass.: Bergin & Garvey.

Smith, F. (1986). *Insult to Intelligence.* New York: Arbor.

Smith, J., and M. Katims. (1979). Reading in the city: The Chicago mastery learning reading program. *Phi Delta Kappan* 59: 199–202.

Smith, N.B. (1965). *American Reading Instruction.* Newark, Del.: International Reading Association.

———. (1986). *American Reading Instruction.* 3rd ed. H. Robinson, ed. Newark, Del.: International Reading Association.

Snow, C.P. (1959). *The Two Cultures.* London: Oxford University Press.

Soltow, L., and E. Stevens. (1981). *The Rise of Literacy and the Common School in the United States: A Socioeconomic Analysis.* Chicago. University of Chicago Press.

Spring, J. (1986). *The American School, 1642–1985.* New York: Longman.

Squires, J. (1985). Textbooks to the forefront. *Book Research Quarterly* 1: 12–18.

Staiger, R. (1958). How are basal readers used. *Elementary English* 35: 46–49.

Stallings, J. (1987). For whom and how long is the Hunter-based model appropriate? Response to Robbins and Wolfe. *Educational Leadership* 44: 62–63.

Stedman, L., and C. Kaestle. (1987). Literacy and reading achievement in the United States, from 1880 to the present. *Reading Research Quarterly* 22: 8–46.

Sumner, W. (1883). *What Social Classes Owe Each Other.* New York: C. Scribner.

Teale, W., and E. Sulzby, eds. (1986). *Emergent Literacy: Writing and Reading.* Norwood, N.J.: Albex.

Theisen, W. (1921). Factors affecting results in primary reading. In E. Horn, ed., *Silent Reading. 20th yearbook of the National Society for the Study of Education.* Part II. Bloomington, Ill.: Public School Publishing.

Thorndyke, E.L. (1898). *Animal Intelligence.* New York: Macmillan.

———. (1906). *The Principles of Teaching Based on Psychology.* New York: A.G. Seiler.

———. (1918). The nature, purposes and general methods of measurements of educational products. In S. Courtis, ed., *The Measurement of Educational Products. 17th Yearbook of the National Society for the Study of Education.* Part II. Bloomington, Ill.: Public School Publishing.

Thorndyke, E.L., and R. Woodworth. (1901). The influence of improvement in one mental function upon the efficiency of other functions. *Psychological Review* 8: 247–61, 384–95, 553–64.

Tönnies, F. (1957). *Community and Society (Gemeinschaft und Gesellschaft).* East Lansing, Mich.: Michigan State University.

Tulley, M. (1983). *A Descriptive Study of the Intents of State Level Textbook Adoption.* Ph.D. diss. Indiana University. Bloomington.

Veatch, J. (1967). Structure in the reading program. *Elementary English* 44: 252–56.

Venezky, R. (1987). A history of the American reading textbook. *Elementary School Journal* 87: 247–65.

Weber, M. (1964). *The Theory of Social and Economic Organization.* New York: Free Press.

Weber, R.M. (1985). Questions during reading lessons. A paper presented at the American Educational Research Association (April), San Francisco, Calif.

Weich, K. (1978). Educational organization as loosely coupled systems. *Administrative Science Quarterly* 21: 1–16.

Wells, G. (1987). Apprenticeship in literacy. *Interchange* 18: 109–23.

Whipple, G. (1949). Desirable materials, facilities and resources for reading. In A. Gates, ed., *Reading in the Elementary School. 48th Yearbook of the National Society for the Study of Education.* Part II. Chicago: University of Chicago Press.

———, ed. (1920). *New Materials of Instruction. 19th Yearbook of the National Society for the Study of Education.* Part I. Bloomington, Ill.: Public School Publishing.

———, ed. (1921). *Second Report of the Society's Committee on New Materials of Instruction. 20th Yearbook of the National Society for the Study of Education.* Part I. Bloomington, Ill.: Public School Publishing.

Wigdor, A., and W. Garner, eds. (1982). *Ability testing: Uses, consequences, and controversies.* Parts I & II. Washington, D.C.: National Academic Press.

Wilkins, W. (1976). The concept of self-fulfilling prophecy. *Sociology of Education* 49: 175–83.

Willis, P. (1977). *Learning to Labor.* Lexington, Mass.: D.C. Heath

Wilson, H. (1919). Foreword. In E. Horn, ed., *Fourth Report of the Committee on Economy of Time in Education. 18th Yearbook of the National Society for the Study of Education.* Part II. Bloomington, Ill.: Public School Publishing.

———, ed. (1915). *Minimum Essentials in Elementary School Subjects— Standards and Current Practices. 14th Yearbook of the National Society for the Study of Education.* Part I. Bloomington, Ill.: Public School Publishing.

———, ed. (1917). *Second Report of the Committee on Minimum Essentials in Elementary School Subjects. 16th Yearbook of the National Society for the Study of Education.* Part I. Bloomington, Ill.: Public School Publishing.

———, ed. (1918). *Third Report of the Committee on Economy of Time in Education. 17th Yearbook of the National Society for the Study of Education.* Part I. Bloomington, Ill.: Public School Publishing.

Winograd, P., and L. Smith. (1986). Improving the climate for reading comprehension instruction. A paper present at National Reading Conference (December), Austin, Tex.

Wise, A. (1979). *Legislated Learning: The Bureaucratization of the American Classroom.* Berkeley, Calif.: University of California.

Wittick, M. (1968). Innovations in reading instruction for beginners. In H. Robinson, ed., *Innovation and Change in Reading Instruction.*

67th Yearbook of the National Society for the Study of Education. Part II. Chicago: University of Chicago Press.

Wixson, K., and C. Peters. (1984). Reading redefined: A Michigan Reading Association opposition paper. *Michigan Reading Journal* 17: 4–7.

Yaden, D. (1984). Children's Questions about Reading. A paper presented at the National Reading Conference (December), St. Petersburg, Fla.

Yoakam, G. (1954). Unsolved problems in reading. *Elementary English* 31: 427–30.

Zimet, S. (1983). Teaching children to detect social bias in books. *Reading Teacher* 36: 418–21.

Zirbes, L. (1927). *Teachers Guide to the Keystone Primary Set.* Meadville, Penn.: Keystone View.

———. (1928). *Comparative Studies of Current Practice in Reading, with Techniques for the Improvement of Teaching.* (Teachers College contributions to Education, No. 316). New York: Teachers College, Columbia University.

———. (1937). The teaching of reading: A second report. *Curriculum Journal* 8: 220–21.

———. (1951). The experience approach in reading. *Reading Teacher* 5: 1–2, 15–16.

Index